EARLY CHRISTIAN, BYZANTINE AND ROMANESQUE ARCHITECTURE

SIMPSON'S HISTORY OF ARCHITECTURAL DEVELOPMENT

New Edition

Volume I

ANCIENT AND CLASSICAL ARCHITECTURE

by

Hugh Plommer

Volume II

EARLY CHRISTIAN, BYZANTINE AND ROMANESQUE ARCHITECTURE

by

Cecil Stewart

Volume III

GOTHIC ARCHITECTURE

by

Cecil Stewart

Volume IV

RENAISSANCE ARCHITECTURE

by

J. Quentin Hughes

and

Norbert Lynton

Volume V

NINETEENTH AND TWENTIETH CENTURY ARCHITECTURE

by

Thomas Howarth

Simpson's History of
Architectural Development
Vol. II

EARLY CHRISTIAN, BYZANTINE AND ROMANESQUE ARCHITECTURE

by

Cecil Stewart

LONGMANS

LONGMANS, GREEN AND CO LTD
48 GROSVENOR STREET, LONDON W1
RAILWAY CRESCENT, CROYDON, VICTORIA, AUSTRALIA
AUCKLAND, KINGSTON (JAMAICA), LAHORE, NAIROBI
LONGMANS SOUTHERN AFRICA (PTY) LTD
THIBAULT HOUSE, THIBAULT SQUARE, CAPE TOWN
JOHANNESBURG, SALISBURY
LONGMANS OF NIGERIA LTD
W. R. INDUSTRIAL ESTATE, IKEJA
LONGMANS OF GHANA LTD
INDUSTRIAL ESTATE, RING ROAD SOUTH, ACCRA
LONGMANS GREEN (FAR EAST) LTD
443 LOCKHART ROAD, HONG KONG
LONGMANS OF MALAYA LTD
44 JALAN AMPANG, KUALA LUMPUR
ORIENT LONGMANS LTD
CALCUTTA, BOMBAY, MADRAS
DELHI, HYDERABAD, DACCA
LONGMANS CANADA LTD
137 BOND STREET, TORONTO 2

This Edition first published 1954

Second Impression by photolithography 1959
Third Impression by photolithography 1962

Made and printed by offset in Great Britain by
William Clowes and Sons, Limited, London and Beccles

CONTENTS

PLATES

EXPLANATORY NOTE TO THIS REVISED EDITION

Frederick Moore Simpson was born in 1856. He died in 1928. Of his life between these years there is a surprising dearth of information, and the customary duty of an editor to provide a brief, eulogistic biography is therefore hard to fulfil, except in terms of brevity. He was awarded a Royal Academy travelling studentship in 1884, took the Chair of Architecture in Liverpool in 1894, occupied that of London University in 1903, and was responsible for the design of a number of uninspiring structures, the best known being the setting for Queen Victoria's statue in Liverpool. In 1879 he made his first journey abroad, and twenty-nine years later wrote: 'I cannot remember a year since when I have not been abroad at least once, sometimes more often.' The object of these journeys was the study of architectural history, and in 1905 he published the first volume of his *History of Architectural Development*; in 1908 the second, and in 1911 the third. He then wrote: 'I cannot say that I know every building in these volumes, but there are very few that I have not seen.' It is not surprising, therefore, that he had little time to practise architecture, and that his reputation today stands almost entirely upon these three great volumes.

The publishers have decided that these should be brought up to date chronologically and factually. This means not only the addition of a new volume dealing with architecture since the accession of Victoria, but also a readjustment of the divisions of the work. This readjustment involves a new Volume II, including Early Christian, Byzantine and Romanesque architecture, derived partly from Volume I and partly from Volume II of the original edition. The task imposed upon me has been to edit this new Volume II.

The Shorter Oxford Dictionary defines the verb *edit* as 'to prepare, set in order for publication literary material', and 'to garble, or "cook"'. Which of these definitions applies in this particular case, it is obviously the duty of the critic to judge. To me, there seemed to be two alternatives: either to leave the bulk of the work as it stood, with the correction of such minor errors as occurred to me and the addition of such new material as seemed necessary to bring it up to date; or to revise it entirely, adding new chapters and new illustrations, but, in order that the character of the original should not be lost, retaining the method and technique which especially distinguish Simpson's *History* from others. The latter alternative was chosen.

Wherever possible, a scale of 50 feet to 1 inch has been adopted for the plans and sections, so that the reader may judge at a glance the relative size of the buildings described. In many cases, where buildings are of exceptional size, this has proved impracticable and a scale of 100 feet to 1 inch has had to be used. Such departures from the rule have been noted below the illustrations. Every effort has been made to secure accuracy of scale, and the sources of the drawings have been indicated.

I have omitted north points on the plans, because although after the year 386 the altar was generally placed towards the east, there are many variations arising out of particular topographical conditions, and it seemed to me that references to, say, the 'south-east end' of a church instead of the conventional 'east end' would lead to confusion. For the same reason I have retained, in certain cases, titles such as S. Mark's, Venice, and San Vitale, Ravenna, in preference to the Church of S. Mark, Venice, and the Church of S. Vitale, Ravenna, because it is by the former titles that these churches are commonly known in England. In the case of the Byzantine Cathedral of Constantinople, I have adopted Lethaby's title of Sancta Sophia, because the cathedral was dedicated not to a Saint Sophia but to the Divine Wisdom (Ἅγια Σοφία), or Word of God.

It is possible that some of the buildings referred to no longer exist. For example, I have not been able to find out whether or not certain churches in Russia and parts of Germany suffered destruction. They are still included here, however, because if they were omitted this history of architectural development would be less comprehensible and certainly less comprehensive.

I wish to thank Dr. Thomas Howarth, Mr. Eric Jarrett and Mr. R. Furneaux Jordan for reading the typescript and giving me their helpful criticisms and advice. My thanks are also due to those who have allowed me to reproduce original photographs. The sources are indicated in the list of plates.

Cecil Stewart
1953

CHAPTER I

INTRODUCTION

THE student of the early developments of Christian architecture is faced with the difficult task of determining the date at which his studies may be said to begin. Some writers consider that A.D. 313 is such a date, the year when Constantine and Licinius together issued the Edict of Milan, which granted toleration to Christians and consequently encouraged the erection of public places of worship. Others prefer the year 326, the date of the foundation of Constantinople—a centre for the development of a distinct style of architecture which was the fusion of influences from both East and West. Some consider that the abdication of the last Roman Emperor in 476 marks a turning point in style between classical and Christian architecture. Others prefer 800, the year of the coronation of Charlemagne, by which time a new architecture, far removed from the interests of the classical archaeologist, was being developed in the West. But the researches of scholars in Italy during the last two decades have shown very clearly the importance of art and architecture in the centuries between the Edict of Milan and the coronation of Charlemagne, for it was during this period, which we name Early Christian, that the foundations of Romanesque architecture were laid. And even before the Edict of Milan in 313 there was some Christian architecture; there was also a great deal of Christian art which, far from being unimportant, or decadent like so much late Roman work, provides a significant clue to the architecture which developed in Europe and in western Asia. It is, however, often exceedingly difficult to distinguish the first indications of a new style from the more obvious signs of a dying and decadent one; but it now seems advisable that some notes should be made of the early manifestations of Christian art if we are to understand the significance of later developments.

The Fire of Rome. On the 19th of July, A.D. 64, a great and devastating fire broke out in Rome and destroyed many of the historic buildings. Up to this time we have no evidence of the existence of a Christian community in the capital. In the eyes of the Romans, the Jews and the Christians seem to have been one people, but now, apparently for the first time, a distinction is made. In the first instance the Jews were assumed to be the incendiaries, but in their place the Christian sect was formally accused and, under the order of Nero, was condemned on the charge of incendiarism and massacred in the imperial circus on Vatican Hill, close to the site of the present Church of S. Peter. From that time until 313 the Christians suffered almost continual persecution, and the Christian movement was literally driven underground to the great catacombs on the outskirts of the city.

The Catacombs. It is here that we can best trace the germination of that art and decoration which is so important a feature of Early Christian architecture. The catacombs served two purposes: the provision of burial grounds and the furnishing of chapels for Christian worship. The earliest of these chapels, and one of the most interesting, is the *Capella Greca*, in the Catacombs of S. Priscilla. It is ascribed to the second century, and here we can see certain forms which were later to become characteristic of Christian architecture in the West. It is rectangular in shape, has an apse over the chief tomb at one end, and is decorated with symbolic paintings of various episodes from the Gospel of S. John. Another chapel, in the Cemetery of S. Sotere, has the three main divisions—nave, chancel and apse—which became so typical a feature of Early Christian architecture. Yet another, in the Catacombs of S. Callistus, has classical columns, capitals and cornices, and an episcopal chair in the centre of the apse. The decoration of nearly all these chapels is extremely crude, and much of it is pagan in style and character; for the art of the Roman Empire in the first three centuries A.D. showed little trace of Christian influence. Tritons and nereids are represented alongside Christian symbols, and the figure of Christ follows classical portrayals of Orpheus or Apollo.

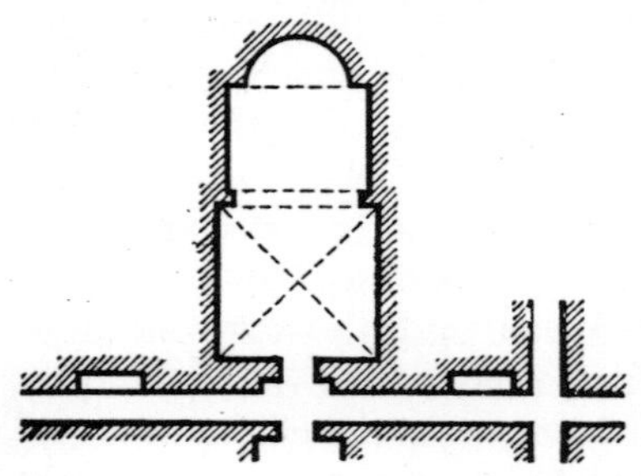

After De Rossi.

Chapel in the catacombs of S. Sotere.
Scale 50 ft. to 1 in.

Functional Requirements. The extent to which the church plan was conditioned by the requirements of ritual and the Liturgy is difficult to determine. It is possible that to some degree the form of service was dictated by the environment provided in the catacombs and in private houses which may have been used for worship. Neither the Founder nor any of His immediate successors laid down specific directions as to the form of worship to be adopted or the kind of building that was necessary. In its early days the Church was regarded as a divine institution rather than as a building, an institution ruled not by men but by the Holy Spirit. But by the second century appointments had been made to fill the offices of bishops, presbyters and deacons, and orders of worship had been framed. Their development need not be traced in detail here. The general tendency was, on the one hand, towards elaboration and growing magnificence (especially after the Church had become a state institution) and, on the other, towards increasing solemnity and mystery, of so sacred a character as to prohibit admission to outsiders. The divisions of the church were arranged to cater for three classes : the officers of the Church, those who had been admitted to Communion, and those who had been excluded and were returning, through repentance, to the right path. To the first class the most sacred part of the temple (the sacrarium, bema or sanctuary) was open. The second had access to the middle of the temple—the nave and aisles—and the third was admitted only to the shelter of the portico, or narthex, from which the services could be heard through the doors which led to the nave. Women were generally segregated, either in the aisles or, in many of the early churches, in galleries accessible from the narthex, from which they could watch the service. In front of the church was a cloistered yard, or atrium, which contained a fountain used for washing before service. The fountain was later abolished, chiefly to avoid resemblance to Mohammedan custom, and holy water stoups were introduced near the entrance to the church.

Baptism by water was a fundamental feature of the Christian institution, and was at first performed at riversides. In the early development of the Church, this required no architectural setting, nor did it involve any serious inconvenience in the warm East, but in the West the desire for privacy, particularly during times of persecution, together with adverse climatic conditions, made special arrangements desirable. The ceremony was therefore transferred indoors and, upon the official recognition of the Church, it is not surprising that the warm rooms of some of the Roman baths should have been converted. Such circular buildings proved ideal for this purpose, though the ceremony was still somewhat arduous for the neophyte and was ultimately simplified by the introduction of the font, which could be conveniently kept at the western end of the church.

Early Christian Architecture. It will be noticed that the functional requirements of the early Church involved no remarkable architectural innovations. Nevertheless, the result was a building form which had marked characteristics. Architecturally, the dominant features were a forecourt or atrium, a portico or narthex, and a long processional nave with aisles, terminating in an apse at the sanctuary end. Geographically, the architecture was not limited to Rome or Italy; examples are to be found in Egypt, Syria, Greece and Constantinople. Historically, this architecture persisted, especially in the West, up to the end of the ninth century.

Division of the Empire. The division of the Empire into two parts, eastern and western, led to remarkable changes in the character of architecture in the East, which makes the work that is to be described difficult to arrange satisfactorily. One style was no longer general over the whole of the civilised world. Local traditions influenced architectural development to a far greater extent than had been possible in the days when the imperial stamp was set on all buildings, whether in Rome itself, at Palmyra in the east, at Nîmes in the west or at Trèves in the north.

At first there was little or no difference between the architecture of western and eastern Europe, Asia Minor and Egypt. The type of architecture that we have classified as Early Christian persisted; but towards the end of the fifth century Greek artistic feeling found opportunities for free expression in Constantinople, under Eastern Emperors, far greater than had been previously permitted. In the Eastern Empire, imperial power extended equally over state and Church; the Emperor was God's Vicegerent on earth, and the ceremony of worship became a state affair, with all the formality fitting to the imperial court. From the narrow underground cells which provided a precarious setting for the prayers of the newly converted in Rome, we come to an architectural magnificence at Constantinople that has never been surpassed. In place of the crude figures which were sketched on the tufa walls of the catacombs, we are presented with a glorious procession of Apostles and Saints, in glittering mosaic, attired with all the solemn dignity of imperial senators.

The contrast between the architecture of the East and that of the West is remarkable. From the fifth to the eighth century

Constantinople was the guardian of civilisation, while Rome and Italy were suffering a long series of disasters. The Eternal City had long before lost her prestige. Under Theodoric, King of the Ostrogoths, who ruled Italy between the years 493 and 526, there was a lull in the fighting and a slight revival of the arts; but the peace he brought did not last long. In 586 the Lombards, a barbarian race, overran the greater part of the country, and for two hundred years the whole of Italy, except Rome, Ravenna and portions of Venetian territory, remained in their possession. In addition to this disaster, plagues and famines, towards the end of the sixth century, swept away a large number of the inhabitants. The end of the eighth century saw the fall of the Lombards, the unification of the different European nationalities under Charlemagne, and the rise of papal power under the Popes Adrian I and Leo II (772–816). Charlemagne was crowned by the latter in 800 under the title of Emperor of the West. The architecture in Italy which followed this event might almost be called papal, since the recrudescence of building activity was largely due to the influence of the Popes, although the revival was assisted by the more settled state of the country under Charlemagne's rule.

Out of this confusion it is surprising that so much was built and still remains. In the East, matters were very different. There the full glory of the Empire had been recreated, with almost oriental magnificence, and the architecture had about it something of the mystery and drama of the Church triumphant, something of the grandeur of oriental state, and something that was purely aesthetic, a spatial concept which was far removed from the load-bearing materialism of Imperial Roman architecture, or the almost monotonous regularity of Early Christian architecture.

Byzantine Architecture. For the purpose of this work, Byzantine architecture is taken to be that type of building first perfected at Sancta Sophia,[1] Constantinople, in which the dome, upheld by pendentives, is the dominant motif. Geographically, the area that is covered includes not only that under the direct control of the Emperors, which varied considerably over the centuries, but also areas outside the Empire, such as Venice, Russia, Sicily and France, in which the Byzantine technique was developed. Historically, the field of study is normally taken from the foundation of

[1] W. R. Lethaby's lead has been followed in giving the title *Sancta*, not *Saint*, since the cathedral was dedicated not to a Lady Sophia but to the Divine Sophia—the Wisdom of the Logos, or Word of God.

Constantinople in 326 until its capture by the Turks in 1453. But the characteristic architecture did not appear until Justinian's reign, in the sixth century, and the influence persisted long after the fall of the Empire. This persistence of Byzantine culture is proof of its remarkable vitality. In Russia, in 1547, Ivan the Terrible, claiming kinship with the last of the Byzantine Emperors, declared Moscow as Third Rome, assumed the title of Caesar (Czar) and developed with Slavonic variations the Byzantine style of building, which prevailed in Russia for many centuries. In Rumania—at Sukavita and Voronet—churches were built in the Byzantine style long after the Empire had fallen. Throughout the Islamic world the legacy of Constantinople was followed in the building of mosques often almost equal in size and magnificence to Sancta Sophia, but never with the same refinement. In many parts of Greece, and especially at Mount Athos, the mode of building has prevailed up to the present day.

Monasticism. The century which followed the establishment of Christianity as a state religion was marked by an isolationist movement, in which a number of men chose to break away from the worldly Church and follow more closely the ascetic life of Christ by giving up all they had and living in solitary retirement, far from the great cities of the Empire. The examples set by these early hermits soon attracted numerous imitators, and in certain districts of Egypt and Syria their numbers were such that some degree of centralisation seemed desirable, for it is difficult for multitudes to live lives of pure individualism. By the end of the fourth century, these men were already organised in communities and building for themselves common meeting places, and the movement had spread to western Europe. S. Benedict (*c*. 500), to whom the growth of monasticism was chiefly due, defined certain rules which revolutionised the Church and laid the foundation for the later development of architecture in the West. He eliminated the elements of oriental asceticism and extreme bodily austerity. The individual was sunk in the community, which was to be self-sufficient and in which the monks had to work as well as pray. This righteous institution soon earned wealth and power, defeating its original purpose but substituting another—the spread of Christianity. Monasteries were established throughout the Western world, all built upon the same lines. New Orders were founded—Carthusian, Cistercian and Augustinian—and each prescribed minor variations of design and layout for their settlements.

Romanesque Architecture. Fundamentally, the architecture which developed was the same throughout the West. It was, basically, a development of Early Christian architecture, having in place of the bema a choir of considerable dimensions to accommodate the monks, and numerous outbuildings to provide living-quarters. There were the long processional nave, the constant use of the arch, and the stone vault which, for various practical reasons, had superseded the timber roof of the Early Christian basilica. Geographically, this architecture covers nearly the whole of the western world—Italy, France, Germany, the Low Countries, northern Spain and Britain. Historically, it covers the period from the coronation of Charlemagne to the beginning of the twelfth century, when a revolution in structural methods occurred which, combining the use of stone ribbed reinforcement to the vault with the pointed arch and the flying buttress, completely changed the appearance of architecture and is called 'Gothic'.

MAP SHOWING CENTRES OF EARLY CHRISTIAN & BYZANTINE BUILDING
AIX-LA-CHAPELLE
KIEV
FONTEVRAULT
VORENET
SUCAVITA
ANGOULEME
PERIGUEUX
CAHORS
MILAN
PADUA
VENICE
& TORCELLO
PARENZO
RAVENNA
ROME
MOLFETTA
ROSSANO
PALERMO
SYRACUSE
SALONIKA
MOUNT ATHOS
CONSTANTINOPLE
METEORA
DAPHNI
ATHENS
MISTRA
MONANVASIA
TREBIZOND
ANI
KALAT SEMAN
ROUEIHA
EZRA
BOZRA
JERUSALEM
DAIRBARAMOUS
CAIRO

CHAPTER II

EARLY CHRISTIAN ARCHITECTURE

History, Characteristics and Style

THE architecture of early Christianity is at the same time nascent and decadent. It is the product of a growing faith and a dying civilisation. The highest expression of structural ability and artistic skill had been reached in Rome in the time of Trajan; and the extent of the decline in the following two centuries can be measured by comparing the sculptured reliefs which Constantine, the first Christian Emperor, took from the demolished Arch of Trajan, to those adjoining, which were expressly designed for his own triumphal arch. We cannot, therefore, in Early Christian architecture, look for the crude and early stages of design with which we associate the beginnings of a style, but instead we can trace a gradual decline in skill and in craftsmanship as Christianity developed, which was coincident with the subsidence of the Empire itself. On the other hand, one cannot help noticing one fundamental difference in outlook which distinguished all Early Christian buildings from classical precedents: the Christian temple, unlike the Greek, was designed to house and to inspire the congregation inside, not to attract the attention of worshippers outside; it was as though the Greek temple were turned inside out. The colonnade, which was a characteristic feature of the larger Greek temple, was also the distinguishing feature of the Christian church; but in the Greek building it surrounded an insignificant cell, whereas in the Christian church it defined the important spaces of the interior—the aisles and the nave—and led the eye dramatically towards the altar.

An important difference between the buildings of the pagan Empire and those now under consideration is that most of the former were secular, whereas the latter were built almost entirely for the purposes of the new religion. Only in the growing centres of population, such as Syria, were new houses and civic buildings necessary. In Rome and in other Italian cities the existing buildings were more than sufficient to provide for a diminishing population. The result is that the only buildings of the Early Christian period in Italy which have been preserved are churches, baptisteries and tombs.

Early Christian architecture was almost wholly dependent for its forms and details upon Greek, Roman and oriental traditions. From a technical point of view there were no significant innovations. Its development, especially in Rome, was determined largely by the poverty of the latter-day Roman Empire, which prescribed the most economical methods of building in preference to the monumental lavishness of Imperial Roman times. To speak of development at all may be misleading, because it seems from existing evidence as though the Christian type of basilica came into being as a fully developed architectural form as soon as Christianity was recognised, and this form persisted without change from the fourth to the ninth century. This does not necessarily prove the incompetence of architects to devise new forms, but suggests that the basilican plan entirely satisfied the needs of the Church in the West.

It is possible that the basilican plan had a long, though unrecorded, history during the centuries of persecution. The idea that no Christian churches were built before the legalising of Christianity is a mistaken one, which is proved by the edicts published by different Emperors, notably one by Diocletian in 303, commanding that all churches should be destroyed and all Christian books burned. Further, it cannot be assumed that the basilican church form was particularly Christian. The remarkable discovery of a pagan temple, 50 feet below the ground near the Porta Maggiore, Rome, dating from the first century and having all the essential features of a Christian basilica—nave, aisles and apsidal end—indicates that this form was already established in Rome before Christianity had taken root.

Origins. The origin of this particular form has been the subject of much controversy. In consequence of its similarity in plan to some of the old Roman basilicas, it has been supposed that converted basilicas formed the earliest Christian churches, but Texier and Pullan, in their *Byzantine Architecture*, state: 'We know of but one instance in which the Roman basilica was transformed into a church. This was the Licinian basilica, at Rome, which was converted in the year 370.' Scott[1] ridiculed entirely the idea that

[1] Sir George Gilbert Scott, *Essay on the History of English Church Architecture.*

basilicas were used for Christian worship. He advanced the practical objection that they were as necessary as before for the purposes for which they were built. He said: 'Christianity unfortunately could not abolish the litigious instincts of our nature, and after fifteen centuries of the Gospel the legal profession still flourishes.' Nevertheless, many points in plan and construction were the same in both basilica and church: the apse at the end, the wooden roof, and the columns dividing the nave and aisles. But it must not be forgotten that temples, which were undoubtedly converted into churches, also possessed many of these characteristics. Roman temples often had the apse, the larger Greek temples the wooden roof and the division into nave and aisles. Moreover, if what Scott contended were true, that the central portions of some of the large Roman basilicas (such as the basilicas Ulpa and Julia) were not covered at all, then the likeness between them and the early churches would be slight. The term 'basilican church' was never used by old writers, and probably its later adoption arose, not so much from any resemblance between the early church and the Roman basilica, as from the erroneous idea that the early church was the basilica converted. Be that as it may; much may be said for the term if properly defined and restricted; but if used loosely, as it sometimes is, and applied to any large church which has nave and aisles, irrespective of other features, it becomes worthless and meaningless. It is absurd to apply it to buildings as different as S. Paul Outside the Walls, Rome, Amiens Cathedral and the Renaissance Church of S. Peter, Rome.

A second, and more attractive, theory is that the basilican form was in some way a development from the classical dwelling house, since in the times of the persecution a private house would be a natural and safe place of assembly for the early Christians. The typical house of the second and third centuries had only one space —the peristyle or atrium—which could have provided sufficient accommodation for any large meeting. The atrium was a colonnaded court surrounded by rooms, with the tablinum at one end of the main axis—which was obviously the place for the clergy. Immediately in front of the tablinum stood the ornamental stone table, the only reminder of the ancient sacred hearth; this is precisely the position of the Christian altar. The worshippers would stand along the aisles. The central part of the atrium was, as a rule, open to the sky, so that it differed to some extent from the nave of the Early Christian basilica. It must be assumed, if we accept the theory, that in adapting the central area of the Roman house to the use of a church, one of the first changes would be its complete roofing.[1] In order to obtain light and air such a roof would have to be raised well above the side aisles to allow for clerestory openings : this was the method invariably adopted in all Christian basilicas. The extension of the main axis in most

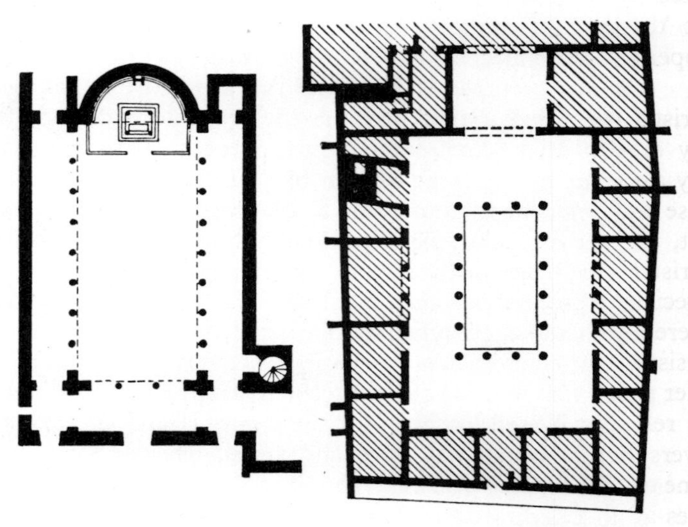

After Hubsch and Lowrie.

Basilica of S. Agnese and plan of a classical house.
Scale 50 ft. to 1 in.

Christian churches can be explained partly on aesthetic grounds, and partly by the wish to provide more accommodation. The omission of the colonnade at either end was one of the very few features in which the private house plan seems to have differed fundamentally from the church plan after the recognition of Christianity. But even so there were some exceptions, for in the Churches of S. Agnese and S. Lorenzo, Rome, the side columns which divided the nave from the aisles were returned across the entrance, and in many cases the other end of the nave was sepa-

[1] Such an enclosure is not unknown. In the Casa de Chirurgo and one or two other examples of Pompeii, the atrium was roofed and had no impluvium (a basin at the centre to catch rainwater from the roofs over the surrounding colonnade).

rated from the apse by a screen, or by an arch known as the 'triumphal arch', so that the resemblance to the house plan was very close.

A third theory—that the basilican church was simply a development of the temple plan—is supported by the knowledge that certain old temples were converted to Christian worship. But this is not likely to have happened until some time after the official recognition of Christianity. For the first century or two after Constantine only a few of the temples, and those probably the least important, would be available for Christian worship. This was especially the case in Rome, where the old pagan religions persisted longer than in any other part of the Empire. The old religions still had their followers, and it is likely that for some time there would be prejudices against the use of temples for the new faith. However, as these died out no reason existed why temples should not be converted. Even the Parthenon at Athens was transformed into a church, and faint traces of fresco paintings of saints on the cella walls can still be seen. Only small alterations, as a rule, were necessary to render a temple suitable for Christian use.

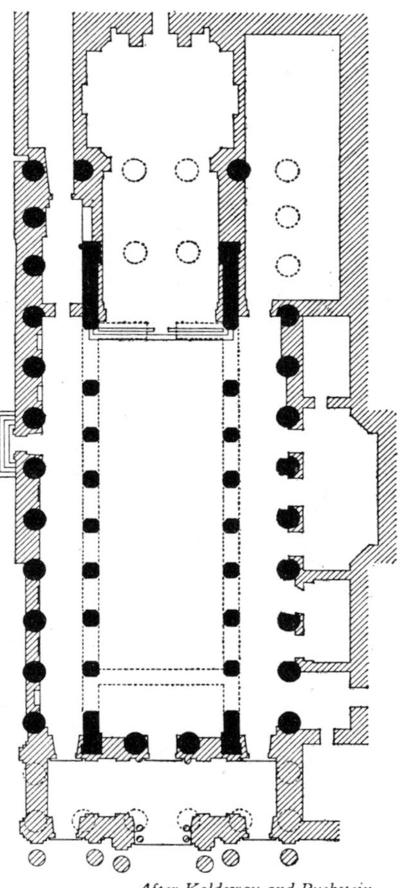

After Koldeway and Puckstein.

The cathedral at Syracuse. Original Greek temple shown in black and dotted lines; 7th century alterations in hatched lines.

Scale 50 *ft. to* 1 *in.*

The Cathedral at Syracuse. The most interesting example of such a conversion is probably the present cathedral at Syracuse, in Sicily. This was reconstructed in the seventh century. The principal alterations were the building of a wall between the columns of the external peristyle at the sides, so as to enclose the old ambulatory which was thus transformed into aisles, and the piercing of narrow, low, semi-circular-headed openings through the walls of the cella in order to connect the aisles with the central part, which became the nave; in addition, the columns of the pronaos were removed, and the cella walls continued eastward to form a chancel. On the north side, the old marble columns of the peristyle, with their Doric capitals, showed externally as well as internally, and above them were portions of the original entablature.

The changes made in other temples, as a rule, were similar. An exception is the temple at Aphrodisia, in Asia Minor, which, according to Texier and Pullan, was greatly enlarged on its conversion in the fourth century by the complete demolition of the cella walls and by the building of aisles *outside* the external peristyle, which thus became the internal colonnade.

The Basilican Church. New churches also had to be built, and these were planned and constructed in such a way as to accommodate the greatest number of people at the smallest possible expense. Whether they were copied from basilicas, temples or classical houses is, perhaps, not particularly important; what is certain is that by the fourth century the form of the basilican church had been finally established. It may be defined as oblong on plan, not cruciform, any lateral projections that might occur being very slight and at the extreme east end. Further, it was divided into nave and aisles by columns, not by piers; it was covered by timber roofs, higher over the centre than over the sides, and had an apse at the end of the nave called the presbytery. The walls were only of sufficient thickness to keep out wet, heat and cold, and to carry the roof, and were not strong enough to support a vault. The entrance was marked by a portico, or narthex, for the use of catechumens, penitents and others, who were not eligible for admission into the church itself but who, through the three doors opening into the church, could hear portions of the service. Such alterations and additions as were made from time to time in the plan were, in nearly all cases, due to ritual developments and to the ever-increasing number of the clergy, who required additional accommodation. In large churches a transept, or 'bema', which stretched across from north to south without a break, was introduced between the apse and the body of the church. It was generally the same height as the nave, from which it was separated by a 'triumphal arch'. A possible reason for this transept was the demand for extra altars, which were placed sometimes at the ends, sometimes at either side, of the central apse.[1] In many of the later churches in Rome, each aisle, as well as the nave, terminated in an apse, making the end tri-apsidal. This plan was common in the Coptic churches of Egypt (see p. 36) from a very early period, but was not introduced into Italy until the eighth century. S. Maria in Cosmedin, Rome, is one of the earliest of the Italian examples.

The Chancel. In early churches, semi-circular tiers of marble or stone seats for the clergy were built around the main apse; these ranged from one to three tiers. The throne for the bishop or chief priest occupied a central position and corresponded to the magistrate's chair in the apse of a Roman basilica. This arrangement still exists at Torcello, near Venice, although much spoilt by modern restoration, and in many of the Coptic churches in Egypt. The lesser clergy and choir were accommodated in front of the principal altar in a portion of the nave which was enclosed by low walls. Examples of this disposition occur at S. Clemente (Pl. 4) and S. Maria in Cosmedin, Rome, which will be more fully described later, but the desire of the clergy for increased privacy led gradually to the chancel's becoming entirely distinct from the nave. In S. Ambrogio, Milan, the east end of which dates from 824 to 829, and in the church at Alliante, Brianza, of about the same period, the portion reserved for the clergy is completely enclosed at the sides. This segregation was further emphasised by the introduction of the raised chancel which followed on the custom of burying the dead in crypts.[2] An early example of

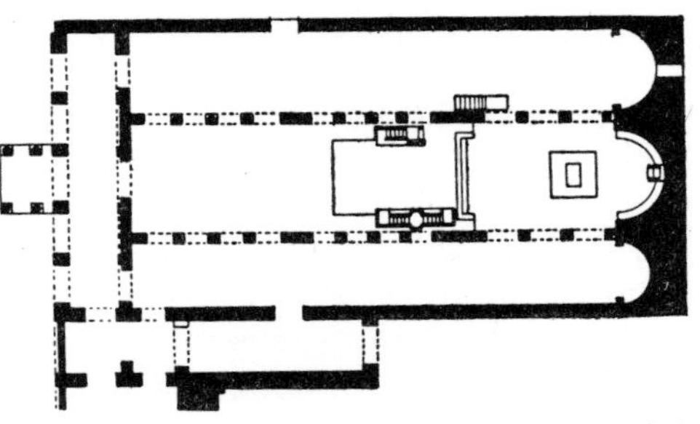

After Hubsch.

S. Maria in Cosmedin.
Scale 50 ft. to 1 in.

[1] The Italians, in most of the later churches, adhered to this eastern position for the transepts, whereas in churches in England, France and Germany the transepts were more central and projected beyond the aisle walls, making the plan cruciform.

[2] Burial in crypts became general in the sixth century.

this most effective feature occurs in the Church of S. Apollinare in Classe, near Ravenna, built in the sixth century.

Atria and Baptisteries. In front of each church was generally a courtyard, or atrium, surrounded by cloisters of which the narthex formed one side. In the centre of the courtyard was the fountain which, in early days, had been used for ablutions. Many of these courtyards have been destroyed, but that of S. Clemente, Rome, still remains (see p. 28). Occasionally, at the end of the courtyard opposite the narthex, a baptistery would be incorporated, as at Poreć, in Istria (p. 32) and Novara, in northern Italy. Baptisteries in this position also exist at Pisa and Florence, but in both these examples there is no intervening atrium and only an open space remains. At Torcello, near Venice, the baptistery was immediately in front of the west door of the church, from which it was separated only by the width of the narthex. Baptisteries, however, did not always occupy this frontal position. Sometimes they were at the sides, as at Zara in Dalmatia and at Grado in Istria, in which case they were generally connected with the church by a passage.

The Nave and Aisles. The essential characteristic of the Early Christian basilica is an oblong plan divided lengthwise into a nave and aisles by rows of columns, or piers, which support a low-pitched wooden roof above the nave, and lean-to roofs over the aisles. Occasionally these rows of columns are duplicated to provide additional aisles parallel with the nave. At the Sanctuary end the nave terminates in an apse, covered by a semi-dome, which projects beyond the rectangular plan, and occasionally additional apses mark the ends of the aisles. The nave roof is always raised sufficiently to admit of clerestory lighting along its length. The windows are large and numerous, and were filled originally with a lattice work of bronze, or with pierced slabs of marble, alabaster or plaster. Some of these slabs still exist in S. Maria in Cosmedin, Rome, and in many churches in south Italy. When glass was substituted in the ninth or tenth century, many of the windows became redundant and were blocked up.

Old columns and capitals were often used for the nave arcades—though not at Ravenna and Torcello—and this accounts for the unsatisfactory proportions so conspicuous in many of the basilican churches. The columns and capitals are often fine in themselves, the capitals being of marble beautifully carved, and the columns monoliths of either marble or granite; but the latter rarely agree with one another, either in height or diameter, and the differences have to be made good, in some cases by raised bases, in others by omitting the bases altogether. The capitals are often of different Orders; it is not uncommon to see Corinthian and Ionic capitals side by side in the same church, and even when all are of the same Order they are often strangely dissimilar. In a very few churches piers instead of columns are introduced at regular intervals. In S. Clemente, Rome, a single pier on either side divides the arcade into two sections of five bays each (p. 28), and at S. Maria in Cosmedin each arcade has three divisions of four bays each, separated by two piers (p. 15). The reason for the piers is not quite clear; they may have had something to do with the ritual arrangement, or perhaps they were introduced because long ranges of columns were considered to be monotonous. Probably, however, they were built to take the thrust of cross-arches which would give a more permanent structural link between the two sides than was possible with the timber truss. This was undoubtedly the reason for their introduction at S. Prassede, Rome, where, in the twelfth century, some of the old columns were converted into piers and arches were built across the nave and aisles.

The openings between the columns and piers are sometimes spanned by lintels, sometimes by arches. Of churches in Rome, old S. Peter's, S. Maria in Trastevere, S. Maria Maggiore and S. Lorenzo are examples of the former, and probably earlier, method; and S. Paul Outside the Walls, S. Agnese and S. Sabina of the latter. The lintels are generally moulded so as to form entablatures, proportionate to the height of the columns, as in S. Maria in Trastevere. When the spaces are arched, cornices, and sometimes whole entablatures, follow the curve of the arches as in late Roman work.

Greek Influence. Much of the building from the fifth century onwards was directed by Greek workmen, and Greek influence was even greater than had been the case in the days of Imperial Rome. Although most basilicas were constructed on Roman lines, they contained many examples of fine Greek craftsmanship. The early Christians freely made use of old material, especially of columns and capitals, and when no more was available Greek workmen were called upon to supply the deficiency. As carvers of capitals, sarcophagi, screens and other fittings, they were supreme, and although in the eighth or ninth century Italian craftsmen attempted to imitate their work, the differences between the two are great and easily discernible. To the Greeks was due the introduction of the 'dosseret', or block over the capital from which the arch springs. This was essentially a Byzantine device, employed first in the East to overcome the difficulty of supporting a wall whose width was greater than that of the capital below (p. 57). In Rome it was first used in the Church of S. Stephano Rotondo in the fifth century, and it was also largely employed in Ravenna, a centre of Byzantine influence in Italy.

Mural Decoration. The basilican churches, especially those in which lintels instead of arches were used, offered a great expanse of unbroken wall surface for decoration. The broad band between the windows and the entablature, and the spaces between the windows themselves, were either covered with paintings, or divided into panels which were often filled with mosaic pictures, as at S. Maria Maggiore. The portion of the wall at the end of the nave over the triumphal arch, and the apses with their semi-domes, also provided fine opportunities for mosaic decoration which were rarely neglected. Some of the most notable mosaics are in the Church of S. Pudenziana and the octagonal tomb of S. Costanza, both of the fourth century, and in the Church of S. Prassede, of the ninth century. In the last the white figures on a gold ground, relieved by a little red and black outlining, are among the most beautiful in the capital. Good mosaics also exist at S. Agnese, S. Maria Maggiore and S. Sabina, but none of the Roman mosaics is comparable to those at Ravenna (Pl. 2). Much of the mosaic work is of Greek craftsmanship. This art had its origin in the East, and although it had been practised by the Romans in the days of the Empire, the great extent to which it was employed in Italian churches was due to the predilection of the Byzantine Greeks for this most effective and durable method of decoration. The earliest work, that of the fourth to sixth centuries, was the finest; for a time afterwards the art declined, but in the ninth century there was a revival which almost equalled this first great flowering of Christian art.

At S. Sabina another extremely effective method of decoration was used: the spandrels of the arches were filled with small slabs of green marble and porphyry, arranged in patterns, and framed in by white marble. Whether or not this work is of the fifth century, when the church was built, is uncertain.

Ceilings. The timber roofs were always of low pitch, and of simple construction. They are now concealed inside by flat, deeply coffered ceilings, richly painted and gilded, most of which date from the fifteenth to the sixteenth centuries, but there is every reason to believe that they were originally ceiled in a similar manner and that the trusses were never intended to be seen from the inside. This would be in accordance with the old Roman traditions.[1]

Floors. The floors at first were of ordinary marble mosaic, such as was common in Rome in Imperial days; but about the twelfth century many were relaid with 'Opus Alexandrinum'. This consists of large slabs, surrounded by bands made up of small cubes of marble of different colours which form delicate patterns; these in their turn are framed in by broad bands of white marble (Pl. 3). The contrast between the small patterns and big slabs is very striking, but the secret of the success of these floors lies in the value of white as a framework for colour—a recipe that does not apply to floors alone. This work was especially popular in Rome, because that city possessed large stores of marbles, mostly broken and chipped, which could be sawn into slabs or shaped into minute cubes. Some of the slabs are of great size; in the Church of S. Maria in Cosmedin, one porphyry roundel is nearly eight feet in diameter. The finest floors of this type in the capital are in the Churches of S. Maria Maggiore, S. Maria in Trastevere, S. Clemente, S. Maria in Cosmedin and S. Lorenzo. Many of the fittings in the churches (screens, pulpits, etc.) are also inlaid with Opus Alexandrinum. Particularly good examples are to be found in the chancel screen at S. Prassede and in the pulpit of S. Lorenzo.

Exteriors. The churches externally possessed little of the richness of the interiors, since the walls were generally plastered and only occasionally were mosaics introduced. Of architectural ornamentation there was very little, but the aisle and clerestory walls of the Church of S. Apollinare in Classe, Ravenna, were arcaded, the arches springing from slightly projecting pilasters. This arcaded treatment afterwards became universal, and the churches of the eleventh and twelfth centuries in all parts of Europe present many effective varieties of it. Like most other features of Romanesque work, it owes its origin to ancient Rome.

Orientation. The orientation of many of the early churches is the very reverse of what is now customary. Until the beginning

[1] In the provinces roofs were generally open with timbers showing and no ceilings.

of the Middle Ages, there does not appear to have been any rule. The variety of direction is especially great in Rome, where nearly every point of the compass is represented. It was very rarely that a church lay exactly east and west. Only two churches, S. Paul Outside the Walls and S. Peter *ad Vincula*, have Sanctuaries at the east end, whereas sixteen, including such important churches as S. Peter's, S. John Lateran, S. Maria Maggiore, S. Clemente and S. Maria in Trastevere, are directed towards the west or north-

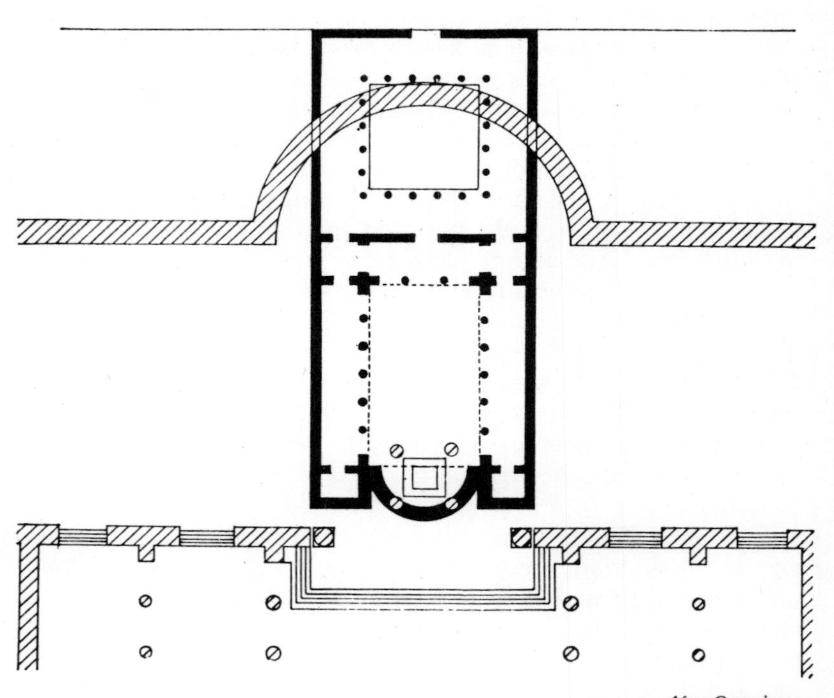

After Cummings.

Basilica of S. Paul Outside the Walls, showing, in black, the original church as completed in 330 with the high road to Ostia at the top; and shaded, a portion of the later basilica. The tomb of the Martyr was not removed when the church was rebuilt and re-orientated.

Scale 50 *ft. to* 1 *in.*

west. In the case of S. Paul Outside the Walls, the original church faced west, but in the rebuilding of 386 the orientation was reversed. Possibly the variety may be accounted for by the direction of the ancient streets. Generally, when the apse was at the east end, as at Ravenna, it was pierced with windows; but in Rome, where so many of the churches had an apse at the west end, windows were omitted. The regulation in regard to orientation seems to have been followed more closely in the Eastern Empire than in the Western, though even in the former some of the earlier examples were directed towards the west.

CHAPTER III

EARLY CHRISTIAN ARCHITECTURE

Churches and Baptisteries

AFTER the recognition of Christianity, Rome was soon provided with churches, and there remain some thirty basilicas which in foundation belong to the Early Christian period. Most of them, unfortunately, have been considerably altered, and in some cases rebuilt entirely, so that the field of useful study is very restricted. Of the three large double-aisled basilicas[1] built or founded by Constantine in Rome, the largest, S. Peter's, was pulled down when the present great cathedral was built on its site in the sixteenth century; S. Paul Outside the Walls was, unhappily, almost entirely destroyed by fire in 1823; and S. John Lateran, which was slightly smaller but much the same in conception, was rebuilt four times before 1362 and has since been so radically altered by almost every Pope that it is now completely uninteresting to the student of Early Christian architecture. In all the basilican churches of Rome, the chief object was to provide an inexpensive building which could be raised in the shortest possible time. The construction was therefore very simple, and the decoration, which would be chiefly mosaics or paintings, could be added at any time when funds permitted.

CHURCHES IN ROME

S. Peter's. S. Peter's (324–330) was the oldest and finest of all the Early Christian basilicas, and although it has entirely disappeared, the careful sixteenth-century measurements and drawings make it possible to say something about its general design and arrangement. There was a large forecourt or atrium, over 200 feet square, leading to the church itself which, covering an area of 80,000 square feet, was larger than all mediaeval cathedrals except

[1] By a 'double-aisled' basilica is meant a church which has a central nave with two aisles on each side; a 'single-aisled basilica' means a church which has only one aisle on each side of the nave.

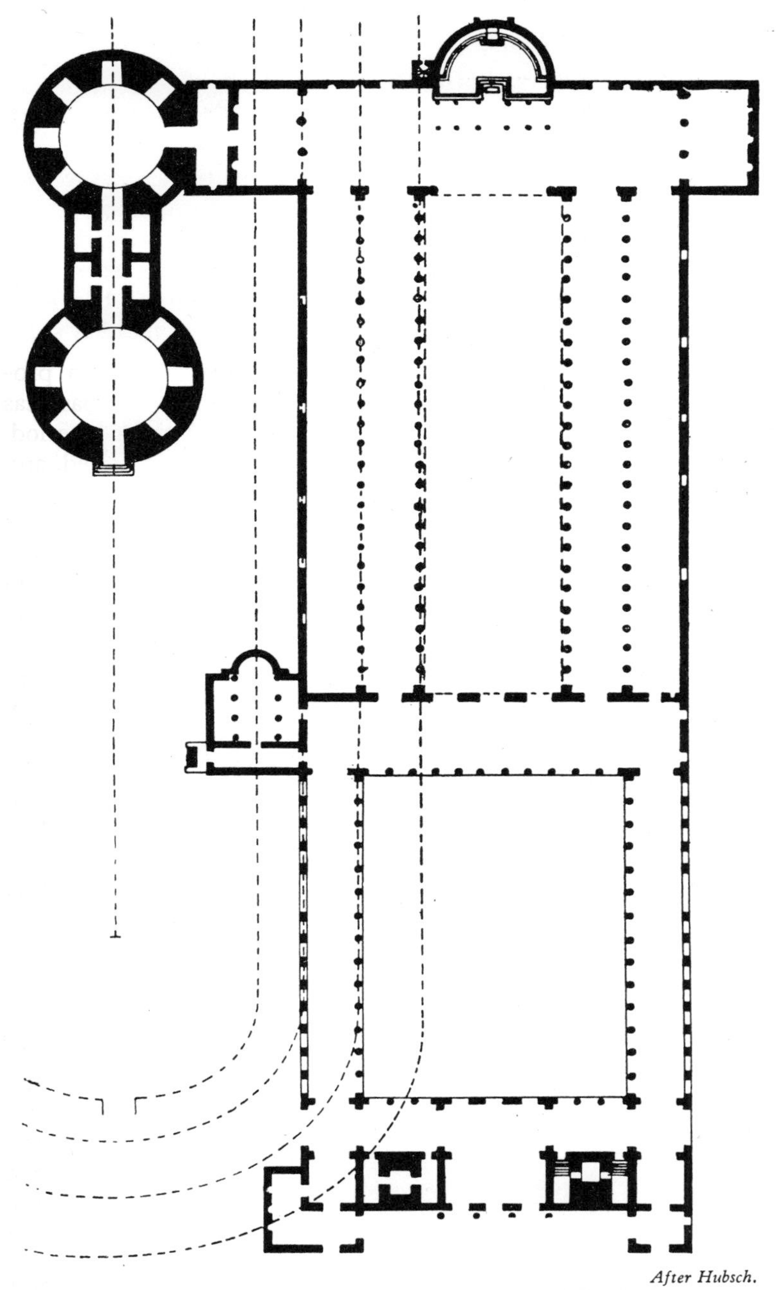

After Hubsch.

Basilica of S. Peter, Rome, showing relation to Nero's Circus.

Scale 100 *ft. to* 1 *in.*

Milan and Seville. The nave was nearly 80 feet wide, which is double the average width of a Gothic nave. The central colonnades which defined it carried a horizontal entablature, above which the wall surface was panelled with pictures. Over this arose the clerestory, and finally, the great trussed roof. The ranges of columns which divided the double aisles were surmounted by archivolts, a characteristic of later Roman work.

An unusual feature, only found in the double-aisled basilicas, was the provision of a large open space, projecting on either side, between the Sanctuary apse and the nave arcade, which some authorities regard as rudimentary transepts. It is certainly possible that the great importance of these early churches, together with purely architectural and symbolical considerations, may have impressed the cruciform scheme upon the minds of the designers of Romanesque cathedrals. In the three great double-aisled basilicas, however, this space was in effect a horizontal addition to the small sanctuary, and was reserved for the clergy. In S. Peter's the southern end of this 'bema' led to a pair of rotundas, placed on the main axis of Nero's circus and, according to mediaeval tradition, erected as mausoleums upon the exact places of martyrdom of the early Christians after the Fire of Rome.

S. Paul Outside the Walls (Pl. 1). The present Church of S. Paul Outside the Walls, although modern with the exception of portions at the chancel end, is so essentially a copy of the original that it may be fairly considered as an example of an Early Christian basilican church. It is an almost exact counterpart of S. Peter's in design and dimensions. The only important differences are that the bema is wider and that the columns along the nave carry arches instead of a horizontal architrave. It has thin walls, incapable of carrying more than its simple wooden roof; and its height, 100 feet, is considerably less than that of a French cathedral which has not more than half its width. Notwithstanding this, few churches convey such an impression of great size, fine scale and stately dignity. The nave has twenty-one bays of excellent proportion—far more than in any Romanesque or mediaeval cathedral. The thirty-six-foot columns have finely-carved Corinthian capitals which, seen from the west end, appear to form a rich band the whole length of the church. A pleasant contrast to these is afforded by the lofty Ionic columns, as high as the cornices over the main arcades, which carry the triumphal arch. Even in its

S. Paul Outside the Walls, Rome

Plate 1

Plate 2

S. Apollinare in Classe, near Ravenna; apse

S. Apollinare Nuovo, Ravenna

Marble mosaic from S. Prassede, Rome

Byzantine carving from altar rail, Torcello

S. Clemente, Rome

Plate 4

Mausoleum of Theodoric, Ravenna

S. Apollinare Nuovo, Ravenna

restored form, the church is still the most interesting, if not the most beautiful, of the Christian basilicas in Rome.

S. Maria Maggiore. Although S. Maria Maggiore is the largest of the single-aisled basilicas, its size is less than a third of the two great double-aisled basilicas mentioned above. The outside has been so altered that there is little to show that the walls enclose a very fine example of an early basilican church. The nave, like that of S. Paul, has twenty-one bays, but the intercolumniation is only about seven feet, and it was therefore easy to carry the nave walls upon lintels, instead of upon arches as was necessary at S. Paul. The introduction in the sixteenth century of wider arched spaces between the columns at the Sanctuary end has destroyed the very satisfactory rhythm that was characteristic of nearly all the older basilicas. The marble columns are rather squat and form part of the fifth-century

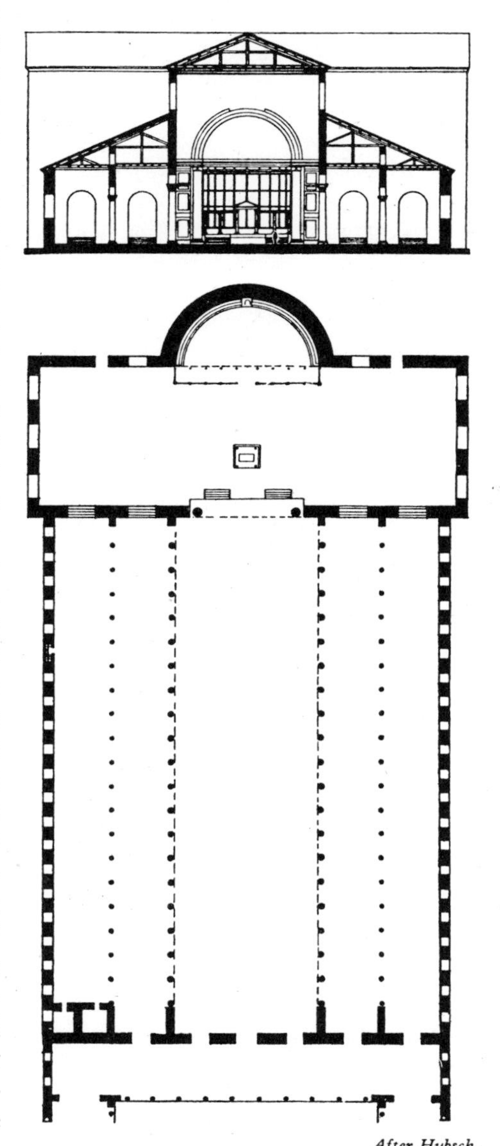

After Hubsch.

Basilica of S. Paul Outside the Walls, Rome.

Scale 100 *ft. to* 1 *in.*

church; there are some mosaics on the walls which are also of that time. The ceiling (*c.* 1585) is panelled with great richness, and although late in date probably conforms in character to the general design of the more prosperous of the early churches.

S. Agnese and S. Lorenzo. S. Agnese and S. Lorenzo, both outside the walls, are the only churches in Rome to have a gallery over the aisles. This feature is more common in early Byzantine architecture, where it was the custom to provide upstairs accommodation for women. Indeed, there is much that is Byzantine in character about both churches. The treatment of the apsidal arch in S. Lorenzo, with its mosaic representations of Bethlehem and Jerusalem, and the two alabaster windows above which have been incorporated purely decoratively; the seventh-century mosaic which fills the semi-dome at S. Agnese; the adoption in both churches of the dosseret block, to carry arches which are considerably wider and deeper than the tops of the antique capitals; all these are features which may be paralleled in the architecture of the Eastern Empire.

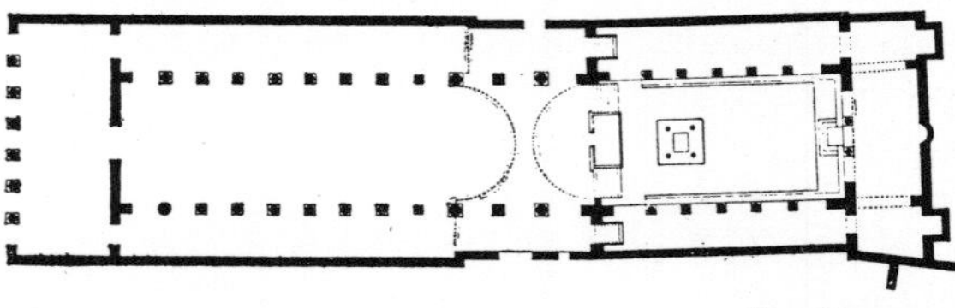

After Cattaneo.

S. Lorenzo, Rome, showing (right) the original fourth-century church of Constantine, and (left) the larger fifth-century church.

Scale 100 *ft. to* 1 *in.*

The Church of S. Lorenzo has a most interesting history. The original building was erected by Constantine and, like S. Agnese, consisted of nave, aisles, a returned aisle at the entrance (in this case at the east), and an apse at the west. In the fifth century Pope Sextus III built another and larger church with the entrance at the opposite end, the west, and an apse at the east; so that the two apses were back to back, as in the Temple of Venus and Rome. In this state the two churches remained, more or less separate from one another, until the beginning of the thirteenth century, when Honorius III destroyed the two apses and threw the two churches into one, adding three more columns to each side. The later church then became the nave, and the earlier the chancel. The floor of the latter was, however, very much lower than that of the nave, and Honorius, in order to avoid descending to the altar, inserted a new floor, supported on piers, over the old one at a level about three feet above the nave floor, and utilised the space underneath as a crypt. The new floor, of course, cut across the middle of the columns at the sides, but notwithstanding this the effect of the raised chancel, flanked and backed by galleries, with the crypt visible below, is extremely fine. The marble Ionic capitals of the narthex are particularly well carved, but what makes them of especial interest is that they are, as Cattaneo says, 'indubitably the work of Honorius III, 1216–37'. This fact makes it clear that in Italy, in the thirteenth century, workmen could be found to execute classical details, and to execute them well, at the very time of the building of Amiens Cathedral in France and Salisbury Cathedral in England.

S. Clemente (Pl. 4). The Church of S. Clemente now consists of two buildings one above the other. The lower is the original church, dating between 514 and 523, which was partially destroyed before the twelfth century, when the present upper church was built. The plan of the original building is somewhat difficult to make out, but it was certainly considerably larger than that which took its place. Some of its old columns are built into the piers which support the walls of the upper church. The rebuilding occurred about 1108 and so, chronologically, it belongs to the Italian Romanesque period, but architecturally it presents so many of the characteristics of the old basilica that it may be regarded as belonging to the Early Christian style. It has all the original fittings and internal arrangements of an Early Christian church, including the low marble screen wall which projects into the nave in front of the altar and encloses the chancel. Most of this screen belongs to the old church, and it is practically certain that it was reconstructed in the same place as before and may therefore be regarded as an example of the arrangement common to churches of the fifth and sixth centuries. From the two ambones, or pulpits, at the sides of the chancel, the Gospel and the Epistles were read. Behind a railing which marks off the bema is the altar, its canopy supported on four columns, and behind this, in the apsidal end, is the bishop's throne, with seats for the attendant clergy on either side. The rest of the inside of the church has suffered as did other Roman churches in the fifteenth century, but the antique columns, some fluted and some plain, which separate the nave from the aisles, and the mosaic decoration of the apse, still remain. The outside is perfectly plain, with little of architectural interest except for the old cloistered atrium in front, which is one of the earliest in Italy and one of the very few which have survived.

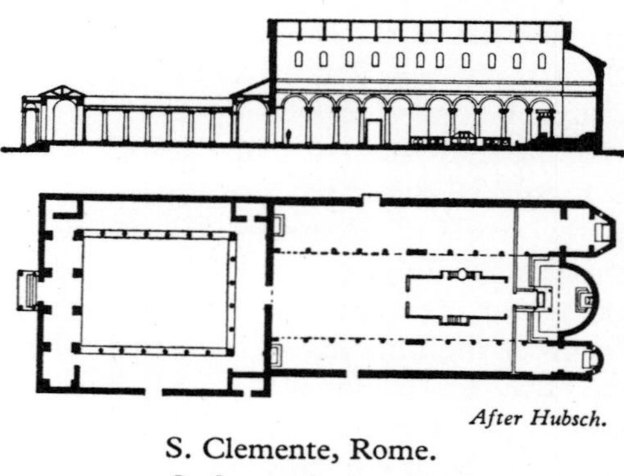

After Hubsch.

S. Clemente, Rome.
Scale 100 *ft. to* 1 *in.*

CHURCHES IN NORTH ITALY

Ravenna, after Rome, contains the most interesting remains of Early Christian work in Italy. These belong to three periods. The first extends from the beginning to the middle of the fifth century and includes buildings which, though designed for the Western rulers Honorius and Galla Placidia, are Byzantine in character (see p. 61). The second extends from 493 to 539, when the town formed part of the kingdom of Theodoric the Ostrogoth, and the third from 539 to 752, during which time it belonged to the Byzantine Empire and was the seat of an exarch, or governor, who ruled the territories along the Adriatic.

There is not much difference, architecturally, between the last two periods, since eastern and western methods of building occur in both. The workmen throughout were Greeks, whether under Roman, Byzantine or Gothic rule. Owing to the conflicting influences, however, all the buildings cannot be placed under one heading. The purely Byzantine, in which the dome was the central motif, will be considered later; but the others, which are of ordinary basilican construction, although Greek in detail and execution, will be included here. Similar to those in Ravenna are the churches in Istria, south of Trieste, which was subject to the same changing government for exactly the same periods as Ravenna, and the cathedral at Torcello, near Venice.

Characteristics. In plan these churches resemble those in Rome, except that there is never a horizontal bema and the colonnades invariably have arches instead of lintels. One small peculiarity which denotes Byzantine influence is especially noticeable: the apses are polygonal on the outside, the semi-circular form being retained inside; in Roman buildings, antique and Christian, they were always semi-circular externally as well as internally.

The basilican churches in north Italy are superior to those in Rome in that the incongruities and bad proportions of so many of the colonnades of Roman churches have been avoided. In Rome the columns, capitals and bases were often pilfered from older buildings, but in north Italy, while the columns themselves may have been antique, the capitals and bases were designed and worked for the positions they occupied, and the church interiors were enriched by carvings as fine as Greek workmen could make them. In refinement of design, the capitals of S. Apollinare in Classe, Ravenna and of Poreć Cathedral, and the low marble screen at Torcello, are not excelled by any carvings in Constantinople, and they are far superior to any of similar date in Rome.

S. Apollinare Nuovo (Pl. 2). The two most important basilican churches in Ravenna are S. Apollinare Nuovo, in the centre of the town, and S. Apollinare in Classe, outside the gates. Both were built by Theodoric, the former being completed in 526 and the latter not until 549, after the town had passed to the Byzantine Emperor Justinian. S. Apollinare Nuovo is much more richly decorated than the other, but its general proportions and detail are not so fine. The column capitals are much coarser, probably because they are slightly earlier in date. In the sixth century, when architectural progress was very rapid, a difference of only twenty years was enough to account for a marked change in quality. The soffits of the arches are coffered, with a flower in the centre of each panel in true Roman fashion.

The principal attraction of the church is the mosaic decoration, which is of two periods. Above the clerestory are the original mosaics of Theodoric—a series of twenty-six panels representing the miracles of Christ and episodes of the Passion; and below are the mosaics executed after the capture of Ravenna by the Byzantines, which provide a magnificent procession of angels and martyrs, all remarkably alike, attired in white robes upon a gold background. The function of these mosaics is wholly decorative, and they have a rhythmic quality which emphasises the length of the nave and makes them, therefore, an important feature in the whole composition.

S. Apollinare in Classe (Pl. 2). The Church of S. Apollinare in Classe, standing solitary in the plain beyond Ravenna, is built of thin bricks with wide mortar joints in the manner of the Byzantine builders. Inside, the finest mosaic decoration is concentrated at the apsidal end, the nave being severely plain apart from a frieze of eighteenth-century medallions above the colonnade. The columns are surmounted by identical capitals, and all have dosserets. They are similar in character to those of the Church of Sancta Sophia, Salonika, built about 485 (see p. 74). The chancel is approached by a wide flight of steps which stretches across the end of the nave, and underneath is a small crypt. On the north side, but detached from the church, is a circular tower. A similar tower stands at one end of the narthex at S. Apollinare Nuovo (Pl. 4). These are possibly the earliest examples of belfries in western Europe, and they have no counterparts in Byzantine architecture.[1]

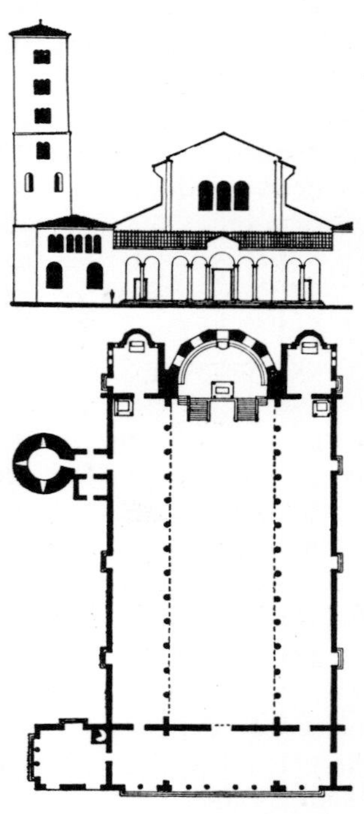

After Hubsch.

S. Apollinare in Classe, near Ravenna.
Scale 100 *ft. to* 1 *in.*

Torcello. Two churches of great interest stand side by side in the little hamlet of Torcello, which was once a large town in the Venetian lagoons. One, the cathedral, is basilican; the other, S. Fosca, is cruciform in plan and is described under Byzantine work on p. 90. The two are connected by a narthex which runs across the west front of the basilican church and around S. Fosca. The

[1] An exception is the tower of the Church of Pantanassa, Mistra, in the Peloponnese, but that is much later in date and may have been the result of Frankish influence.

basilican church was begun in the seventh century, rebuilt in the ninth and again in 1008. The central apse, which is the oldest part of the church, contains six rows of seats, of which the uppermost two are concentric with the wall, the rest being of a more shallow curve. In the centre is the bishop's throne, approached by a straight flight of steps. Under the seats, a narrow staircase leads to a tiny crypt. Altogether, of all the examples of the furnishing of the apse that have been preserved, this is one of the best. A row of six columns divides the choir and presbytery from the nave. Between these columns is a low marble parapet, or chancel rail, carved with animals and birds of purely Byzantine character (Pl. 3). The main body of the church and the aisles belong to the last rebuilding. The proportions are fine: the total

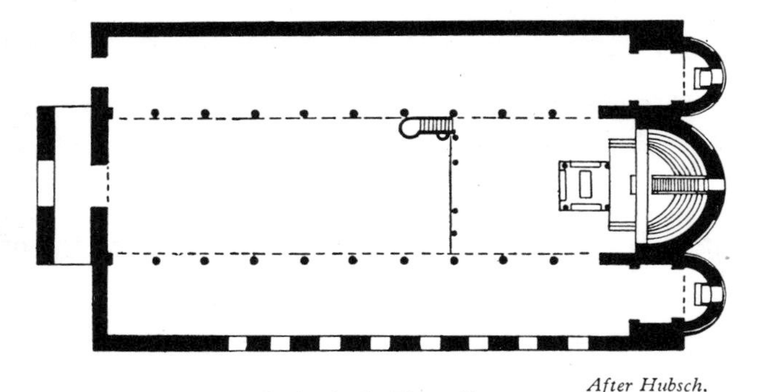

After Hubsch.

Cathedral, Torcello
Scale 50 *ft. to* 1 *in.*

width is about 70 feet, which is divided in the usual way—half to the nave and the other half to the two aisles. The capitals of the columns are the work of Byzantine carvers who, at the end of the tenth century and the beginning of the eleventh, were almost as skilled as their forefathers had been in the sixth. The capitals are free copies of Corinthian style, no two being exactly alike but all extraordinarily delicate, with deep undercutting. The remains of the baptistery may be traced in front of the west door immediately outside the portico. It consisted of an octagon of the seventh century, surrounded by a square, of later date, with niches at the corners.

Istria. The peninsula of Istria contains a number of basilican churches, of which the most interesting are the Cathedrals of Poreć and Grado. The former was built between the years 525 and 543 (contemporary with Sancta Sophia, Constantinople), and the latter about forty years later. Poreć Cathedral still retains its old atrium, a cloistered walk some 70 feet square, at the end of which is an octagonal baptistery, with a campanile of a later date beyond. Opposite the baptistery three doors lead directly into the basilica which, with its closely set ranks of marble columns, is very like S. Apollinare in Classe, though slightly smaller. 'The church at Parenzo,' [Poreć] according to Jackson,[1] 'is inferior to those of Ravenna in size alone; in beauty of execution it is quite their equal, while in the completeness of its plan, its atrium and baptistery, it surpasses them.' At the end of each aisle is an apse in the thickness of the wall—a favourite arrangement in Byzantine churches—while the central apse projects and is polygonal exter-

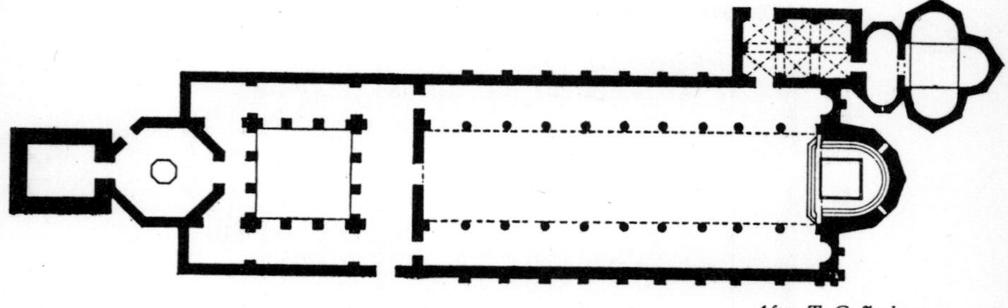

After T. G. Jackson.

Cathedral, Poreć.
Scale 50 ft. to 1 in.

nally, and, rather unusually, has four windows instead of three. It still retains its semi-circle of marble seats for the clergy and its episcopal throne at the centre. The lower wall surfaces are entirely covered with panelling of variegated marble, porphyry, serpentino, onyx and discs of mother-of-pearl. Above, the decoration is completed by glass mosaic, which in detail and composition is pure Byzantine.

The Cathedral of Grado is very different from that of Poreć. There is no atrium, and the baptistery is at the side. There is only one apse, the inside walls are severely plain, and the column capitals are nearly all classical Roman which have suffered considerable mutilation. The glory of the church is in its mosaic pavement of the sixth century, which extends over the greater part of the nave. It is very different from the 'Opus Alexandrinum' of the churches in Rome, being composed entirely of small tesserae

[1] T. G. Jackson, *Dalmatia, Quarnero and Istria*, Oxford, 1887.

of different colours which form inscriptions in Greek and Latin. The wide bands, large slabs and roundels which play so important a part in pavements of Roman churches do not occur here. The church was thoroughly examined at the end of the last century by Jackson, and among his discoveries was that the one original fretted window still surviving was not carved in marble or stone but was constructed in a kind of concrete, cast from a mould for repetition throughout the church (see p. 58).

CHURCHES IN CONSTANTINOPLE AND SALONIKA

Constantinople. It might have been expected that some of the earliest examples of Christian architecture would be found in the capital which was built by, and named after, the first Christian Emperor; such, however, is not the case. Nothing remains at

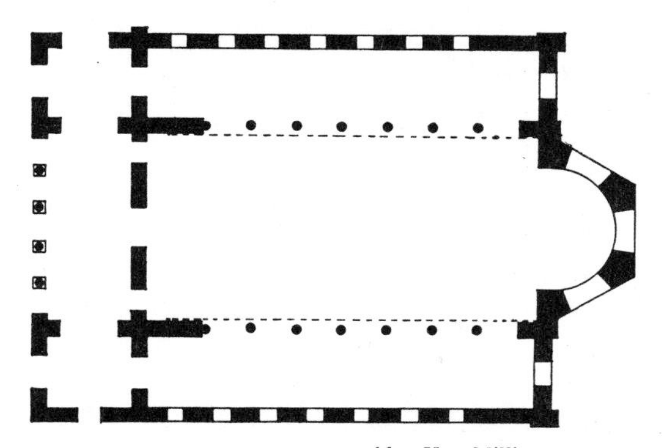

After Van Millingen.

S. John Studion, Constantinople.
Scale 50 ft. to 1 in.

Constantinople of buildings erected by Constantine, or his immediate successors, that have any connection with Christianity. The oldest existing church in that city was not built until 463, nearly a century and a half after the foundation of the city. It was basilican, not domed, and remained comparatively intact up to the present century, when, under an unusual weight of snow, its wooden roof collapsed. This church was dedicated to S. John and was attached to the Monastery of Studion. Its general disposition was similar to that of S. Agnese in Rome in having galleries over the aisles and a single apse. Today interest centres on the floor mosaics, which depict in extraordinarily beautiful detali little animals, birds and foliage.

Salonika. Salonika is far richer than Constantinople in early churches. Two of the earliest of basilican type are S. Demetrius, which has recently been rebuilt, and S. Paraskevi, which has now been cleared of Turkish additions. Texier and Pullan state, in their *Byzantine Architecture*, that both were originally of the fifth and sixth centuries. This shows that at that time the old Roman traditions were still strong in the East and had not yet been superseded by Byzantine methods of construction; although, if the Church of Sancta Sophia, in the same town, was really built in 495 as some authorities contend, it would be clear that, as at Ravenna, opinions differed as to the most suitable plan. The Church of

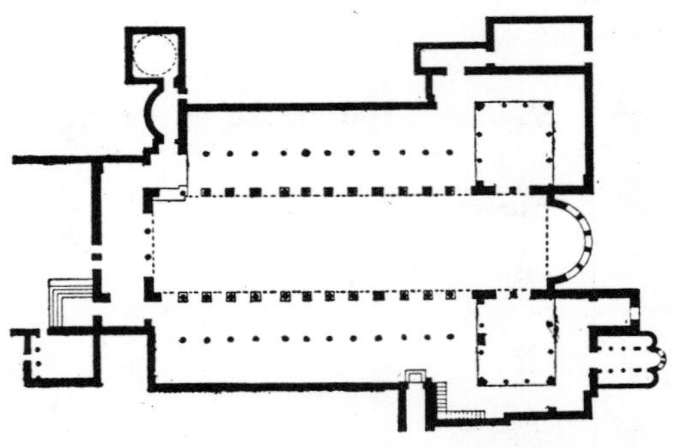

After Texier and Pullan.

S. Demetrius, Salonika.
Scale 100 *ft. to* 1 *in.*

S. Demetrius has a tragic history. It was captured by the Crusaders in 1185 and pillaged of all its treasures. It was converted into a mosque after the Turkish conquest in 1430, and in 1917 was completely devastated by fire. Since 1936 somewhat drastic steps have been taken towards its restoration.

Unlike S. Paraskevi, S. Demetrius had double aisles, and the columns returned at the west end to form a western aisle, or inner narthex. There was a large apse, which followed the Roman plan in being semi-circular externally as well as internally. The church had transepts at the east end that were unusual in that they were colonnaded and separated by the nave arcade, which continued the entire length of the church. There was thus no triumphal arch. Over the aisles were galleries for women. These stopped against the transepts, which were carried up the full height of the nave. The nave arcades were separated by piers into divisions of four or five bays each, as in the Churches of S. Clemente and S. Maria in Cosmedin, Rome. S. Demetrius is some two centuries earlier than they, so the probability is that this arrangement originated in the East.

COPTIC CHURCHES IN EGYPT

Egypt was a most flourishing centre of Christianity in the third century, and even later. Here developed the Coptic Church, whose beliefs in the Monophysite doctrine (that Christ was the indissoluble union of a divine and a human nature) led to a schism in the universal Church and the election of an independent Coptic leader—the Patriarch of Alexandria. With the spread of Mohammedanism, many of the Coptic churches were destroyed, or so thoroughly altered as to make it difficult to assess their relative importance. A number are earlier in date than the churches already described in this chapter, and it is more than probable that they suggested many of the features found in Italian churches. They are basilican almost without exception. The columns of the internal arcades are generally returned at the west end, as at S. Agnese, Rome, S. John, Constantinople, and S. Demetrius, Salonika. At the east end are always three altars, which are placed either in apses or in square recesses built into the thickness of the wall. The central and most important apse is called the 'haikal'. This tri-apsidal arrangement was evidently customary in Egypt long before it appeared in Italy. The seats for the clergy are generally arranged around the haikal, as are those at Torcello and Poreć, and behind the bishop's chair, in the centre, is a little niche in the wall for an ever-burning lamp. The east end is separated from the body of the church by a screen of wood with doors, sometimes inlaid with marbles and ivory and often covered with paintings, like the iconostasis of the Greek Church. Over the west end and the aisles are galleries for women. Most of the openings in the gallery fronts are now walled up, but originally they were filled with pierced screens, which allowed the worshippers behind them to follow the services but effectively shielded them from the view of the men below.

Most of the churches differ from the normal basilican church in that the nave is generally barrel-vaulted in stone, instead of having a timber roof. These barrel vaults, except in the earliest examples, are *pointed*. Many of the arches between the columns are also pointed, showing that this form was employed by the Copts in their churches long before it appeared in the West. Another important difference is that there are generally three domes, side by side, over the east end. This use of the dome does not necessarily indicate Byzantine influence. Some of the churches were built before the Byzantine era, and the dome had for centuries been a feature in the East. The early Coptic builders were well acquainted with its construction and probably used it before Constantine went to Byzantium; certainly long before Justinian built Sancta Sophia.

The exteriors of the churches are generally very bare and plain. Those built on the upper reaches of the Nile and in the desert differ very little in appearance from the ancient temples, since nothing shows on the outside except plain walls, crowned by a form of Egyptian gorge moulding, with perhaps one or more domes appearing behind. Some, indeed, were built inside old temples, as at Denderah. When the earlier churches were built in Cairo, some architectural expression was doubtless given to them externally, but after the Saracen invasion the Christians, as Dr. Butler states in his *Coptic Churches in Egypt*, were naturally concerned to avoid attracting the attention of the Mohammedans, and therefore surrounded their churches by other buildings to such an extent that from the outside they are completely uninteresting.

Inside they were decorated in much the same manner as the churches in Italy, and many of these decorations still remain. The walls are veneered with marble, or else covered with marble—not glass—mosaic, the designs of which are often very complicated. Occasionally the walls, piers and fittings are painted, but these paintings are generally of later date than the churches.

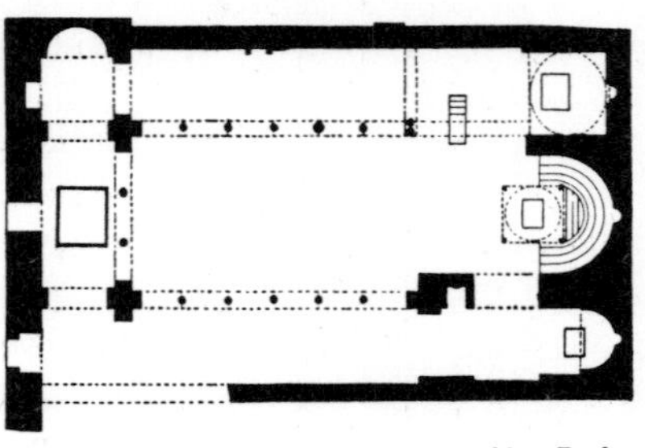

After Butler.

Church of Abou Sargah (S. Sergius).
Scale 50 ft. to 1 in.

Cairo. There are six churches within the ancient Roman fortress called Babylon, which is a part of the district of Old Cairo, and although they differ in many respects the Church of Abou Sargah, or S. Sergius, built in the eighth century, may be taken as representative. It is a fairly large church, with the nave arcades returned at the west end to form a narthex. Sunk in the floor of the narthex, on the central axis of the nave, is a baptismal tank known as the 'Epiphany tank', such as is frequently met with in other churches in Egypt. Over the narthex and aisles runs a gallery, and two of the apsidal ends still retain their brick domes, which are plastered outside. Below the central dome is a small crypt.

Desert churches. The desert of Nitria, north-west of Cairo, is famous as the first place to which the anchorites in the early days of Christianity retired from the world. It was here that monasticism began, and many of the Coptic monasteries in this region

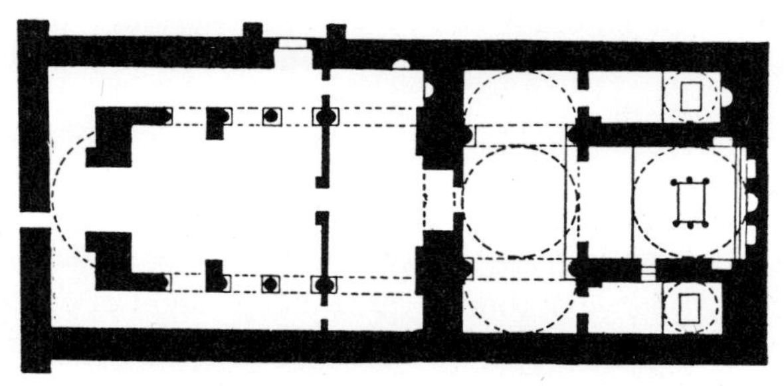

After Butler.

Dair-as-Suriane, Egypt.
Scale 50 ft. to 1 in.

were founded over early chapels or oratories close to the Mediterranean. The majority of the churches follow the basilican plan described above, but one, the monastic church of Dair-as-Suriane, which was founded by Greeks from Syria in the sixth century, has a number of interesting features. The arches of the arcade are pointed, and so is the barrel vault which covers the nave. Over the centre of the transept is a dome, supported on the north and south sides by transverse arches, beyond which are semi-domes.[1] The Sanctuary is screened off by folding doors, which Dr. Butler states are of the eighth century and the oldest of their type in Egypt.

[1] The arrangement is not unlike that in Sancta Sophia, Constantinople, built in the same century, except that there the semi-domes are east and west instead of north and south.

In the Church of Dairbaramous, which is smaller, the pointed arch is also used throughout for the nave arches and vaults, the latter being strengthened by transverse ribs built across from pier to pier. The principal dome over the haikal is carried on stalactite pendentives, such as were afterwards common in Mohammedan work. A. Gayet, in his *L'Art Copte*, states that it was from the Coptic churches that the Saracens learned the use of the pointed arch and the stalactite vault; or rather, that as the Saracens compelled the Coptic workmen to build for them, the Copts naturally followed, in the mosques, the methods they had been accustomed to employ in their own churches.

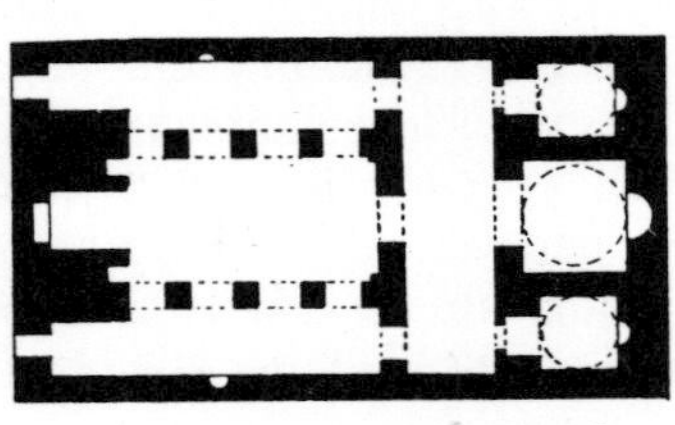

After Hamilton.

Dairbaramous, Egypt.
Scale 50 *ft. to* 1 *in.*

CHURCHES IN SYRIA

The story of Syria, as far as it concerns us here, is almost entirely limited to the fifth and sixth centuries. The country was peopled chiefly by Greeks who, though quite independent of other Christian countries, evolved there a style of considerable ingenuity which might have had great effect on the architecture of western Europe. Unfortunately, however, in 639 the country fell into the hands of the Saracens, who completely put an end to Christian building. The latest date that has been found carved on any church is 609. With one exception—the Church of S. Simeon Stylites at Kalat Seman—all are small, but the planning is often very original. Only two examples are Byzantine in character (see p. 62), the others being oblong, or basilican in plan. A special characteristic is the use of exceptionally large blocks of stone, on which the masons worked architectural features without having any apparent knowledge of their constructional origin or significance. For instance, many of the doorways and windows have arched openings, but instead of constructing these in several voussoirs, the builders preferred to cut the arch out of a single slab, or out of three or five stones laid on their horizontal beds. A similar approach is to be found in the treatment of pilasters, in which the capital and upper part of the shaft are worked in one stone and the lower part of the shaft and the base in another. The detail of carving is very refined and reminiscent more of classical Greek than contemporary Byzantine art; but there is a certain heavy and cumbersome quality about the architecture, and a lack of scale which is caused chiefly by the use of large stones.

Exteriors. The external treatment shows considerably more ornamentation than was the rule in the West. There is always a narthex at the west end, and over this there is often an open gallery, like a loggia, having columns in front. The windows are set back in the wall behind, an arrangement which has an excellent effect. This method was adopted later in some of the Romanesque churches in Italy, of which S. Ambrogio, Milan, is the most famous. The narthex is often flanked by low towers at the ends of the aisles, crowned by pediments, as at Tourmenin. The principal doorway is always at the west end, but one peculiarity of these churches is the number of additional entrances at the sides. The east end sometimes has three apses, but a single apse at the end of the nave is more common, and this is generally built within the thickness of the wall. Some apses are semi-circular inside and out, others are polygonal externally, and one, at Tourmenin, is polygonal on both sides. The projecting apses of S. Simeon are decorated with two tiers of attached columns, which start from the plinth and finish under an oversailing course at the top of the wall. This method of decorating walls, which was doubtless suggested by the columned and arcaded classical remains, also found favour with the later Romanesque builders in the West. In the Churches of S. Trophime at Arles and S. Gilles in Provence a similar treatment is found. Both Syrian and western examples were based on Roman work, and the mouldings of the pediments and archivolts, and the fluting of the pilasters, are identical with what is found, quite independently, in Provence. It is not suggested that the Romanesque builders copied Syrian churches—indeed, they had no opportunity, for Syria was in the hands of the Saracens—but it is interesting, and not a little curious, to note that although some centuries and many hundreds of miles intervened, there is a marked similarity in the work of the different countries. The builders, both eastern and western, drew their inspiration from the same source and employed it in much the same manner. Where Syrian work differed chiefly from the Romanesque was in its greater refinement of detail.

Interiors. The most interesting of the churches are those in which piers, and not columns, are used for the nave arcades, the bays being very few in number and of considerable span. The arrangement is, therefore, closer in general character to the traditional Roman than to the Early Christian basilican churches which we have already described. A further point of resemblance is the introduction of transverse arches, which divide the nave along its length in the manner of the classical Basilica of Constantine.

Roueiha. In the church at Roueiha the arcade consists of three arches on each side, which spring from stumpy piers, about 10 feet high, T-shaped in plan. These piers are about 33 feet apart from

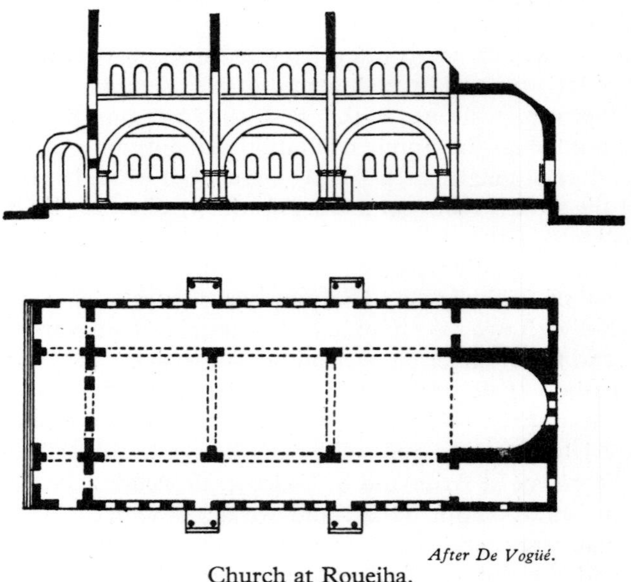

After De Vogüé.

Church at Roueiha.
Scale 50 ft. to 1 in.

centre to centre, and from them transverse arches, slightly less in span, are thrown across the nave. Two porches on each side provide additional entrances. The windows are almost continuous in the aisles and there are four to each bay of the clerestory. Except for these there is little to give the church scale, yet the effect of the long nave, divided into three rectangular bays by the transverse arches, must have been extremely dignified.

S. Simeon Stylites. Of the churches in which columns rather than piers were used, that of the Monastery of S. Simeon Stylites at Kalat Seman is the most remarkable and interesting. It consists of four basilicas, grouped together in the form of a cross, around a central unroofed octagon, about 92 feet across. The eastern arm terminates in a large apse, flanked by two smaller apses which were built later. In the centre of the octagon stands the base of the pillar on which S. Simeon is said to have lived for over thirty years without ever descending. S. Simeon died in 459, and the church was probably begun soon afterwards, but it was not completed until the sixth century. The total length of the church from east to west is about 330 feet, and from south to north 300 feet. The arms are connected by aisles on the canted sides of the central octagon, and opening out of each is a small apse, lit by windows; these apses may have been used as chapels. Altogether this is a most ingenious plan, constituting in effect four churches in one. It is larger than any other church in Syria, and has no counterpart anywhere.

Stone Vaults. The churches in the north, already mentioned, had timber roofs, generally supported by corbels from the clerestory wall, but the churches in the southern part of Syria, in what is known as the Haouran, were vaulted with stone. In the secular basilica of Chaqua, which is of the third or fourth century, the vault was similar to that over the Baths of Diana at Nîmes. Transverse semi-circular arches, about 12 feet apart, spanned the central portion of the building, and on the extrados of these rested long stones which reached from one arch to another and formed a continuous barrel vault. In the church at Tafkha, instead of a barrel vault a flat ceiling was carried in the same way. In the Haouran stone was easily obtainable, whereas wood was exceedingly scarce; for this reason, everything was of stone, even to the doors.

Summary. The most noticeable peculiarity of Early Christian churches generally, when compared with the later Romanesque and Gothic, is their spaciousness. This is owing to differences in proportion. Internally, the basilicas have much greater width and less height than the churches which came after; and also they have their columns much closer together. Few Gothic churches have, like S. Apollinare in Classe, a nave nearly 50 feet wide—York Minster is the only one in England with this width—and not even Milan Cathedral is as wide as S. Paul Outside the Walls. The close spacing of the columns between the nave and aisles necessitates many bays, and this multiplication of bays is most useful in giving direction and scale. No Gothic nave has anything approaching the number of bays (twenty to twenty-four) found in the large Early Christian basilicas. Each bay of the arcade in S. Apollinare in Classe is 12 feet from centre to centre; at Torcello it is 11 feet; and even in the great Church of S. Paul Outside the Walls, Rome, it measures only 13 feet 4 inches. In Gothic England about 20 feet from centre to centre is usual. In France and Germany the intercolumniation is greater, and in Italy it is sometimes as much as 60 feet, as in the cathedrals at Bologna and Florence. The simple cylindrical column of Early Christian architecture almost always achieves a satisfactory effect, and it is doubtful if all the ingenuity displayed by the Gothic architects in their clustered piers ever succeeded in producing a combination which equals in dignity the simple column. It may be urged that a multiplicity of columns is something of a drawback, but, in point of fact, it does not really offer the same obstruction as half the number of piers, twice the size, such as are customary in Gothic work. The one feature which the Christian basilica lacked, and which the later Romanesque designers considered so important, was the sense of height, that aspiring tendency which the mediaeval builders achieved, even at some sacrifice of spaciousness.

CIRCULAR BUILDINGS

Early Christian circular and multangular buildings in Italy, although not so valuable architecturally as those of similar form built under Byzantine suzerainty, are interesting as connecting links between Roman work and the fully developed domical style of the East. They differ from Roman precedents in exactly the same way as the Early Christian basilica differed from the rectangular pagan temple; the columns are transferred from the outside to the inside. In place of the peristyle there is the internal colonnade, little or no attempt being made at external decoration.

This centralised type of building was chiefly devised for baptism and for burial—for those Christian ceremonies which marked the entry to and the departure from the Church on earth. Only a few, if any, were originally intended to be churches. Architecturally, they fall into two classes: those which are constructed with timber roofs, like the basilicas, and those which are domed, in the manner of the early Roman tombs. The buildings of the former class have thin walls, and columns to define the different spaces, and those of the latter have thick walls to carry the dome; in some cases—as in S. George, Salonika—there are no columns inside at all. When there are domes they seldom show on the outside, since they are generally covered with a tiled timber roof.

S. Stephano Rotondo. By far the most remarkable of the circular buildings with timber roofs is that now known as S. Stephano Rotondo, in Rome, built, according to Cattaneo, between the years 468 and 482. A reduced copy of it, now in ruins, was built in Perugia about a century later. Two similar buildings were erected by Constantine at Jerusalem, one to mark the spot of the Ascension of Christ, the other to cover the Holy Sepulchre.[1]

In the Church of S. Stephano two concentric rings of columns define the central area and the surrounding aisles. Much of the outer aisle was destroyed and a wall has been built between the columns of the outer range, except at the east. The central portion is now divided in two by higher columns which were not part of the original design. On the wall over them rest the tie beams of a flat ceiling, and some authorities contend that this central part was originally open to the sky. The accompanying plan illustrates the building in its present and its probable original state. There are twenty-two columns in the inner arcade, with roughly-carved Ionic capitals carrying stone lintels. The outer colonnade is Corinthian and Ionic, and arched. It is divided by piers into eight bays with either five or six columns to each bay. All the columns have been taken from older buildings, and all have a dosseret over. If Cattaneo's date is correct, this is probably the

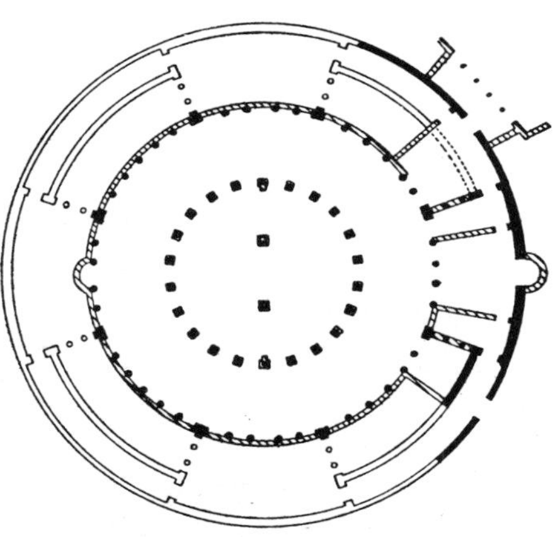

After Cattaneo.

S. Stephano Rotondo, Rome. Shaded portions represent later work.

Scale 50 ft. to 1 in.

[1] This circular plan was perpetuated in the West by the Knights Templar and the Knights Hospitaller of S. John of Jerusalem. Examples in England are S. Sepulchre, Cambridge, S. Sepulchre, Northampton, and the restored Temple Church in London.

earliest example of the use of the dosseret. The floor is level throughout, and there are no signs now that the central part was ever sunk, as it would have been had the building been a baptistery.

Baptistery of Constantine. The Baptistery of Constantine, attached to the great Church of S. John Lateran in Rome, is an octagonal building, divided into a central portion and surrounding aisle by eight massive porphyry columns, which are crowned by capitals of different Orders, with smaller columns over them. The central part has an octagonal dome of timber construction, and the aisle is covered by a flat ceiling level with the springing of the dome; but the building has been so altered at different times that it is difficult to say what was the original design. It is manifest, however, that the upper columns are too slight to carry any heavier construction than that now employed; and the thinness of the outer walls proves that one dome to cover the whole building was never contemplated.

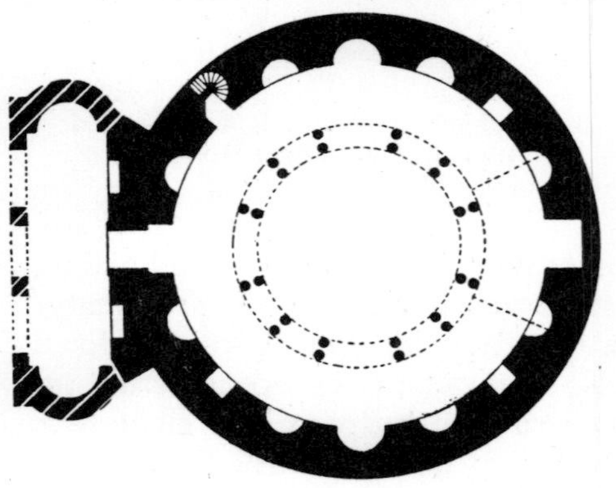

After Hubsch.
Tomb of S. Costanza, Rome.
Scale 50 ft. to 1 in.

Tomb of Costanza. The Tomb of Costanza, the daughter of Constantine, is outside the walls close to the Church of S. Agnese. It was probably built in the fourth century and later converted into a baptistery. It is the most interesting of the domed circular buildings in Rome.[1] The twenty-four internal

[1] At Nocera, between Naples and Paestum, is a building, now a baptistery, of similar plan, with coupled columns, a central dome and vaulted aisles; but it is much later in date.

granite columns, grouped in pairs, are more than sufficient to carry the central dome and to resist the thrust of the barrel vault that covers the surrounding aisle. The building is very Roman in all its characteristics, naturally enough, since it dates from the fourth century. Above each pair of columns is an entablature, from the top of which spring the arches. The barrel vault over the aisle is similar to those covering the galleries in the great theatres and amphitheatres, and is enriched with fine mosaics contemporary with the building itself. The central dome does not appear outside, since a circular wall is carried up around it to support a timber roof.

S. George, Salonika. S. George, Salonika, is an interesting example of the type of church, consisting of a circular nave and an oblong, apsidal-ended bema, or chancel, which afterwards became a favourite in Germany, Italy and other countries. Whether the two parts of the building were built simultaneously is uncertain; probably the circular portion is Roman and the bema, which has much thinner walls, is a Christian addition. The former is 80 feet in diameter, and is surrounded by a wall 18 feet thick, into the lower part of which are set eight big niches, like those of the Pantheon, except that they are all rectangular in plan. Two of these niches form entrances to the church, and a third is cut through to afford access to the chancel. Over the semi-circular dome is a low-pitched roof, and the outside wall, considerably thinned, is carried up above the springing of the dome to support the tie beams and rafters, as at S. Costanza. This arrangement, whether Roman or Early Christian, must be regarded as an early example of the custom, afterwards common in mediaeval churches in the West, of covering a vault or dome with a protecting timber roof, the vault itself being quite thin, and very different from the

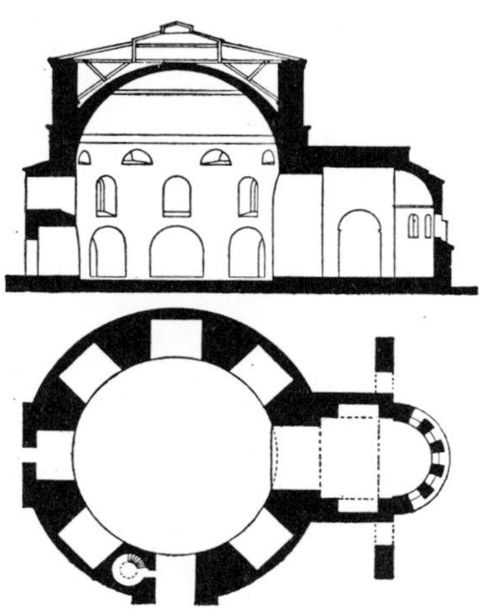

After Texier and Pullan.

S. George, Salonika.
Scale 100 *ft. to* 1 *in.*

thick, concrete vaults of the Romans. The wall being carried up, its weight exerts a vertical pressure, and counteracts to some extent the lateral thrust of the dome. The church is lit by lunettes in the dome, just above the springing, and by wide, semi-circular-headed lights below.

CHAPTER IV

BYZANTINE ARCHITECTURE

History, Characteristics and Style

At Constantinople, the East joins with the West, and here it was that the first of the great Christian styles had its rise and reached its zenith. From the East it inherited a love for colour and a delight in rich materials for interior decoration, which contributed greatly towards its success; from the West, fine scale and bold construction. For its development it was largely dependent on Greek craftsmen, who were released from the limitations which had hampered their work in the days of the old Roman Empire. They were on their native soil, and the old Greek artistic instinct awoke to new life in the greater freedom of a new city, a new religion and, to some extent, a new construction.

The city of Constantinople was founded in 326 by Constantine the Great, who enlarged the old Greek settlement of Byzantium, and was inaugurated as the new seat of imperial government on the 11th of May, 330. To signify its political importance, it was at first called New Rome, but later it was renamed to commemorate its founder. The creation of a new capital in the East was the result of many causes, and had some forty years earlier been foreshadowed by the policy of the Emperor Diocletian in making his capital at Spalato on the Dalmatian coast. It was already recognised that the wealth of the Empire lay in the East, and that the western provinces, besides being a source of considerable expense, had little material wealth to contribute to an overgrown court. No longer were there dreams of conquest and extension. The Empire had reached, indeed had passed, the limits of administrative convenience. The urgent requirements at the close of the third century were the maintenance of the wealthy grain-producing eastern provinces, and the repulse of the persistent assaults of the Persians. Rome had long ceased to be the centre of political gravity. In these latter days, that vast assemblage of buildings had largely housed an impoverished population of slaves and beggars, and had become a serious drain on the public purse without having even commercial importance. When Constantine established the new centre of government at Byzantium he was only following a policy, laid down by his predecessors, which seemed essential to the preservation of Roman supremacy in the East. Constantine was astute in selecting that particular point where Europe and Asia nearly met, and in appreciating the desirability of associating the new Christian religion with surroundings relatively free from pagan connections.

The importance of Constantinople as a cultural and economic centre cannot be over-emphasised. It was not only situated on a promontory of enormous strategic value, controlling the caravan route from Persia and India, and the sea and land routes from China (via the Caspian and Black Seas) to the Mediterranean, but it was also the artistic focus of the known world. From east and west travellers and traders, artists and architects, flocked to the new city. Constantinople absorbed the distinctive qualities of them all—Greeks, Romans and Orientals—and disseminated throughout the Empire that fusion of styles which we call Byzantine. In this New Rome it was natural at first that the Roman style should predominate, but before a couple of centuries had passed the new and coherent Byzantine style had evolved.

Periods. Byzantine architecture is divided into three periods, each of which possesses distinct characteristics. The first and greatest period is that of the sixth century, when, under Justinian (527–565), a new and powerful movement, culminating in the building of Sancta Sophia, Constantinople, set a standard and an ideal which influenced all work for many centuries, not only in the Empire around Constantinople but also in Italy and France. After the death of Justinian, the Empire was involved in struggles with the Persians and later with the Saracens, so that little survived of the architecture or art. There followed a long-continued dispute known as the Iconoclastic Controversy, which raged around the questions of image-worship, encouraged the destruction of much interior decoration and drove many of the most skilled workers out of the Empire.

The second period began in the ninth century when, under the dominion of the House of Macedonia (867–1059), an artistic revival dawned. This revival was especially marked in Venetian territories, where S. Mark's rivalled Sancta Sophia in the magnificence of its architecture; but it was not until some years later, under the Comneni (1081–1185), that its revival bore fruit.

Most of the existing churches in Constantinople, in Armenia and in other parts of the Empire, belonged to this latter part of the second period. Meanwhile, power in the West was growing, and the Byzantine Empire, already involved in struggles to regain its possessions in Asia Minor from the Seljuk Turks, was subjected to attacks from the Normans and the Venetians. The Empire had by this time shrunk to less than half its size, and the Fourth Crusade provided the western powers with the opportunity to attack the capital itself. In 1204 Constantinople fell to the Crusaders and the city was looted on a scale hitherto unparalleled. The immediate result was a great revival of the arts in the West and a decline in the East.

The third great period was associated with the family of Paleologus, who assumed control in 1261 after entering into a treaty with Genoa, which now rivalled Venice as a trading power in the Mediterranean. The Paleologus period (1261–1453) represented the last great flowering of Byzantine architecture. The shrunken Empire was confined to Constantinople, Salonika and Greece. It was no longer wealthy, and the quality of its architecture had to depend on simplicity rather than on expensive materials and enrichment. The Empire was now faced with the gradual advance of the Turks, and piece by piece the Empire was lost, until in 1453 Constantinople fell to Mohammed the Conqueror. So terminated the history of Constantinople as a source of inspiration to European art and architecture, but the seeds already sown flourished with surprising magnificence even beyond the limits of the original Empire: in Russia—at Kiev, Novgorod and Moscow—the splendours of the Empire were reproduced; in Rumania, the painted churches of Sukavita and Voronet rank among the most remarkable examples of Byzantine achievement, although built two centuries after the collapse of Constantinople. Throughout the Balkan world, the Byzantine style continued to make itself felt, and even in Constantinople the Mohammedan successors copied its essential structural principles in the building of mosques for the Faithful.

The Pendentive. The essential characteristic of Byzantine architecture is the carrying of a dome over a square space. This is generally achieved by the use of pendentives, which are curved triangles composed of bricks or stone laid between supporting arches. They are, in effect, the portions of a hemisphere which remain when its sides are cut vertically and its top horizontally, the diameter of the hemisphere being equal to the diagonal of the square below. While the Byzantines could not claim to have invented this method, since there were buildings of an earlier date in which it was adopted, they must be given credit for being the first to use it on a large scale. The origin of the pendentive is still uncertain; Choisy[1] claimed that it originated some centuries before, in Asia Minor, but recent excavations at Ur in Mesopotamia suggest that it may even have been adopted some four thousand years before Christ. G. T. Rivoira, in his *Lombardic Architecture* (1910), maintained with a wealth of documentary evidence that the use of the pendentive could logically be traced from Etruscan times and that the Romans, and later the Byzantines, were simply continuing a well-established practice. Nevertheless, wherever the pendentive may have originated, it remains that the Byzantines were the first to grapple with the problem of its use in a building as vast as Sancta Sophia; for to raise a dome, 107 feet in diameter, on piers and arches, so that it should spring some 150 feet above all the other parts of the building, demanded a constructional skill far beyond anything that had been achieved before.

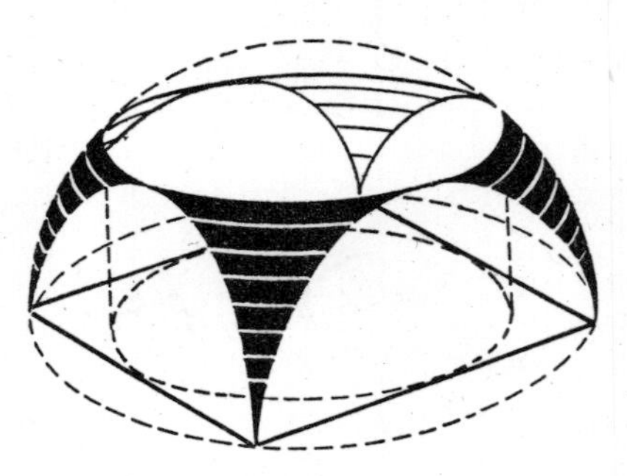

Pendentives.

The Squinch. The pendentive was not the only method adopted in effecting the passage to a circle. In place of pendentives, the Byzantines sometimes substituted corbelling. This was generally employed over an octagonal plan, the stones being laid across the corners to make sixteen sides, then a second course laid so that the plan became thirty-two-sided. From this the change to a circle presented no difficulty. A second expedient, commonly called the 'squinch', or pseudo-pendentive, was more common and more satisfactory. This consisted of an arch which, springing across the angles of the square, changed the space to be domed into an octagon; in small buildings, the dome

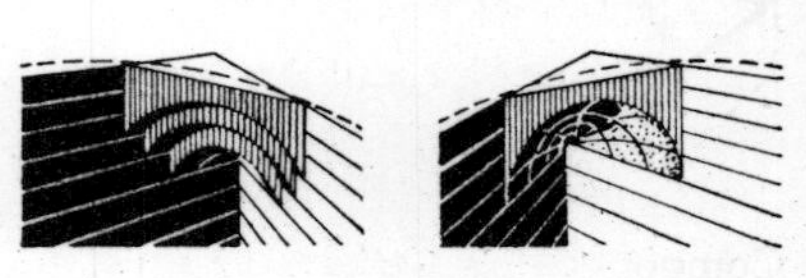

Squinch.

[1] *L'Art de bâtir chez les Byzantins*, Paris, 1883.

might be placed directly upon this, but in large buildings small pendentives were introduced above to transform the octagon into a circle upon which the dome could rest. The area on the underside could be treated in two ways: either by a series of smaller arches (see Pl. 7), or by the creation of a hood-shaped angle niche.

Simple and Compound Domes. Domes were of two kinds: simple and compound. In the simple dome, the dome and pendentive were in one, both being parts of the same hemisphere and the height of the dome being only a little greater than that of the side semi-circular arches.

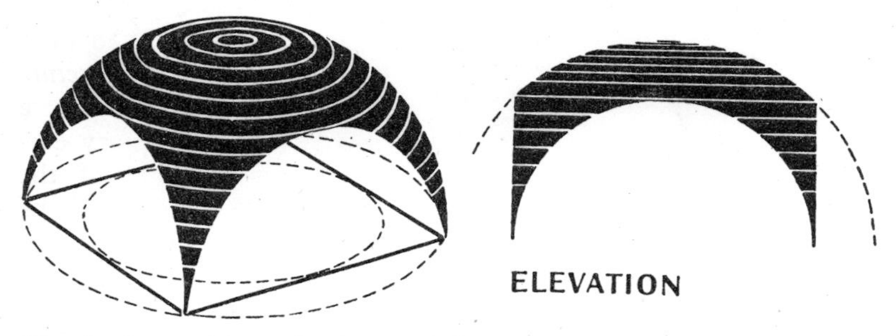

Simple dome, the pendentives and dome being part of the same hemisphere.

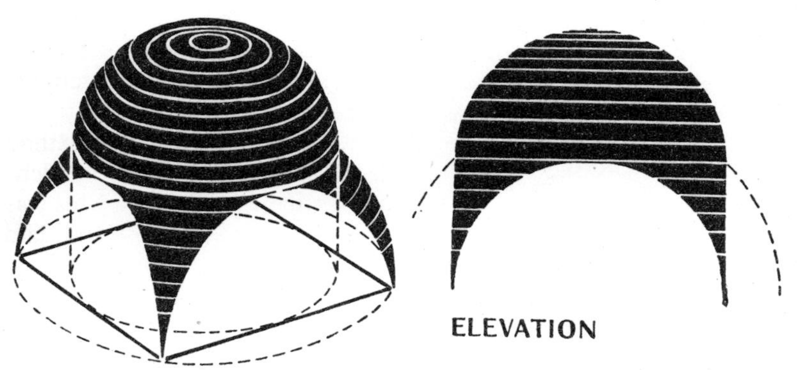

Compound dome, the dome being a hemisphere set above the pendentives.

In the compound dome, three methods were followed; all gave greater height, and were consequently used in all important buildings. In the first period (sixth century), the dome was either a simple hemisphere or melon-shaped,[1] starting directly

[1] Melon-shaped: this is the usual term given to domes having convolutions similar to those of a cantaloup.

from the top of the circle formed by pendentives or from the octagon formed by squinches. The melon-shaped dome was reinforced by the convolutions, which acted as ribs and to some

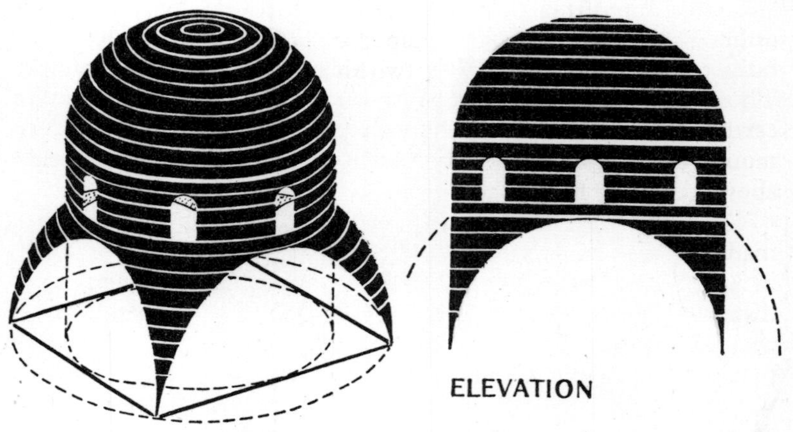

Compound dome with drum.

extent did away with the need for pendentives. In the later periods (eleventh and fourteenth centuries), the dome was raised upon a cylindrical wall or drum, enhancing the external appearance and providing a vertical surface for windows and decoration.

Lighting of Domes. In churches having domes over drums, the windows were always in the drum, leaving the surface of the dome unbroken; where there were no drums the windows were in the dome itself, immediately above the springing. In some cases the lower part of the dome was thickened for half its height by a vertical outer face, which formed on the outside a pseudo drum. The carrying up of this face was a good expedient constructionally, for it provided weight above the haunches of the dome and helped to neutralise its thrusts. The drums were seldom circular in plan externally, but many-sided, and the angles were often enriched by marble shafts. In the second and third periods there was no radical change in the plan of the church, but there was a

Section through the dome of the Church of S. Luke of Stiris, showing thickening of lower part of the dome to form pseudo-drum.

marked decrease in size, and a tendency for the drums to become much taller and the windows so elongated that they became mere slits.

Construction of Domes and Vaults. Byzantine domes and vaults, unlike the Roman, were of no great thickness, and were generally built of brick, although in some cases cut stone was employed. The domed buildings in Ravenna were constructed of hollow earthenware jars or urns, so formed that one jar fitted into the mouth of another. Such domes had low-pitched timber roofs above them to protect them from the weather.

To avoid the use of wood centering, the Byzantines adopted many expedients, most of which they learned from the workmen in Asia Minor who, having little or no timber, had been obliged to dispense with it almost entirely. For their small domes of stone, the only centering consisted of a revolving central post, with rods fixed at the top which could be moved at will to wherever support was required. One rod defined the inner radius of the dome, the other the outer. The stones were laid with quick-setting cement, and the work on the construction of the dome probably proceeded in a leisurely manner, one course being allowed to set before the next was added. In their brick domes, the beds of the bricks did not radiate from the centre of the dome, but approximately from points on the springing line opposite. A little 'coaxing' was required at the apex to close the aperture, but otherwise there was no difficulty. In their barrel vaults, only the lower courses would be built with centering and laid to radiate in the usual manner; above these the bricks or stones would be laid in a series of arches or layers, as in the Assyrian and Egyptian vaults, each inclining towards a back retaining wall.

Altogether, Byzantine construction was more skilful than Roman; there was less of brute strength about it, and more science. Copper or lead, and in the final period cement or tiles, were laid on the extrados, so that the dome visible from the outside was the same dome as seen from the inside. The only exceptions were at Ravenna, where domes were covered by a separate tiled roof, as in Early Christian examples (see pp. 43–45), and at S. Mark's, Venice, where lofty, lead-covered, timber-framed cupolas of a distinctly oriental pattern were added in the thirteenth century.

Wall Construction and Materials. The Byzantine builders, although they adopted the plan of few and large piers, seldom employed concrete. The walls and piers were generally of brick throughout, although stone and combinations of stone and brick were sometimes used. The bricks were like those used by the Romans, large and flat; they were about an inch-and-a-half thick, and the mortar joints were generally of the same thickness. Externally, the walls were sometimes faced entirely with stone, but more often, courses of brick and stone were used together in varying proportions. In the magnificent walls and towers which guarded the land side of Constantinople, brick was used in bands of about five courses, with from five to ten courses of stone in between. This technique was simply a continuation of the old Roman tradition. In Constantinople, where a good building stone was not available, the churches were often built in two or three courses of brick and single courses of stone in turn; in the churches of Greece, single courses of brick, and stone or marble, alternated, and bricks on edge were placed in the vertical joints between the stones. This treatment was exceedingly decorative, and many variations were adopted to relieve the flat surfaces of the walls; brick, or marble, was occasionally cut into diamonds, triangles or squares and arranged in bands, or bricks would be set diagonally to provide string courses.

Interior Decoration. Internal finishes were invariably of an applied character; that is to say, the carcase of the building was built first and allowed to settle before the mosaics and marble linings for the doors, windows and walls were added. This was a sound practice, for no injury could result to the decorations through the dampness inherent in new work or through uneven settlement of the structure. In the first and second periods, the lower portions of the walls were panelled with thin slabs of marble, cut and polished so as to show their 'figure' to the best advantage; the upper parts, together with the vaults and domes, were generally covered by glass mosaic. In the third period, when finances were low, the walls and domes were more often plastered and decorated with paintings in oil or tempera.

Byzantine mural decoration was in close harmony with the architecture. Where mosaic was used, it was carried over the vaults and domes without interruption. The various surfaces were used to provide a series of pictures of Biblical incidents and characters to teach and assist the illiterate, and to overawe the spectator with the splendour and richness of their design and execution. The arrangement of the decoration, and all details of design, had to conform to a standard pattern laid down by the ecclesiastical authority. The majestic head of Christ Pantocrator gazed down from the dome, the four Evangelists, manuscripts in hand, occupied the pendentives, while the Virgin stood, or was enthroned, in the conch of the apse. And all around, every available space was filled with episodes in the life of Our Lord, and with a procession of saints and martyrs, each having his particular character inscribed in coloured letters on a golden background. The figures were tall and dignified, simple in outline and clad in stiff, highly conventional drapery. Mosaics are ideal for the decoration of curved surfaces, because the glass takes and reflects the light in a far more effective way than can be achieved on flat wall areas, where the light is more likely to be evenly distributed.

In the last period of the Empire, when mural painting took the place of mosaic work, the artists showed much greater freedom in design. There was still no attempt at naturalism, and the craftsmanship was of great refinement and delicacy. In contrast to the western practice of shading, white highlights were used to suggest modelling and form. In all periods the floors of the churches were treated with mosaic work, which followed very closely Roman prototypes, with the incidental introduction of Christian emblems. The designs were generally geometrical in character and composed of many coloured marbles, incorporating horizontal slices from porphyry or marble columns encircled by lacing bands of inlaid cubes.

Carving. Byzantine carving was not deep; it was often little more than incised work, and the modelling was very slight. But it must be remembered that the material used was in nearly all cases marble, and that the deep undercutting suitable for soft stone was inappropriate. The Byzantines loved the interlacing endless knot; they carved it on capitals and on the slabs of pulpits, parapets and other fittings. Although they undercut sparingly, they used the drill freely at all periods to form little holes of deep shadow. The finest mural carving is in the spandrels over the two tiers of arches in Sancta Sophia, Constantinople, but even this is simply an all-over decoration. The oriental outlook which stimulated the iconoclastic movement resulted in a ban on sculptural representation of the saintly or divine form, and encouraged the elaboration of non-representational ornament. Such statues and portrait busts as have survived are of a purely Roman character, and even in the final phase of Byzantine development, when artists appear to have been less restricted by ecclesiastical domination, figure representation showed little attempt at natural expression, the figure being suggested by simple incised lines. The finest Byzantine carving is to be found in miniature works in ivory and steatite, and on the capitals and the stone panels which formed a base of the iconostasis—that screen which extended across the eastern end of the church and cut off the High Altar from the nave (Pl. 3).

Capitals. The variety in the capitals was endless. It is true that in the finest churches—Sancta Sophia, San Vitale and S. Mark's—capitals in reciprocal positions were substantially alike,

After Texier and Pullan.

Byzantine column capitals; on the left, wind-blown acanthus. From S. Demetrius, Salonika.

slight differences being due to the fact that the workmen were left free to interpret the given design in their own way. The result was that a broad effect was produced and a hard, mechanical appearance avoided. Byzantine capitals often had impost blocks, or dosserets, above them. The origin of these is uncertain; it has been suggested that they were simply an expedient to give additional height to Roman columns which were being used second hand from classical buildings (see p. 17). W. R. Lethaby, in his *Mediaeval Art*, suggests, however, that the delicate projecting carving of Corinthian types of capital was relieved of the weight above by the interposition of the plain dosseret block, which was so reduced below as to rest only on the centre of the capital. The use of the dosseret was also particularly valuable when there was a need for a thick or rectangular impost. At Sancta Sophia, the dosseret occurred only over some of the subordinate capitals. Many Byzantine capitals were free renderings of the antique Corinthian; many others followed the Sancta Sophia form, the most effective of the latter being carved in imitation of basket-work.

Columns. The columns were, as a rule, monoliths of marble, like those in Roman work, and had an entasis.[1] Many of the columns in Sancta Sophia have annulets (bands of bronze) immediately under their capitals and above their bases. These are not so much decorative features as a precaution against the columns' splitting or scaling, because of the weight over them and because, being monoliths, they are not placed on their natural bed. A few of the columns are similarly banded in the middle.

Windows. Windows in the first period were semi-circular-headed openings, either single and of no great size, or of considerable width and divided into two or three lights by columns or thin strips of unmoulded marble. These strips might be no more than 3 inches wide, but 12 to 18 inches deep. The mullions in the second period retained the earlier proportions, but were enriched with attached shafts of circular or octagonal section. They were placed in the middle of the opening and had capitals with small projections at the sides, but great projections at the front and back in order to reach to the inner and outer faces of the wall. They might almost be termed corbels, not capitals. The lower portion of each window, to about a third of its height, was often filled with thin marble slabs, sculptured on the outside, which allowed a certain

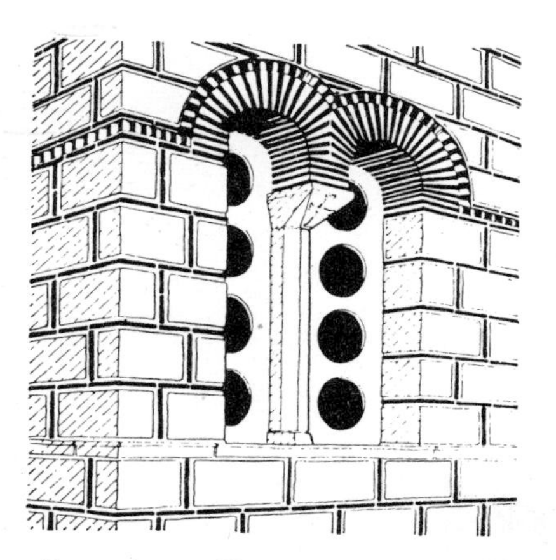

Byzantine walling, showing brick and stone construction.

[1] Occasionally, but very rarely, columns are met with which are not of the usual cylindrical form, but are oval in plan. Such are those in a little tomb at Messina, and in a small ruined church at Olympia.

amount of light to shine through. The upper part was filled with slabs of marble, alabaster, cement or stone, which were pierced with circles, squares or richer patterns. In the third period, windows were very simple, tall, narrow slits, semi-circular-headed and relieved on the outside by brick-work decoration. The pierced openings of the slab infilling were sometimes fitted with glass, sometimes left open. Whether the glass was coloured or not seems uncertain. Lethaby and Swainson, in their work on Sancta Sophia, say that although coloured glass may have been used in the smaller windows of the church, 'it is hardly possible to conceive of the great windows being anything else than white glass.'[1]

After T. G. Jackson.

Byzantine window, from Grado Cathedral.

Plan Types. Plans of Byzantine churches fall into five main categories, the first two being merely developments of already well-established classical forms, and the last three purely Byzantine contributions, involving, as has already been remarked, that essential structural feature—the dome over a square space.

I THE BASILICA

Details of the basilican type of church have been described in previous chapters. The differences between those built in Rome and those built under Byzantine suzerainty are slight. Roman basilicas were chiefly lit by clerestory windows, and the walls of the aisles were blind; but in the eastern examples it was customary to provide additional lighting in the aisles, and in Syria the shortage of timber and the abundance of stone encouraged the development

[1] Simpson did not consider this at all obvious, because the church with its modern glass seemed to him over-lighted. It must be borne in mind, however, that it is exceedingly doubtful if an absolutely clear glass could have been manufactured at the time of the original building, and the use of coloured glass would not have produced an effective lighting for the highly-coloured mosaic decorations.

of barrel vaults over the nave in place of the Roman timber trusses. Internally, the difference lies in the lavish richness of mosaic decoration which was applied in the East, in contrast to the rather severe marble panelling of the Roman basilicas. The basilican type of building was not developed by the Byzantines after the first period, chiefly because it did not satisfy the demands of the Orthodox religion nor the ambitions of the skilled architects of the age.

II THE CIRCULAR OR POLYGONAL HALL

Like the basilica, the centralised domed hall is directly descended from pagan architecture. Circular domed buildings have been found in the East and West, and the Pantheon at Rome is the largest and noblest example of this type. Similar to this is the Church of S. George, in Salonika (see p. 45), which was probably a pagan edifice subsequently transformed into a church. The circular form was not particularly suitable for church ritual, and only two important examples (San Vitale, Ravenna, and SS. Sergius and Bacchus, Constantinople) exist in the Byzantine area, both being built at an early stage of Byzantine architectural history. A rotunda seems to have been considered more appropriate for baptisteries, which were essentially bathrooms and naturally assumed the shape that was common in both public and private baths among the Romans. The pool, or bath, occupied the centre, and as baptism was a private sacrament it did not require space for a congregation.

III THE CRUCIFORM BUILDING

The origin of this form probably lies in the interest in symbolism which had been stimulated by the discovery of the wood of the Cross by S. Helena, mother of Constantine. Yet again, this plan was most inconvenient and unsuitable to the Church ritual, and most examples were designed expressly as mausoleums or memorials. The arms of the cross were generally very short, and the crossing was marked by a dome. The most famous example of the first period was the Church of the Holy Apostles in Constantinople, which had five domes, one over each arm and one over the crossing. This plan was copied at S. Mark's, Venice, and at S. Front, Perigueux, in the second period.

IV THE DOMED BASILICA

The supreme achievement of the Byzantines was the production of an harmonious design which combined the horizontal axis required by ritual with the vertical axis which is determined by the dome. In the Church of S. Irene, Constantinople, which was completed some years before Sancta Sophia, this combination was attempted by the setting of domes on the crossing arches of the basilica. Although one dome was raised higher than the rest, the result was unsatisfactory, since the central space was insufficiently emphasised and the longitudinal direction was too strongly marked. Similar plans were developed in France in the second period, at Angoulême and Cahors, with like results. The solution was found in Sancta Sophia, where the central dome received its longitudinal extension by the support of two semi-domes of equal span. Nothing like it was ever attempted again in Byzantine times; it remains to this day, as Choisy says, 'a marvel of stability, daring, fearless logic and science.'

V THE CROSS-IN-SQUARE

This plan belongs exclusively to the second and third periods, and the examples are numerous but much smaller than those churches associated with the first period. The cross was visible only from above, since the nave and transepts were carried higher than the corners of the square. The central dome, which was raised on a drum, was supported either on piers or on columns, and the angle spaces were roofed either by vaults or by smaller domes. At the eastern end there was a projecting apse and, as a rule, two supporting but smaller apses which were commonly cut in the thickness of the wall in the angle chambers. The whole structure might be little more than 30 feet square, but it formed a compact and unified whole which, with regional variations, continues in south-western Europe as the orthodox form of a Christian church.

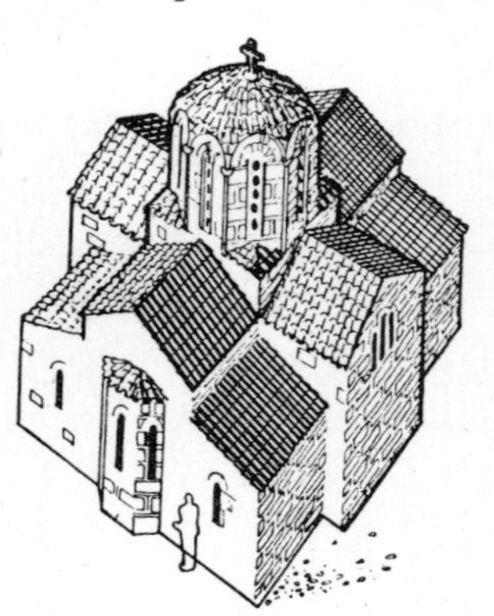

CHAPTER V

BYZANTINE ARCHITECTURE OF THE FIRST PERIOD

THE buildings which belong to the first period, and which led up to a climax in Sancta Sophia, are some of the most interesting and inspiring in existence. They are interesting because they are anterior to, or contemporary with, the great church at Constantinople, and they are inspiring by the rare beauty and originality of their plans and the great charm of their proportions and details. The principal examples were all built between 450 and 550[1] and, apart from the mausoleums of Galla Placidia and Theodoric at Ravenna, they were all churches or baptisteries, and all square or octagonal externally. The interiors generally comprised a large central space divided from an enveloping aisle by piers, between which, in most cases, were semi-circular niches formed by columns. These niches are characteristic of early Byzantine work, and do not exist in the churches of the second and third periods; they seem to have come into being with Justinian's reign—unless, as is suggested in modern restorations, they occurred in the Baths of Gallienus, Rome—and to have disappeared at his death. Their eclipse is to be deplored, for few arrangements are more effective. They were always two storeys in height and finished with semi-domes. By their aid variety was given to the plan, additional space to the central area and scale to the building.

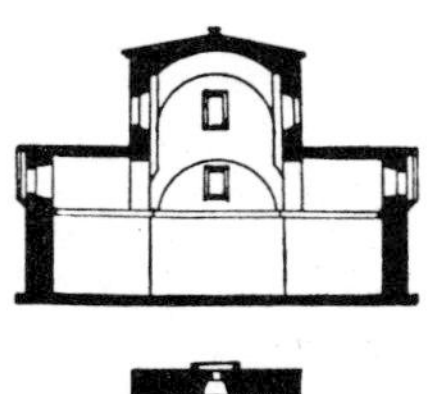

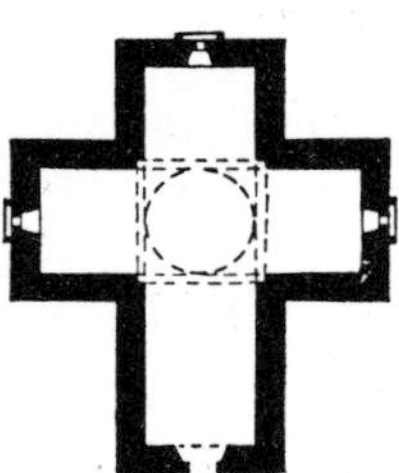

After d'Agincourt.

Mausoleum of Galla Placidia, Ravenna; plan and transverse section.

Scale 50 *ft. to* 1 *in.*

The Mausoleums at Ravenna. These two buildings are the exceptions mentioned above. The earlier (450), which contains the tomb of Galla Placidia, is a brick cruciform building, having a 'simple' dome which rests on square

[1] The basilican churches at Ravenna, which fall within this period, have already been mentioned on pp. 28–30, although often catalogued among Byzantine buildings.

walls above the barrel-vaulted arms of the cross. The interior is covered with particularly beautiful mosaics, in which the groundwork is blue and green and Christ is depicted as a young and beardless shepherd. This treatment is quite different from that of the later periods, where gold is invariably used for the background and the Christ is bearded and awe-inspiring. The Mausoleum of Theodoric (*c.* 520) is remarkable for its dome, which is carved from a solid block of Istrian marble, 107 feet in circumference, 3 feet thick, and 470 tons in weight. Such a dome is simply a dead weight, exerting no outward thrust and resting on the drum as a lid on a dustbin. The building is two storeys high and decagonal in plan. The wall of the lower storey is arcaded and much thicker than that above, which is set back to form an open terrace all around at first floor level. This upper part is circular inside, is 30 feet in diameter, and was originally surrounded by an arcade—the removal of which has probably enhanced the appearance of the building. Altogether, the monumental character of this mausoleum is a striking testimony to the power of Roman traditional design, but the detailed carving of the cornice and doorway is pure Byzantine, and the monolithic drum is entirely original (Pl. 4).

After d'Agincourt.

Mausoleum of Theodoric, Ravenna; (left) elevation and ground-floor plan; (right) section and upper-floor plan. *Scale 50 ft. to 1 in.*

The Syrian Examples. The Syrian churches, rather than the Ravenna mausoleums, must be regarded as the connecting links between the Early Christian domical buildings and those of purely Byzantine type. The cathedral at Bozra (512) and the Church of S. George at Ezra (*c.* 515) are both square externally. The cathedral is circular inside and has four niches to fill the corners of the square. At Ezra the internal shape is octagonal and niches are similarly placed; in addition there is an inner octagon defined by piers. The use of piers is a new development, for hitherto, in buildings of similar plan, columns—either single or coupled—had been employed. This inner octagon is reduced above by corbels to a figure of sixteen sides, carrying the dome, which in section is not hemispherical but pointed. The octagonal drum, pierced with windows, is most unusual and is probably the earliest example of its kind. Another example of a square church is at Kalat Seman (*c.* 550), in northern Syria, in which the square is surrounded by aisles. Inside, the square becomes an octagon by the insertion of niches at the corners in exactly the same way as in the church at Ezra. The church at Kalat Seman is joined by a basilican church, a dual arrangement which was not uncommon. Similar examples still exist at Torcello (see p. 30) and at Trèves, and the oldest domed church in Constantinople, SS. Sergius and Bacchus, originally had a basilican church joined to it which has now entirely disappeared.

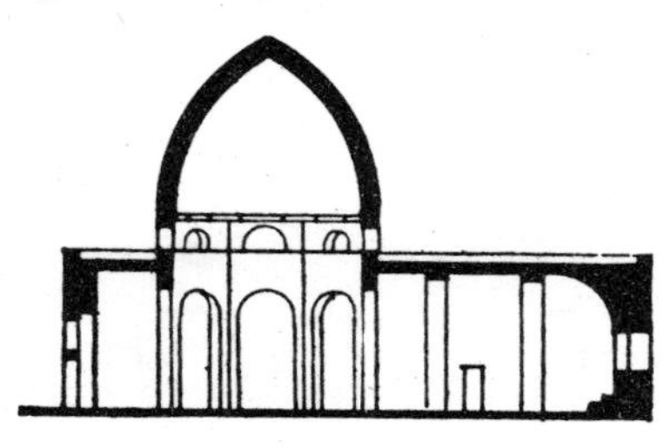

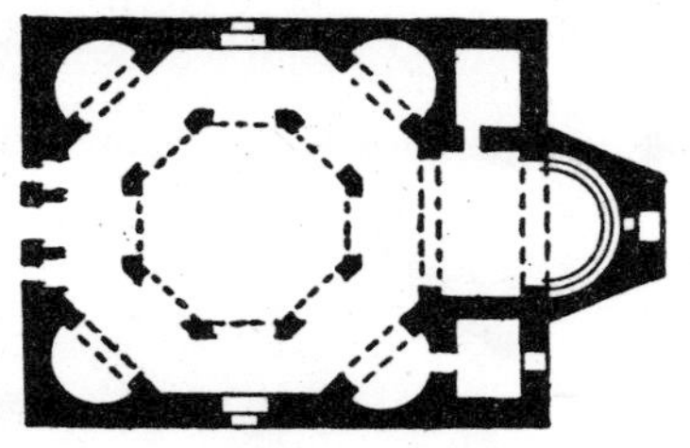

After De Vogüé.

S. George at Ezra.
Scale 50 *ft. to* 1 *in.*

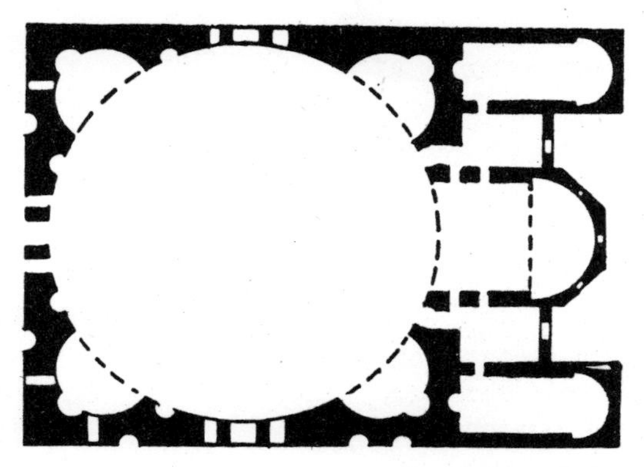

After Texier and Pullan.

Cathedral at Bozra.
Scale 50 *ft. to* 1 *in.*

SS. Sergius and Bacchus, Constantinople. The resemblance in plan between the churches in Syria and the great Church of SS. Sergius and Bacchus (527–535) is obvious. At SS. Sergius and Bacchus the niches are defined by columns, and columns also stand between the piers on the four sides, helping to carry the gallery which runs around the church over the aisles. The early date of the church is shown by the fact that although the columns of the gallery level have arches over them, those of the ground floor support lintels, which form a continuous entablature around the central area.

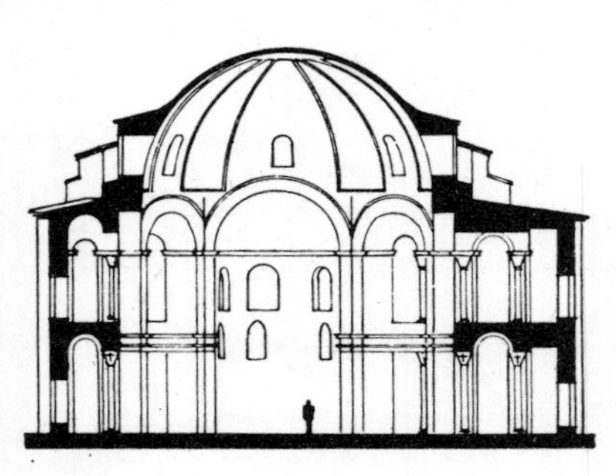

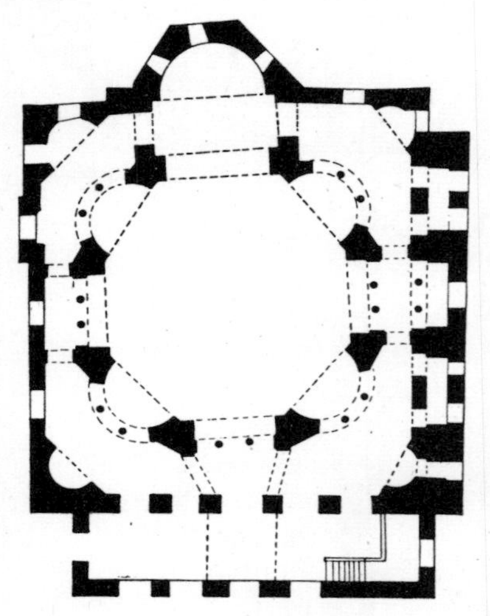

After Van Millingen.

SS. Sergius and Bacchus, Constantinople.

Scale 50 *ft. to* 1 *in.*

The mouldings of this entablature are debased but by no means coarse, and on the frieze is a raised inscription in Greek letters. This is virtually the only example of Byzantine work in which the classic entablature is retained, although an apology for a cornice exists at Sancta Sophia in two or three places. Except in certain parts of Italy and the south of France, where old traditions lingered long, it disappeared entirely, and was not seen again until resuscitated by the Italian architects of the Renaissance in the fifteenth century.

The dome of this church is particularly interesting. It is of the melon-shaped type, and in its application over the octagon no pendentives are employed. Instead, the dome is divided into sixteen compartments, each alternate section coming above the angles of the octagon and the inside surfaces being concave in plan. This is primarily a constructive device, for it provides a form of ribbed reinforcement to the dome. The dome is pierced by eight windows, just above the springing, which amply light the central octagon. Its height from the floor to the apex is about 70 feet.

San Vitale, Ravenna. The design of San Vitale is remarkably similar to that of the Church of SS. Sergius and Bacchus, and there has been much controversy respecting which was the earlier foundation, though it is now certain that San Vitale was later in its completion.[1] San Vitale is slightly larger, but the exterior forms an octagon and not a square. Every side of the inner octagon has its apse, with the exception of that at the east end, which forms the entrance to the bema and is wider than the others; further to emphasise its importance, the gallery stops against it on either side. The columns in the lower storey support arches, rather than the horizontal architrave which was noted at SS. Sergius and Bacchus. The construction of a very light dome by means of hollow pots or terra cotta amorphae enabled the builders to dispense with buttresses. The walls of the church are lined with marble, very effectively arranged in panels of deep red framed by cippolino and other light-coloured marbles. In no other church is the beauty of the 'figure' displayed so skilfully. Above this panelling are mosaics which, by their wealth of design and rich and oriental colouring, make San Vitale the supreme example of Byzantine interior decoration. Altogether, this is one of the most effective interiors in existence, and few churches of even larger size are more imposing.[2] In contrast, the outside, which is built of large

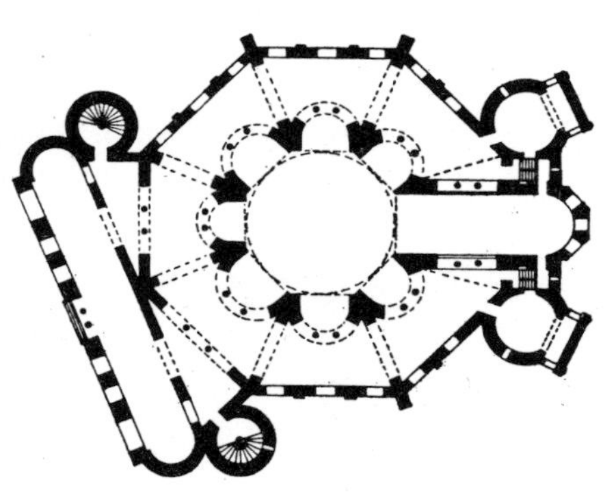

After Cummings.
San Vitale, Ravenna.
Scale 100 *ft. to* 1 *in.*

[1] Van Millingen (*Byzantine Churches in Constantinople*) and Rivoira (op. cit.) both suggest that the design of the church at Constantinople was copied from Ravenna. Fergusson (*History of Architecture*) and Hamilton (*Byzantine Architecture and Decoration*) consider the reverse to be the case.

[2] Simpson was not impressed by the mosaics, for he considered that apart from those in the chancel they had been 'barbarously modernised'. But, although there is evidence of much restoration, this view is not held by most authorities.

flat bricks with thick mortar joints, is very plain. The dome is completely hidden by walls and by the low-pitched roof above. Whether the original roof was similar in design it is impossible to say, but in any case some covering must have been used to protect the dome of pottery below.

S. Lorenzo, Milan. The plan of the Church of S. Lorenzo in Milan bears such a remarkable resemblance to the other examples we have cited that it is included here, although Milan is situated beyond the recognised sphere of influence of Constantinople in the first period. The date of this church is not known, though it certainly must be as early as the time of Justinian. Up to the eighth century it was the cathedral of the city; in the eleventh

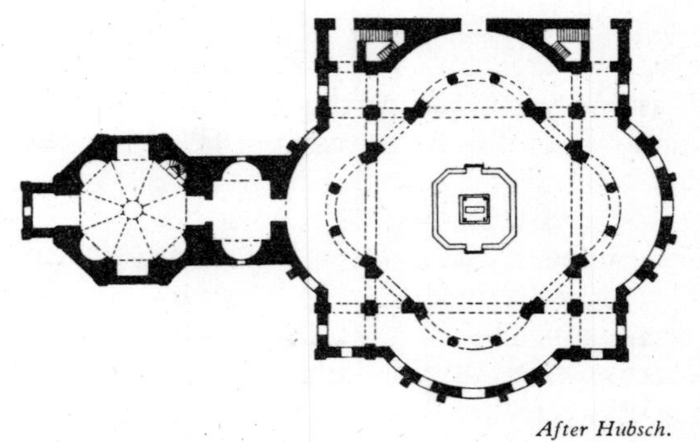

After Hubsch.

S. Lorenzo, Milan.
Scale 100 *ft. to* 1 *in.*

century it was burnt down, and in the twelfth, restored. The dome fell in 1571, and the church suffered rather badly when it was rebuilt. The plan is a square with a projecting apse on each side, built in a rather shallow curve, concentric with the internal colonnaded apses around the central area. The dome as it now stands is octagonal, and is about 70 feet wide; originally, it must have been second in size only to that of Sancta Sophia.

Sancta Sophia, Constantinople (Pl. 5). In the Church of Sancta Sophia we find a synthesis of the various types of architecture already described, but on a scale so startling and with so daring a construction that one might be tempted to regard it as an original conception. But there can be no doubt, from the many buildings which preceded it, that nearly every feature can be traced back. W. R. Lethaby points out the remarkable resemblance of the plan of Sancta Sophia to that of SS. Sergius and Bacchus. 'It may be conceived as formed by dividing SS. Sergius and Bacchus in two, and removing the two halves from one another, then, above the void, raising a still higher dome, supported right and left by ranges of arcades as in a basilica.'[1] By supporting the central dome with two semi-domes, the desired horizontal extension to the plan was achieved. Nothing had been built before equal in extent to the nave of Sancta Sophia; nor in the remaining nine hundred years of the Empire was anything like it attempted again.

Sancta Sophia was built upon the site of a basilican church, also dedicated to the 'Divine Wisdom', which had been totally destroyed by fire at the beginning of Justinian's reign. The architects were Anthemius of Thralles, and Isidorus of Miletus. The construction of the new church was begun in February, 532, and it was completed on the 26th of December, 537. Twenty years afterwards, as a result of an earthquake, a portion of the dome collapsed, and the whole dome was rebuilt with a slightly higher section, in the form in which it now stands.

Plan. In plan, the church is nearly square. At the west end is a narthex, 205 feet long and 26 feet wide, which forms a very fine entrance porch. Above this is the gallery for women, which is linked with galleries over the side aisles. At the east end there is a slightly projecting apse, semi-circular internally and polygonal on the outside. No church in the world can compare with Sancta Sophia in its internal architectural effect. This is not due to the area it covers, but to the originality of its plan, the extent of its nave, and the perfect proportions which exist throughout between its different parts. The side aisles, with the galleries over them, are so separated from the nave by screens of columns and great piers that the nave may be said to stand by itself. It forms a magnificent hall, over 20 feet wider than any of the great Roman halls, and wider by far than the nave of any Gothic cathedral; and although the cathedrals of Rome and Florence have central areas which are wider than the nave of Sancta Sophia, none can boast of an unbroken floor space of over 200 feet in length and more than 100 feet in width. Each end of the nave terminates with a large semicircular apse of the full width, out of which open smaller niches, one on each side. Lethaby and Swainson suggest that this biapsidal arrangement was due to the change in the orientation of churches which took place in the period between the building of

[1] *Mediaeval Art*, 1904.

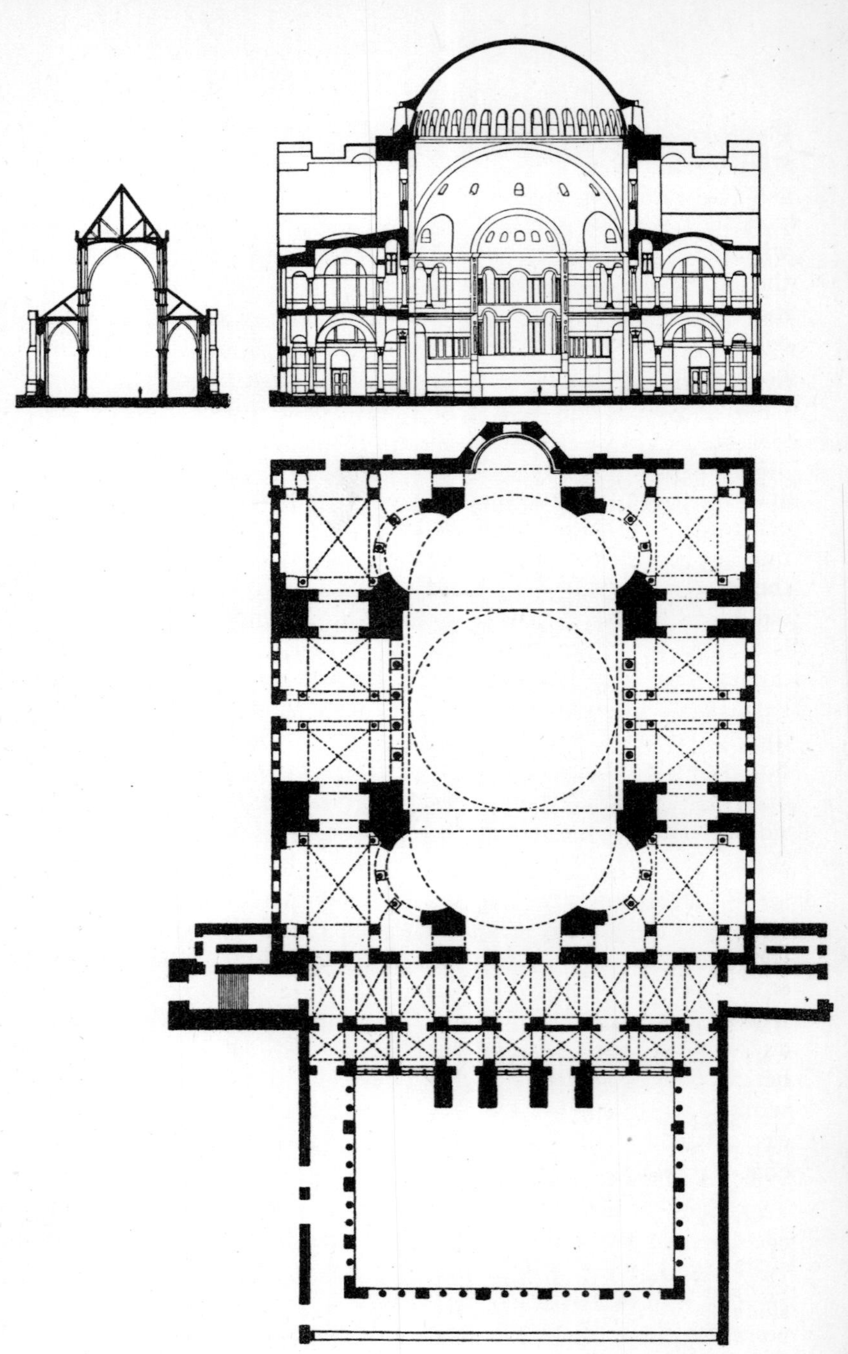

After Salzenberg.

Sancta Sophia, Constantinople. Plan and cross section, with section through Salisbury Cathedral to the same scale.

Scale 100 *ft. to* 1 *in.*

the original Sancta Sophia and that of the existing church, and which would necessitate a reversal of the position of the altar. But even supposing that some use was made of old foundations, the present western apse is not likely to occupy the position of the one which served as chancel to the original church, because not even the old basilica of S. Peter, at Rome, had a chancel apse approaching in width the 100 feet which is the span of the semi-circular ending at Sancta Sophia. The peculiarity in the plan is more probably due to natural development. Buildings with apses at both ends were by no means uncommon in Roman work. An oblong chamber in the Baths of Diocletian, Rome, terminated in that manner, and so did the porches of the Baptistery of Constantine and the Tomb of Costanza, Rome.[1] The conception of this great central hall may, in fact, be claimed to be essentially Roman. At first sight there is not much likeness between a building such as the Basilica of Constantine and this church, but on analysis they will be found to have much in common. In each the central space is divided into three, but at Sancta Sophia a dome and two half-domes take the place of the three intersecting vaults of the Roman basilica. It is, of course, true that there is poetry in the plan of the Eastern church to which the Hall of Justice cannot lay claim; but in the main proportions, in the disposition of piers and external buttresses, and in the columns which divide the centre from the sides, there is considerable resemblance between the two buildings. Where the church is greatly superior is in the heightening of the central portion by a dome on pendentives so that it becomes a crowning feature of the interior, to which all the other parts lead and upon which the eye involuntarily rests immediately on entering.

Supports of Central Dome. The dome is supported on its east and west sides by transverse arches, beyond which, and of the same height, are the semi-domes. These are penetrated by the smaller semi-domes over the side apses, by the central apse at the east end and by the arch over the opening to the gallery at the west end. The semi-dome over the central eastern apse is a trifle

[1] In an early basilican church at Orleansville, in Africa, and in other churches of later date elsewhere, notably in Germany, apses containing altars are found at both ends; but these churches have little in common with Sancta Sophia, which can never have had two altars, because dual altars are contrary to the custom of the Greek Church, and because the position of the narthex, at the west end, effectively disposes of the idea that an altar can ever have been placed there.

higher than those over the side apses.[1] On the north and south sides of the central square are longitudinal arches, the same height as the transverse, and between these four arches are the pendentives, probably the largest triangular pendentives in the world.[2]

Considerable abutment was necessary to take the thrust of the great transverse arches running north and south. This was provided by immense masses of masonry, 75 feet in depth and 25 feet wide, which were carried across the aisles on arches, as in the Basilica of Constantine, and stood up above the aisle roofs. These form the most outstanding features of the outside. Similar buttresses were not necessary to support the longitudinal arches

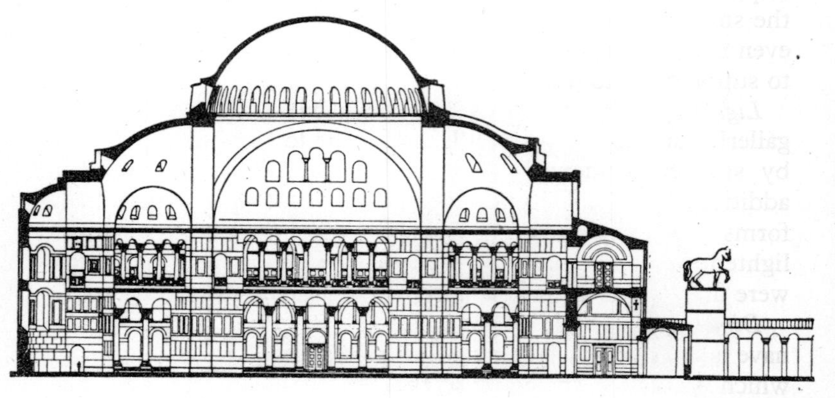

After Salzenberg.

Sancta Sophia, Constantinople. Section through dome and semi-domes.
Scale 100 *ft. to* 1 *in.*

running east and west, for not only were these partially supported by the walls underneath them, but their thrusts were counteracted by the semi-domes at the ends and by the big piers which formed part of the buttresses to the other arches.

Columns. The most original and striking characteristics of the

[1] Simpson considered that the central eastern apse might with advantage have been higher still, in order to emphasise the Sanctuary, but this would have cut into the semi-dome most awkwardly and would have destroyed the rhythm of the three openings.

[2] The domes over S. Peter's, Rome, and S. Paul's, London, start from octagons, and the pendentives have consequently much less projection and are altogether slighter; and in the domes of the Pantheon at Rome and the Cathedral at Florence there are no pendentives at all, for in the former building the plan is circular, and in the latter the walls below the dome, and the dome itself, are octagonal.

interior are the screens of marble columns and arches which support the side walls and galleries[1] under the longitudinal arches. The columns are of great beauty in themselves, but their chief value is that they give scale to the church. There are two storeys, and the columns of the lower storey are more lofty and altogether bigger than those above. Below, there are only four columns on each side, whereas at the gallery level there are six; the upper ones do not, consequently, stand immediately above the lower. This was a most successful device, and does not appear to have been attempted before, although a like multiplication of columns is to be found in the treatment of aisle and triforium arcades in Romanesque churches. Columns and arches of similar proportions form the small apses at the two ends, and here the superimposition is even more remarkable, for each apse has only two columns below to support six above.

Lighting. The church is lit by large windows in the aisles and galleries and in the side walls under the longitudinal arches, and by smaller windows in the large and small semi-domes. In addition, a ring of forty windows lights the great central dome and forms a very remarkable feature. The church is now over-lighted, but this would not have been the case when the windows were filled with pierced slabs or with less transparent glass.

Dimensions. The following are the principal dimensions: the nave is 107 feet wide and 225 feet long; the height to the cornice, which marks the springing of the great arches, is 73 feet, and to the crown of these arches, which are slightly stilted, nearly 130 feet; this is also the height of the big semi-domes.[2] But this last dimension does not convey a true idea of the height of the interior of Sancta Sophia, because nearly half of its central area is covered by the great dome, 107 feet in diameter, the apex of which is nearly 180 feet from the floor.

Exterior (Pl. 5). The exterior at first sight causes disappointment. The brick walls are plastered over and distempered in bands of red and white, and the dome, including the sloping walls between

[1] Some of the finest views of the church are obtainable from these galleries, and especially of the carved marble spandrels and the mosaics in the upper part of the church. A few of these mosaics remain untouched, but most of the wall area has been plastered over and is only now being uncovered.

[2] It is true that this is not so high as the vaults of Amiens, Beauvais, Cologne and Bologna Cathedrals and S. Peter's, Rome, but it is as high as Chartres, Rheims and Notre-Dame, Paris, and is far higher than any of the English cathedrals, which have an average height of only 75 feet.

the windows at its base, is covered with dull lead. None of the rich colouring which one generally associates with the East is seen, but the grand simplicity of the dome, resting on its plain square base, the great scale of the projecting buttresses on the north and south sides and of the great semi-circular arches in between them, each 15 feet 8 inches deep on the soffit, more than compensate for the absence of ornament and colour. Shadow is the cheapest and most effective ornament a building can have, especially in the East, where it is far more telling than in our duller climate; and there is plenty of light and shade on the exterior of Sancta Sophia. The lower portions of the semi-domes of the east and west are hidden by sloping walls, and very little shows of the domes themselves; but that little serves to carry the eye upwards to the central dome, and helps to produce the pyramidal effect so noticeable in this church.[1] The four minarets, added by the Turks in the fifteenth and sixteenth centuries, are unfortunately among the ugliest in Constantinople, but they emphasise the great mass of the church and are therefore of some value.

[1] The piled-up pyramidal outline is even more marked in some of the later Turkish mosques in Constantinople, which are modelled on Sancta Sophia.

Sancta Sophia, Constantinople; interior

Sancta Sophia, Constantinople; exterior

Holy Apostles, Salonika; detail of brickwork

S. Mark's, Venice; Byzantine mosaic decoration

S. Saviour, Constantinople

S. Mark's, Venice; detail of south-west corner

S. Mary of the Admiral, Palermo, showing squinch arches

Plate 7

S. Front, Perigueux; interior

S. Front, Perigueux; exterior

Trinita di Delia, Castelvetrano, Sicily

Typical minor Greek church, Omorphi Ecclesia, near Athens

Plate 8

S. Dimitri, Vladimir

S. Basil, Moscow

CHAPTER VI

BYZANTINE ARCHITECTURE OF THE SECOND PERIOD

THE second period includes the churches built in the eleventh and twelfth centuries, in Constantinople; in Salonika—which, under its old name, Thessalonika, was the second city of the Eastern Empire; in Athens and its neighbourhood; in Armenia, which remained Christian notwithstanding Persian persecutions and Mohammedan invasions; and in Russia, which had been converted by Vladimir, Prince of Kiev, at the end of the tenth century. Under this heading are also included a few churches built beyond the dominion of the Byzantine Empire in northern Italy and in Sicily, as well as the remarkable domed churches which were built in Aquitaine in imitation of Byzantine work. Only two buildings of importance appear to have been built in the centuries between the first and second periods—Sancta Sophia, Salonika, and S. Irene, Constantinople. Because their architecture differs in many respects from that of the first period, and has much in common with that of the second, they have been included in this chapter.

The churches of this period are, as a rule, small;[1] none can compare in size and importance with Sancta Sophia, Constantinople, and only a few are as large as the other examples described in the last chapter. This is due to the diminished strength and importance of the Empire, and to the constantly recurring external wars and internal dissensions which afforded the people little inducement to build extensively. But the old artistic Greek spirit still survived throughout the Empire, and although the churches are small they are often interesting in plan, are always admirable in proportion, and are decorated with a rare richness of marble and mosaic. A characteristic feature is the incorporation of a small drum under the dome, which provides side lighting and leaves an uninterrupted surface for the decoration of the dome.

[1] This is partly accounted for by the fact that in the Eastern Church the greater part of the congregation stands, and does not kneel or sit as in the West.

Plans. No hard-and-fast rules can be laid down for the planning of churches in this period, since there is great variety. The churches differ in many important essentials from those already described, and local characteristics distinguish, to some extent, the churches of one country from those of another. In one respect they all agree: all have that distinctive feature of Byzantine work, the central dome. Some have additional domes, and in such cases the largest covers the crossing and the others are subordinated to it. In none of the churches of this period are found the colonnaded niches, surrounding the central area, which form so fascinating a feature in nearly all early examples.

CHURCHES IN THE EAST

Sancta Sophia, Salonika. Sancta Sophia, Salonika, is ascribed by Texier and Pullan and others to the sixth century. Its details are certainly of that period, but in its plan and general ordinance it resembles the churches of later date; it may have been rebuilt. The internal form is a cross with an oblong, the central portion being covered by a dome and the remainder by barrel vaults. This dome is not a perfect circle, but is slightly flattened on four sides; while this made possible a slight reduction in the overhang of the pendentives, it was not a commendable feature. Between the dome and the pendentives is a low drum pierced by windows, an arrangement which was possibly used here for the first time. The narthex runs around three sides of the church, forming an unusual feature which was later adopted at S. Mark's, Venice. The bema is not quite so wide as the nave, and the central apse is slightly narrower than the bema, so that the vaults over these portions diminish in height at each break. This diminution in height and width at the east end is a characteristic of most Byzantine churches,

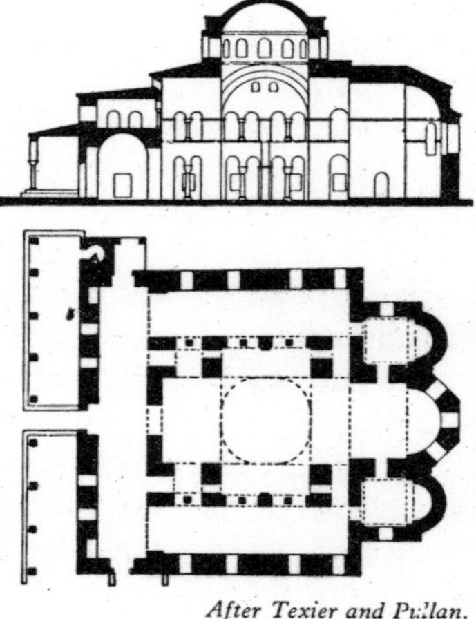

After Texier and Pullan.

Sancta Sophia, Salonika.
Scale 100 *ft. to* 1 *in.*

and a very effective one, because it introduces an element of false perspective by giving the appearance of greater length.

S. Irene, Constantinople. S. Irene occupies the site of a church built by Constantine and rebuilt by Justinian, but the existing church is the result of a second rebuilding in the latter half of the eighth century. To some extent its plan is basilican, for it is divided into nave and aisles, but the church bears more resemblance to the Basilica of Constantine in Rome than to the more common wooden-roofed, Early Christian basilicas. The nave consists of two divisions, the part farther from the entrance being square in plan and covered by a dome which rises above the roof on a drum pierced by twenty windows. The nearer part is rectangular in plan and covered with a simple elliptical vault, in which the domical surface and the pendentives are continuous. Piers on each side mark the divisions of the nave. Between these piers are columns which support the galleries over the aisles. Above the galleries, the walls are carried up between the wide barrel vaults which cross the nave, and have windows similar to those in Roman buildings and in the Church of Sancta Sophia, Constantinople.[1] The church is now, and has been for centuries, used as an armoury, and necessary utilitarian alterations have largely destroyed its ecclesiastical character.

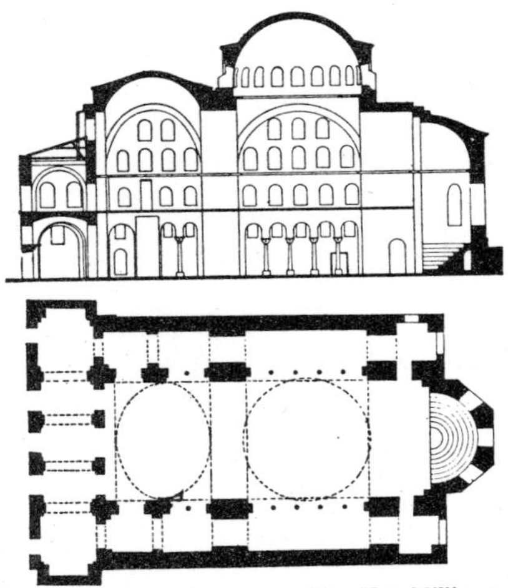

After Van Millingen.

S. Irene, Constantinople.
Scale 100 *ft. to* 1 *in.*

Other Churches in Constantinople. During the second period many important churches were built in Constantinople, of which eleven still survive and three are mentioned here. Nearly all were transformed into mosques, with the consequent defacement or

[1] Simpson considered it possible that the original building may have been built in the first instance as a basilica rather than as a church, and that this accounts for the great barrel vaults across the nave, which are curiously Roman in character and scale. But there is no literary authority for this; indeed, it has always been known as the 'old church', or Ecclesia Antiqua—*Notitia, regio secunda*; Codin, *De aed.* (p. 73).

covering-up of much of their Christian decorations. Most of the churches were built of thin bricks and had brick domes and barrel vaults. Three apses were generally provided, and these were round on the inside and polygonal externally. A similar treatment was usual in the drums of the domes, and the external angles were often decorated with columns linked by arched cornices.

The Church of Theotokos Pammakaristos (The All-Blessed Mother of Christ) was built in the eleventh century, and is interesting in that it provides a link between the domed basilican plan and the later cross-in-square type. The central area is bounded on three sides by a rectangular barrel-vaulted ambulatory with cross vaults at the corners, a feature which is characteristic of many churches in Constantinople. The church is remarkable for its lofty, melon-shaped dome of twelve concave compartments. This, fortunately, still retains its mosaics depicting Christ (in the centre) surrounded by the Apostles, each holding in his hand a scroll with an appropriate quotation from the Scriptures.

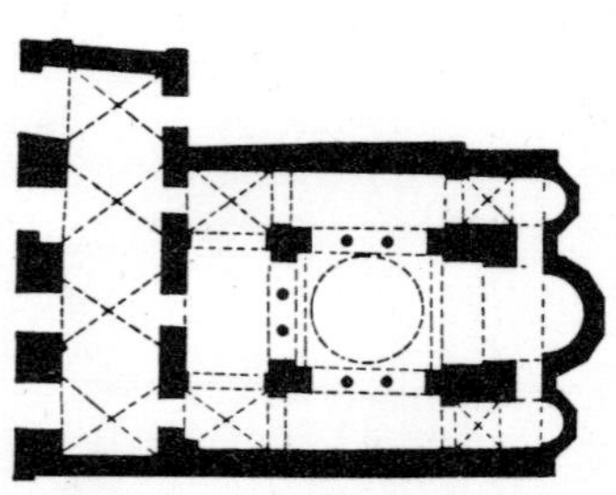

After Van Millingen.

S. Theotokos Pammakaristos, Constantinople.

Scale 50 *ft. to* 1 *in.*

The Church of S. Theodore is of old foundation, but the plan and general design suggest that it was rebuilt in the eleventh century. It is an excellent and early example of the true cross-in-square plan, and shows the great interest in external decoration which developed in the second period. There is a dome over the central area, and three supporting but smaller domes over the terminal bays above the exonarthex. All are raised on richly decorated drums. The roofs of the cross arms are barrel-vaulted and are finished externally as gables.

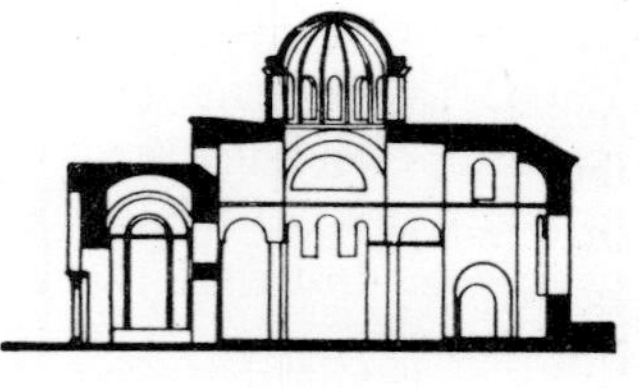

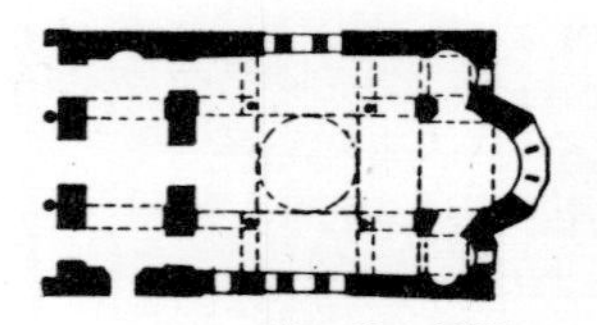

After Van Millingen.

S. Theodore, Constantinople.

Scale 50 *ft. to* 1 *ft.*

S. Saviour Pantepoptes is another example of the cross-in-square type. It was founded, or restored, at the beginning of the twelfth century. The dome is divided by square ribs into twelve bays, and is lighted by twelve semi-circular-headed windows. The arms of the cross are barrel-vaulted, and the angle chambers are covered with cross-groined vaults. There are three apses, expressed polygonally on the outside. It is considered by Van Millingen[1] to be the most carefully built of all the later churches in Constantinople, and it has none of the irregularities of setting-out which are to be found in most Byzantine churches.

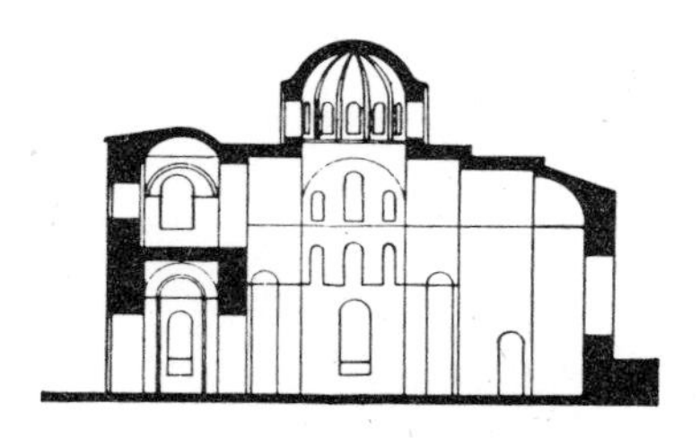

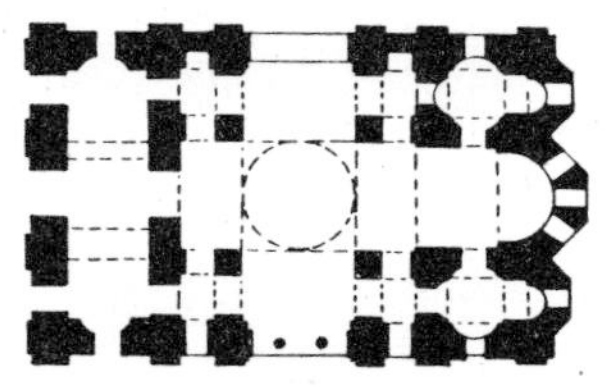

After Van Millingen.

S. Saviour Pantepoptes, Constantinople.

Scale 50 *ft. to* 1 *in.*

Churches in Greece. Greece played only a small part in the development of Byzantine architecture during the first two periods. The country was poor, and its classical cities had become merely provincial outposts of the Byzantine Empire. Apart from Salonika, there was no great city on the Greek mainland. As representative of the second period, there are a few churches in the neighbourhood of Athens, but all are relatively small and only a few have the rich mosaic and marble decoration which was usual in Constantinople. However, they are sufficiently interesting to be worthy of study, and provide a most important architectural link between the second and third periods. Nearly all the churches are square in plan, with no projections other than an apse, or apses, at the east end. A narthex, sometimes open, but more often enclosed so that it becomes part of the church, is generally incorporated at the west end. Two types of design are common; the one was usually employed for larger churches, the other for smaller. In the former, the dome is set on a low drum and its diameter is considerable, since it covers a central space which is the full width of the bema and two side chapels. In the latter, the dome is raised on a lofty drum, but its span is the width of the bema alone. It was this latter type which was to be fully developed

[1] *Byzantine Churches in Constantinople*, London, 1912.

in Greece during the third period, and which is described in more detail in the next chapter. In both types, four equal arms branch from the centre, forming a Greek Cross. The result is a church which is really square in plan, but presents a cruciform appearance externally as well as internally. Although the churches are small, they are striking because of their loftiness. The height of the arms, to the springing of the vaults, is often as much as three times their own width, and that of the apex of the central dome is frequently greater than the total width of the church.

Larger Churches in Greece. The best-known examples of the larger type of building are the Church of Daphni, near Athens, S. Nicodemus, in Athens, and the larger of the two churches in the Monastery of S. Luke in Phocis, north of the Gulf of Corinth.

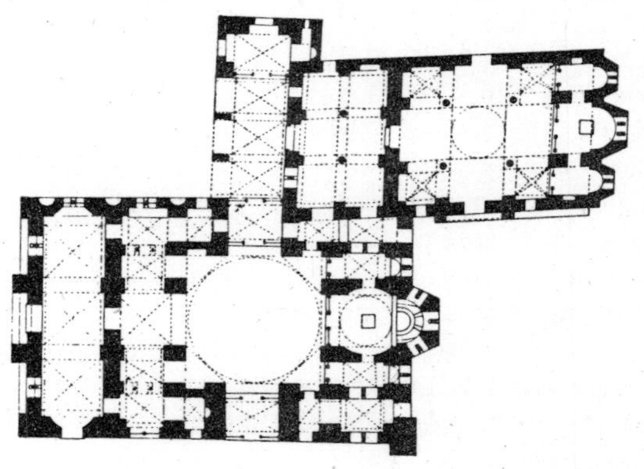

After Schultz and Barnsley.

Two churches of the Monastery of S. Luke of Stiris, Phocis, Greece.

Scale 50 ft. to 1 in.

There is little difference in size between the three, and in each case the transition from the square to the round drum of the dome is effected by squinch arches across the angles of the square, to form an octagon, and then by small pendentives to form the circle. The principal dimensions of the church at Daphni show that it was set out in simple ratios, which are doubtless responsible for the excellence of its proportions. The diameter of the dome is 26 feet, its height just double—52 feet, and the total length of the church, including the apse but excluding the narthex, is 52 feet also. The cross arms are narrow and lofty, their height from the floor to the springing of the barrel vault being equal to the diameter of the dome. The mosaics are among the most lovely in the world, and although they have suffered by restoration they are still the finest examples of their age. The great head of Christ looks down from the dome in magnificent and terrifying majesty. This is not the familiar Lord of loving kindness, but a supreme oriental Over-lord, burdened with all the sins of mankind.

The Church of S. Nicodemus, in Athens, originally built in the eleventh century, was so drastically restored in the nineteenth that little of the original remains other than the plan and, on the outside, some curious cut brickwork in the form of Kufic lettering.

Similar decoration, and a similar plan, are to be found in the well-preserved Church of S. Luke of Stiris, in Phocis, the only difference being that, in the latter, but one apse projects, instead of three. The central area is covered by a low dome, which appears externally as a figure of sixteen sides with a tiled roof. Inside, the church still retains its original inlaid marble floor and a great deal of glass mosaic and marble wall decoration.[1]

Smaller Churches in Greece. Adjoining the large Church of S. Luke is a smaller church, dedicated to the Panagia, which is of a simple cross-in-square plan, and which has a central dome of little more than 10 feet in diameter, carried on four columns. It has in addition a large narthex divided by columns; beyond this is an exo-narthex which also acts as a side porch for the larger church. It is richly decorated outside with saw-tooth brick bands and variegated tile patterns.

The Small Cathedral in Athens is only 40 by 35 feet externally, and is probably the smallest building in Europe honoured with the title of Cathedral. It is also the only church in Greece which is faced entirely of marble, and as nearly all this facing has been borrowed from older classical buildings, it is of considerable archaeological interest. The frieze above the principal entrance consists of an ancient Greek calendar of festivals, with crosses added afterwards. At the corners are embedded Corinthian capitals, and on one face of the single projecting apse is an archaic relief immured upside down. The treatment of the outside of the dome is characteristic of many smaller churches in Greece of the second and third periods. The tiled covering adheres closely to the curve of the dome and continues to the corners of the octagon,

[1] For particulars of this church and its adjoining smaller church, see Schultz and Barnsley's finely illustrated monograph, *The Monastery of St. Luke of Stiris, Phocis*, London, 1901.

down the sides of the semi-circular archivolts over the windows of the drum, and there is therefore no horizontal eaves-projection.

Churches in Armenia. The churches in Armenia resemble, in many respects, those in Greece, but also possess certain distinctive characteristics of their own. When they were built is uncertain, but it is probable that few, if any, of the existing churches are earlier than the tenth century, and it is unlikely that any major contribution to architecture was made after the thirteenth. The tenth century was certainly the richest and most prosperous period of Armenian history, and it is reasonable to suppose that many of the churches were begun during that time, and that by the close of the thirteenth century, when the Turko-Tartarian hordes swept over the land, further development became impossible.

The churches are small, but high, and are generally faced inside and out with fine squared stone. In plan, some of the churches are square and of the usual Byzantine type, but a number are oblong, the western and eastern arms being extended. The cross arms occasionally terminate apsidally on the inside, giving a trefoil or quatrefoil plan. The domes at the crossings are raised on lofty drums like those in the smaller Athenian churches, but the domes do not show externally for they are hidden by steep, conical stone roofs. The other portions of the churches generally have semi-circular or pointed barrel vaults, and are covered with tiles or lead. The exterior is commonly relieved by blind arcading along the walls, and occasionally by the application of low relief decoration and intricate patterning in stone around the door and window openings. The east end has usually three semi-circular apses inside, but on the outside these are polygonal and separated by two triangular niches, the heads of which are arched so that the wall above is flat.

The Cathedral, Ani. The most important examples of Armenian architecture are to be found at Ani, the capital, and the most important of these is the cathedral. It was built, according to an inscription on its walls, in the year 1010. The most interesting features of this building are its pointed arches and vaults and the clustering or coupling of the columns in the Gothic manner. While it does not follow that these arches were built at the beginning of the eleventh century, there is no evidence to suggest that any rebuilding took place, and there is no reason that the pointed form should not have been employed in this period, since it was common in the East centuries before. A tall and graceful blind arcade, similar in character to that at the Cathedral in Pisa—which was built about fifty years later—and pierced by narrow windows, relieves the flatness of the exterior walls and the high circular

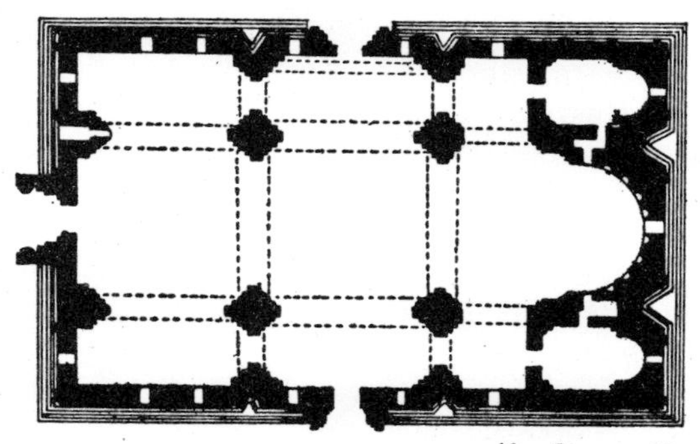

After Strzygowski.

Ani Cathedral, Armenia.
Scale 50 *ft. to* 1 *in.*

drum. The plan is straightforward, being of the cross-in-square form but with the eastern and western arms about twice the length of the side bays.

Churches in Russia. The history of Russian architecture begins with the conversion to Christianity of Vladimir, Grand Duke of Kiev (988). As a direct result, the development of cultural and commercial relations between Constantinople and Kiev were encouraged. Architects from Constantinople were employed in the construction of the first churches, and it was only natural that they should follow, in their designs, the Byzantine tradition. The oldest and most important example of their work was the Church of Sancta Sophia, at Kiev (1036), which was a brick cross-domed basilica, having two additional bays on the west and an extra aisle to the north and south. It was originally nearly square in plan and was roofed by a central dome, 25 feet in diameter, and twelve smaller domes. At a later date four more aisles were

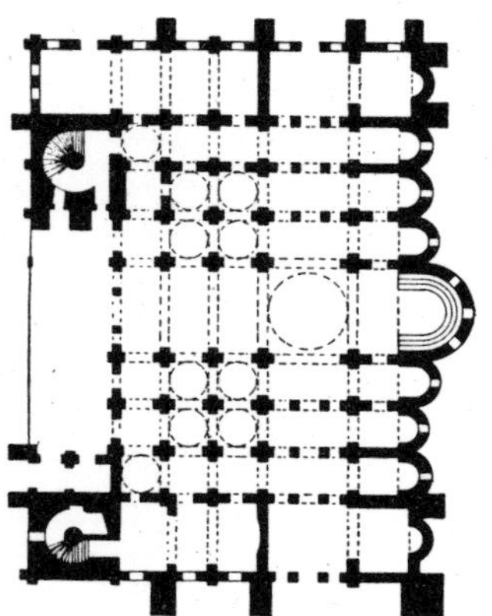

After Loukomski.

Sancta Sophia, Kiev.
Scale 100 *ft. to* 1 *in.*

added, giving an unusual lateral extension to the plan. Each aisle terminated in a round apse.

It was not at Kiev but at Novgorod, some 570 miles farther north, that Byzantine architecture underwent its curious Slavonic change. The Byzantine dome was quite new to Russia, and in Novgorod it was transformed into what became the most striking feature of the Russian skyline. From the simple inverted saucer or hemispherical outline was evolved a shape like that of a Turkish helmet, the top surface of the dome being steepened, partly to throw off snow and partly for aesthetic reasons. In the twelfth century further developments took place. The external diameter of the dome was increased at a point above the springing, thus giving it the onion shape which became a Russian characteristic; the number of domes was increased and, at the same time, the drums assumed a new character: they were heightened to such an extent that they appeared like turrets, high above the roof line of the church. No rule can be laid down regarding the number of domes nor for their location in relation to the planning of the church, since they often appear to have been placed without regard to the internal arrangements. The tall cylindrical drums, surmounted by curious bulbous domes, became mere external decoration to the main structure, but they had, nevertheless, a certain barbaric splendour which was far removed from the classic simplicity of the churches in Constantinople and in Greece.

The Cathedral of Sancta Sophia, Novgorod (1052), was smaller and simpler than the church of the same name at Kiev. In form it was essentially a cube, with three tall, rounded apses at the east end, the whole being surmounted by six domes raised on high cylindrical drums. Many churches were erected in the Novgorod region, all more or less similar in character; the most interesting was the Church of the Saviour at Nereditsa (1198), which had a single bulbous dome to mark the crossing. This church possessed a remarkable series of frescoes, covering every available wall space, which was completed a few years after the construction of the church. The building suffered greatly in the last war, and the destruction of the frescoes was a serious loss.

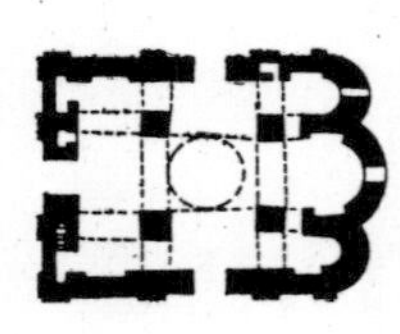

After Loukomski.
Sancta Sophia, Novgorod.
Scale 50 *ft. to* 1 *in.*

Throughout the Middle Ages, Russia was directly inspired by Constantinople in its art and its architecture, but after the fall of that city to the Turks, artists and architects were invited to Russia from Italy and Germany to undertake the principal building activities. These activities were then centred in Moscow, which was rapidly becoming the focus of a new unified Russia. The churches continued to follow the traditional Byzantine ground plan and the traditional mural decoration internally, but were profusely decorated with Renaissance ornament outside. A tall pyramidal structure, derived from the traditional Russian wooden steeple, was introduced over the crossing in place of the central dome. By the middle of the sixteenth century the architecture had become so thoroughly Russianised as to deserve classification as a distinct style of its own. Although this style

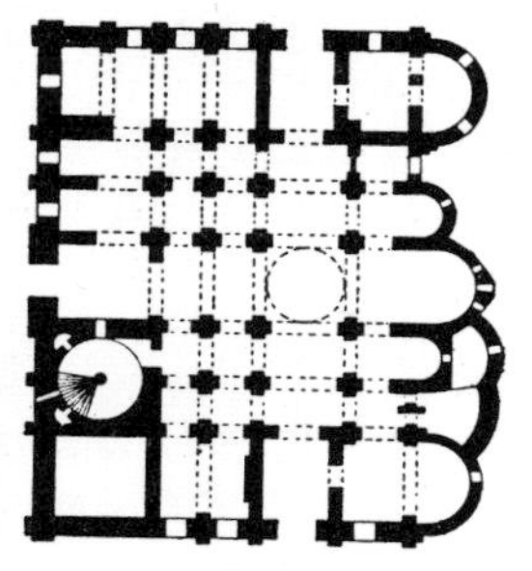

After Loukomski.

S. Saviour, Nereditsa, near Novgorod.
Scale 50 ft. to 1 in.

After Buxton.

S. Basil, Moscow.
Scale 50 ft. to 1 in.

cannot be considered to belong to the second period with which this chapter is chiefly concerned, mention is made here in order to complete this part of the story. One example only will be cited, one which is unique, yet combines nearly all the features that are typical. It is the Church of S. Basil in Moscow, the Vasili Blazhenni, in the Red Square (Pl. 8). It was begun by Ivan the Terrible in 1554 to commemorate the conquest of Kazan, but was not completed until 1679. Nothing like it exists either in the West or in the Byzantine Empire, but most of its forms can be traced back to the Byzantine style. The eight bulb-like domes are each different and painted in the most brilliant colours. It has an almost symmetrical plan, consisting of nine variously shaped chapels surrounding a larger, centrally-planned church, all being linked by an intricate series of corridors and passageways. Altogether it is a most bizarre and complicated building—the most fantastic development of Byzantine architecture imaginable.

CHURCHES IN THE WEST

The boundaries of the Byzantine Empire varied considerably throughout the centuries. During the reign of Justinian (527–565) they were extended as far west as Spain and included the whole of Italy and Sicily. Apart from the churches in Ravenna, described in the last chapter, there are no significant monuments of that period in the West. By the eleventh century, although the Empire had dwindled and no part of Italy remained under its control (despite close commercial ties), and although the government in Sicily lay in the hands of Norman conquerors, there was a distinct flowering in art and architecture that was essentially Byzantine. To some extent this was the product of growing trade and commerce in the Mediterranean, but in a much greater degree it was a result of the Crusades. The troops of the first three Crusades travelled via Constantinople, and those taking part in the Fourth Crusade (1204) concentrated their energies on the sacking and looting of Constantinople itself. The plunder which was carried back to western Europe, and the travellers' tales of the glories of the city, undoubtedly excited the imagination of western artists and had a palpable influence on art and architecture. In Venice and Sicily the 'new' architecture may have been merely a return to the art of Justinian's time, but in central France—where numerous domed churches are to be found—nothing like it had been experienced before.

S. Mark's, Venice. The original Church of S. Mark was built at the beginning of the ninth century upon a basilican plan and of proportions similar to those of the church at Torcello (see p. 31). It was partially burnt down during an insurrection in 976 and restored two years later. Thus it remained until about 1063, when important alterations were made which completely changed its plan and appearance.[1] The present plan was entirely the work of Byzantine architects. It would appear, from a description by Procopius, that it reproduced Justinian's Church of the Holy Apostles in Constantinople.[2] The alterations by which a basilican church with wooden roofs was transformed into a church of Greek cross plan, with domes, can be understood by reference to the plan. The nave columns were removed, and at the newly-formed crossing four big piers, each the full width of an aisle, were built, with corresponding piers at the west end. Each pier is penetrated by openings, the arched heads of which correspond with the arcades between the piers in the nave and transepts. From these piers there spring barrel vaults which, branching out on all sides, support the pendentives and the domes. There are five domes, the two larger being placed over the nave and crossing. The domes over the transepts and chancel are narrower by the width of the coupled columns which are placed against the big piers—a particularly happy method of obtaining the diminution in width before mentioned as characteristic of Byzantine churches (see pp. 74–75). The larger domes are 40 feet in diameter, and their crowns nearly 100 feet above the floor; the lesser domes are 33 feet wide, and their crowns slightly lower.

Although S. Mark's is in many important respects different from Sancta Sophia, Constantinople, the two churches are often compared, because the same Byzantine spirit animates both. S. Mark's looks like a large church, but it is relatively small and, but for the transepts and narthex, the whole of it could be put inside the nave alone of Sancta Sophia. The arcades between the piers in the nave and transepts perform the same duty as do those in Sancta Sophia, of giving scale to the interior, but there the resemblance ends. In Sancta Sophia they have a constructive as well as

[1] Of the basilican church only the lateral and west walls remain, and possibly portions of the walls of the east end.

[2] This church was destroyed by the Turks in 1464.

an aesthetic value; in S. Mark's they merely carry mean little galleries, less than 3 feet wide, which lead from one great pier to the other. This feature is undoubtedly one of the principal defects in S. Mark's, whose galleries contrast very unfavourably with their spacious counterparts in eastern churches. In Venice, large

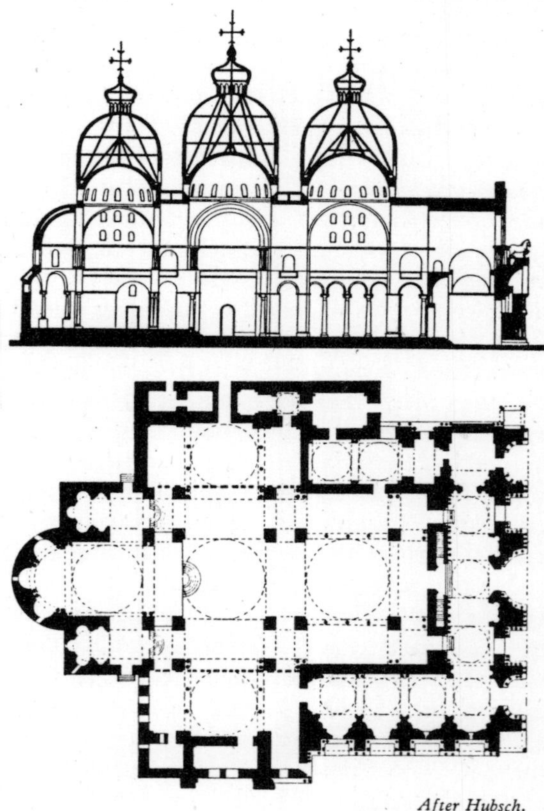

After Hubsch.

S. Mark's, Venice. Heavy dotted line indicates the limits of the original basilica.

Scale 100 *ft. to* 1 *in.*

galleries would have served no practical purpose, since in western countries the sexes were not separated to the same extent as in the East; but these apologies for galleries were probably retained because the Greek architect wanted an excuse for side columns, which he knew from experience to be extremely effective in a design. The aisle walls have round-headed windows, and are carried up the full height of the church to the underside of the barrel vaults, as at S. Irene. The principal lighting, however, is by windows in the domes, sixteen in each, arranged, as in Sancta Sophia, just above the springing. There are no drums, which is proof that drums were by no means universal in later Byzantine churches. The chancel is raised a few feet above the rest of the church, and beneath the chancel and a portion of the nave are the crypts, parts of which belong to the original church.

The Internal Finishes. As in other Byzantine churches, mouldings are very sparingly used. Nothing more than slight string courses or very small cornices are introduced to break the surfaces of the vaults, pendentives and domes, or to define the division between the marble veneer on the ground storey and the mosaics covering the upper surfaces. Some of the mosaics are very beautiful, others are regrettable—according to whether they are early or late in date. The earlier, mostly of the eleventh or twelfth century, are the work of Greek craftsmen from Constantinople, and nothing could possibly be more effective, in a decorative sense, nor could the design be more suitable for this material. The single figures, or groups of figures, are clearly defined, and are separated by vast expanses of plain gold mosaic, dimly lit by the small semi-circular-headed lights in the domes. The later mosaics were designed by Renaissance painters, and are simply bad painting transmuted to mosaic. Nothing could be less effective, nor, upon a Byzantine structure, less suitable.

The capitals of the columns show great variety of design and much skill in execution. The principal capitals are modified Corinthian, crowned by the impost block, or dosseret, already referred to (p. 56). There is more carving inside S. Mark's than is customary in Byzantine churches, since slabs of various dates, many from the old basilica, have been inserted in the gallery fronts and as wall linings in other parts of the church. Many are like those in Constantinople, with their interlacing bands and flat decorative design of peacocks and other birds. The fittings are very rich and include the iconostasis with the figures of the Virgin and the Apostles; the pulpits, one of which is crowned by a bulbous dome of eastern outline; the *pala d'oro* (now modified to form the altar-piece), an exceedingly delicate example of Byzantine workmanship covered with gold and silver plate, which was executed in Constantinople in the beginning of the twelfth century; and the famous marble floor, with its mixture of large slabs and small tesserae arranged in an intricate pattern.[1] Although S. Mark's has suffered much from alterations and additions, it is still a Byzantine church, and within its richly furnished interior it is still possible to recapture, even more than in Sancta Sophia, the atmosphere of almost oriental mystery which pervaded so much of the architecture of the Eastern Empire.

The Exterior. It is easy to find fault with the outside of S. Mark's; to ridicule its bulbous domes, its gingerbread ornament, its objectionable mosaic 'pictures' of inflated Renaissance cherubs, and the huge expanse of glass in the upper part of its big central window. What the church was like in the thirteenth century is seen in the enchanting mosaic over the door in the north-west corner, which depicts the arrival of the remains of S. Mark to their final resting place, the saint's haloed head peeping over the edge of the coffin to see and bless his funeral escort; in the background is portrayed the church, devoid of all the marble *bijouterie* of the late Renaissance. And yet it may be claimed that this long, low building has, even now, the most fascinating façade in Christendom. It has a glamour which is felt at first sight, and which increases with each visit. S. Mark's is, as Ruskin said, 'a vast illuminated missal, bound with alabaster instead of parchment, studded with porphyry pillars instead of jewels, and written within and without in letters of enamel and gold.'

The charm of S. Mark's is due partly to its situation, partly to its colour (especially in the delightful contrast between the porphyry columns and green marble jambs surrounding the central doorway), and partly to the fact that, while there is sufficient resemblance between the different parts to produce a symmetrical whole, the variety in the detail and the modifications in each division afford endless interest. The casing of the external walls with marble was begun in the thirteenth century, at which time, also, most of the columns which flank the doorways were added. These were for the most part brought from earlier buildings of different periods, the impost mouldings which surmount them, and the square plinths on which they rest, being specially worked to receive them. A curious, but a most effective jumble they make. Columns rarely stand directly over one another, or underneath the arches they are apparently intended to support; in

[1] Probably nobody today holds the opinion that was once so warmly championed: that the irregularities of its surface are due to design and were meant to symbolise the waves of the sea.

fact, they are arranged with a glorious disregard of structural custom which is quite refreshing, and which emphasises thoroughly their unconstructional, decorative character. Only a Greek from Constantinople, who had observed the superimposition of columns at Sancta Sophia, could have felt able to disregard traditional criteria by placing, at the corners of a building, six columns over one solitary shaft.

Little of the original face of the exterior shows, except at the sides, where in places the plain brick arches and walls, customary in Byzantine work, are still visible. In the thirteenth century the low brick domes which still show internally were surmounted by bulbous cupolas of an oriental pattern. The effect they produce is bizarre but not unpleasing, although very contrary to what one expects in a western church. But Venice can hardly be regarded as a western city. It occupies such an exceptional position, as the port for the East, that it is only natural that with the merchandise it imported, and with the plunder that it acquired as a result of the Crusades, there should have come eastern art forms and ideas. S. Mark's, Venice, is unique in its style and its setting. No other cathedral can boast of an atrium comparable with the Piazza of S. Mark's, which has a charm of its own and is probably the only large square in Europe in which greenery is totally lacking.

S. Anthony, Padua. S. Mark's was not without its imitators. It was copied in the Church of S. Front at Perigueux in Aquitaine

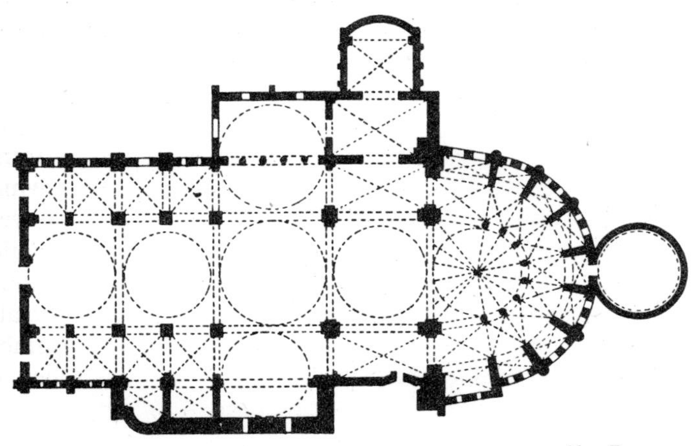

After Fergusson.

S. Anthony, Padua.
Scale 100 *ft. to* 1 *in.*

(see p. 94), and was the model for the Church of S. Anthony, Padua, which was built at the end of the twelfth and the beginning of the thirteenth century. At Padua, additional length was apparently sought, for there are seven domes instead of five, and the vaulted aisle runs round the apse. The Church of S. Anthony is a very confusing building, however; round and pointed arches are used indiscriminately, and there is a sad want of skill in the adjustment of details. The interior is striking chiefly because of its height, but as the domes are simply whitewashed, the effect is rather hard and cold when compared with the rich gold mosaic finish of S. Mark's. Externally, the Church of S. Anthony is a bewildering jumble of domes, to which are added two tall, minaret-like spires which give the whole an almost oriental quality.

S. Satiro and S. Fosca. Two other churches in north Italy possess peculiarities in plan which bring them under the head of Byzantine. The first is the little chapel of S. Satiro, in Milan, built in 879; and the second the Church of S. Fosca, at Torcello, near Venice, built in 1008. The Milan example has been altered considerably externally, and is partially enclosed by a wall of later date. Originally it was square in plan, with an apse on three of its sides—and possibly on the fourth—an arrangement doubtless suggested by the earlier and more important S. Lorenzo, of the same city (see p. 66). Internally, it becomes cruciform, like so many small churches in Constantinople, Greece and Sicily, and the squares in the corners are vaulted. A somewhat similar arrangement is followed in the Church of S. Fosca, but the plan here is more elaborate, for the east end is lengthened and divided into a chancel and side aisles of two bays each. Three tiers of squinches are used in the angles of the square, in order to arrive at a circular base for a dome that was never built; instead there is a timber roof, set upon a broad round drum. This church, and probably the basilican church alongside it, described on p. 31, were the work of the Byzantine Greeks who helped in the first restoration of S. Mark's, Venice, after the fire at the end of the tenth century.

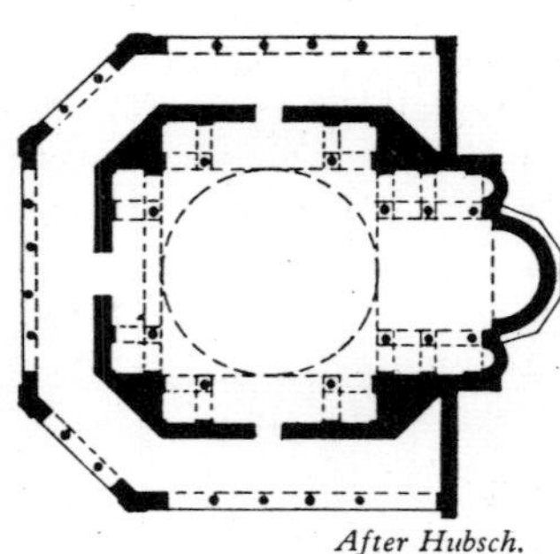

After Hubsch.

S. Fosca, Torcello.
Scale 50 ft. to 1 in.

Churches in Sicily. Early in the eleventh century, Sicily and the south of Italy were governed by Normans who, in 1038, had gone to the assistance of the Byzantines in an endeavour to drive out the Saracens. Under Norman kingship, the Byzantine-Saracenic inheritance was developed to produce an architecture that had a peculiar hybrid quality, in which Norman characteristics were singularly absent. Nothing remains of the architecture of the period of Justinian, when Sicily was part of the Byzantine Empire, nor are there any relics of Saracen times. But these deficiencies are amply compensated for by the number of churches of the Norman period which are chiefly the work of Greek artists and Mohammedan craftsmen. All the examples are in or near Palermo and all have domes, except two large basilican churches bedecked with Byzantine mosaics (see pp. 191–3). The domes are invariably raised on squinches, and are unlike any in the Byzantine world. They rise above the square walls of fine ashlar like great bubbles, plastered, and painted a dull reddish-brown. There is no definition of a drum, but instead the domes are stilted to allow for occasional window openings at the base.

The earliest church in Palermo is S. John of the Hermits (1132), which has five domes set on squinches, two over the nave and three —smaller—over the choir and transepts. The north transept is heightened to form a domed bell-tower. All the arches and windows are pointed.

There are three other important churches in Palermo which exhibit Byzantine features. The first is the Church of the Martorana (1143), which was originally named S. Mary of the Admiral. It is of the cross-in-square type, with four Corinthian columns to carry the dome. In 1588 the main front was pulled down and the western arm prolonged to form a Latin cross. Inside there are some fine Byzantine mosaics, cheek by jowl with some sweetly sentimental Renaissance frescoes (Pl. 7). The second church is the Capella Palatina (1143), in the Palace, which has been called the most beautiful Chapel Royal in the world. It has a nave of five bays, with a dome raised high on squinch arches at the eastern end. All the wall areas above the marble dado are covered with the finest mosaics in western Europe. Thirdly, there is the Church of S. Cataldo (1161), which has a cross-in-square plan and three domes defining the nave, crossing and choir. Only one apse

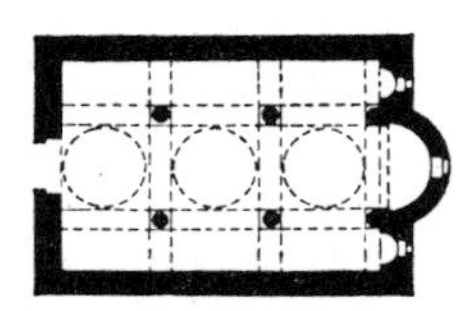

After Henderson.
S. Cataldo, Palermo.
Scale 50 ft. to 1 in.

projects at the eastern end, and the cross-in-square plan is disguised on the outside by the heightening of the corner bays.

Two other buildings must be mentioned. One is significant, not only because it is particularly delightful architecturally, but also because it is one of the very few examples of secular architecture in the Byzantine tradition that have survived. It is La Piccola Cuba, a little garden kiosk which was situated in the Royal pleasure park, now an orange grove. It consists quite simply of four pointed arches, which form a square and carry a stilted dome, beneath which, originally, a fountain played. The other building, once the Church of Trinità di Delia, Castelvetrano, is now a mausoleum. It is a cross-in-square building with three round apses, having a central dome set above squinches and carried on four columns, with antique capitals, which mark the crossing. Apart from a Renaissance tomb it is quite bare inside. Outside it is very pleasant; golden-coloured, rather solid in appearance, relieved only by a series of flat, pointed arches and the dome which crowns the composition. The windows are fitted with fretted plaster screens, Saracenic in character (Pl. 8).

Domed Churches in Southern Italy. The influences which moulded the civilisation and the art of southern Italy are identical with those which affected Sicily. Greeks, Romans, Byzantines, Saracens and Normans in turn played their part. Nothing remains of the period of Byzantine dominion, but many of the buildings have the same mingling of Byzantine and Saracenic influences that we have noted at Palermo. Most of the surviving examples, however, are slightly earlier than those at Palermo, being ascribed by C. A. Cummings[1] to the middle of the ninth century. Two churches—La Cattolica at Stilo and S. Mark at Rossano—have true cross-in-square plans; and two others—the cathedral at Molfetta and the small Church of the Immaculati at Trani—have naves with three domes in line, like S. Cataldo at Palermo.

The little Church of La Cattolica, which measures only 25 feet square, is thoroughly Byzantine in structure and plan, but lacks the customary interior decoration. Four columns, without bases and with roughly-blocked capitals, support twelve arches which divide the interior into nine bays, each about 5 feet square. The central bay is covered by a dome raised high on a drum and capped by a low-pitched conical roof. The four corner bays are similarly covered by domes, but on lower drums. Almost identical in

[1] *Architecture in Italy*, London, 1928.

dimensions, structure and plan is the Church of S. Mark at Rossano; but instead of columns to carry the arches there are piers, and in front of the church there is a small atrium. Both are dramatically sited on high rocks, and both are remarkable monuments to the diffusion of the cross-in-square—that most perfect

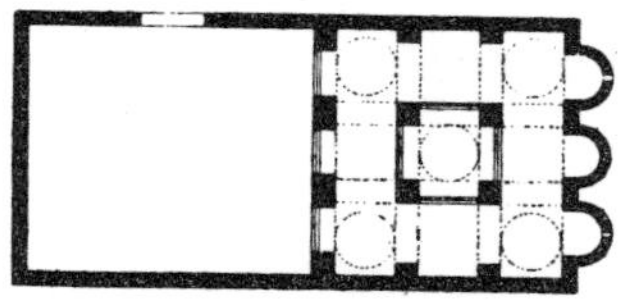

After Cummings.

S. Mark, Rossano.

Scale 50 *ft. to* 1 *in.*

form which is typical of so much Byzantine architecture of the second and third periods.

In the cathedral at Molfetta the nave is separated from the aisles by three broad round arches, which spring from cruciform piers, each composed of four half-columns. The domes over the nave

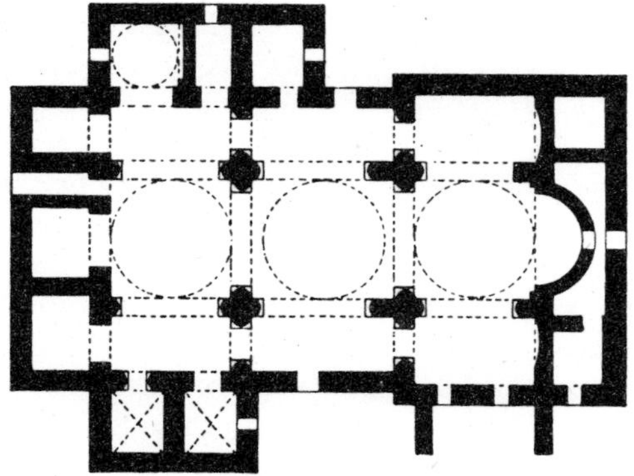

After Fergusson.

Molfetta Cathedral.

Scale 50 *ft. to* 1 *in.*

are carried on squinch arches, and the aisles are covered by half-barrel-vaults. An unusual feature is the parabolic section of the central dome. The other two are hemispherical; but all three are octagonal outside and covered by low-pitched, conical, tiled roofs.

Domed Churches in France. The remarkable group of domed churches, built during the eleventh and twelfth centuries in the heart of France, are mentioned in this chapter because they bear such a close relationship to Byzantine architecture, and because they are of a style which was not later developed in the evolution of Romanesque and Mediaeval architecture.

Perigueux may be taken as the centre of the region. In this town there are two domed churches: S. Etienne, built, in part, about 1050, and the great five-domed Church of S. Front which, excepting portions of an earlier church which form a kind of narthex at the west end, was rebuilt after a fire in 1120 (Pl. 7). The similarity in plan and dimensions between S. Front and S. Mark's, Venice (see p. 86), cannot be accidental. S. Mark's was copied from the Church of the Holy Apostles at Constantinople, which was still standing in 1564, and it is therefore possible that the architects of S. Front may also have gone there for their inspiration. The early Crusaders were largely directed by Frankish leaders, and upon their return they may well have desired to reproduce in their homeland something of the style and magnificence which they had seen in Constantinople. It has also been suggested that the existence of a Venetian colony of merchants and artists in Limoges, sixty miles from Perigueux, may have stimulated the development of a new type of architecture in the region. By 1120 S. Mark's was completed, so far as its main structure was concerned, and the idea of copying its plan may have had some appeal to the builders in the south of France who, according to R. Phené Spiers,[1] had for more than a century been building churches with domes, and who had already devised a method, peculiarly their own, of building a dome on pendentives over a square space. On the other hand, French authorities are inclined to the belief that S. Front was built earlier than S. Mark's, that it was, in fact,

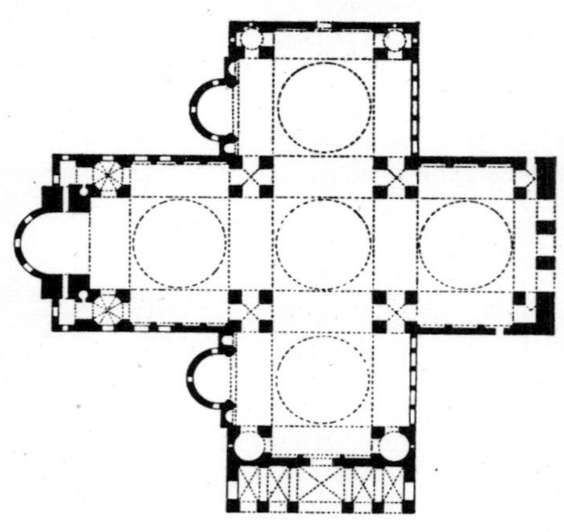

After Spiers.

S. Front, Perigueux. Compare with plan of S. Mark's (p. 86).

Scale 100 *ft. to* 1 *in.*

[1] *Architecture East and West*, London, 1905.

founded about 984 and only repaired in 1120, and that the method of construction adopted there was followed in later examples at Angoulême, Cahors and Fontevrault. The conflict between the different theories is further complicated by the fact that the Church of S. Front was, after 1856, almost entirely pulled down and rebuilt by *M.* Abadia, an architect who, instead of copying the old work, was inclined to introduce 'improvements' of his own in order to bring the resemblance to S. Mark's closer than it may have been originally.

Comparison Between S. Mark's and S. Front. The five domes of S. Front, like those of S. Mark's, rise over each arm and over the crossing, but unlike S. Mark's they are all of the same diameter, about 40 feet, and there are no detached shafts against the piers, as in the transepts and choir of S. Mark's, to reduce the span and therefore the diameter of the domes. This in itself is an argument against Byzantine workmanship; for no architects closely associated with Byzantine architecture could have failed to notice the fine effect such breaks produced, or would have omitted them in the design of any building similar to S. Mark's. In S. Front the domes are all carried on pointed transverse and longitudinal arches, which spring from four heavy square piers pierced with narrow, semi-circular-headed openings. S. Front lacks the arcading between the big piers which helps to give the scale of S. Mark's, and because of this omission and the complete absence of any wall decoration, it does not look so large as its prototype. In S. Front the three apses are placed at the east end of the choir and on the eastern walls of the transepts, whereas at S. Mark's the triple apse of the old basilica is retained. The most remarkable differences are, however, to be found in the detail construction of the pendentives and domes. The pendentives in S. Front are constructed with horizontal beds, like corbelling, across the angles of the square instead of radial to the curve. Nor are these pendentives simply a part of a sphere, for, in order to reduce the overhang of the topmost courses, they have a curve of double flexure. It is obvious that the designer was unhappy about the stability of the pendentives, and not thoroughly at home with the construction he had adopted, for instead of allowing the domes to spring from the face of the pendentives in the Byzantine manner, he set them well behind the topmost course to form a gallery. At Angoulême and Fontevrault, both built a few years earlier, the domes spring naturally from the pendentives, as in all Byzantine work, but at

S. Etienne, Perigueux, and Cahors Cathedral, the domes begin as in S. Front. The domes are not, as a rule, spherical, but ovoid, with a considerable thickening of masonry at the top to provide a steeper outer surface. The reason for this steepening was probably that the outside could then be protected with tiles laid directly on to the surface; in the Byzantine tradition lead covering was usual and therefore no increase in the pitch of the dome was necessary.

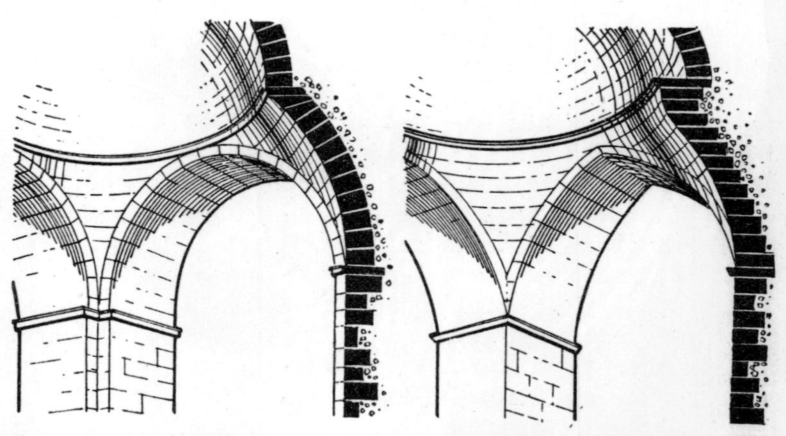

Comparison between Byzantine (left) and French (right) methods of dome construction.

Aisleless Domed Churches. S. Front can hardly be said to be without aisles, but they are merely the width of the great piers supporting the domes, and are in no way cut off from the rest of the church. Most of the other large domed churches in the area are aisleless. Some of the smaller churches, such as those of Mouthiers and Berneuil, have only one dome, which generally separates the barrel-vaulted nave and chancel. However, in all the larger churches (Angoulême, Fontevrault, Solignac, Souillac) the naves, which are from two to four bays long, exclusive of the bay at the crossing, are domed.

The Cathedral of Angoulême (1101–1119) may be taken as a typical example of an aisleless domed church In plan it is a Latin cross. The transepts have considerable projection and terminate in square towers. Between each tower and the crossing is a narrow bay which finishes with an apse on the east wall. Around the chancel the apses are somewhat unusually placed, the arrangement being similar to that in Issoire Cathedral, Auvergne, except that there is no ambulatory aisle. Only the dome over the crossing can be seen from the outside, for the chancel and the narrow transept bays are barrel-vaulted and the nave domes are hidden by the covering timber roof. This roof precludes win-

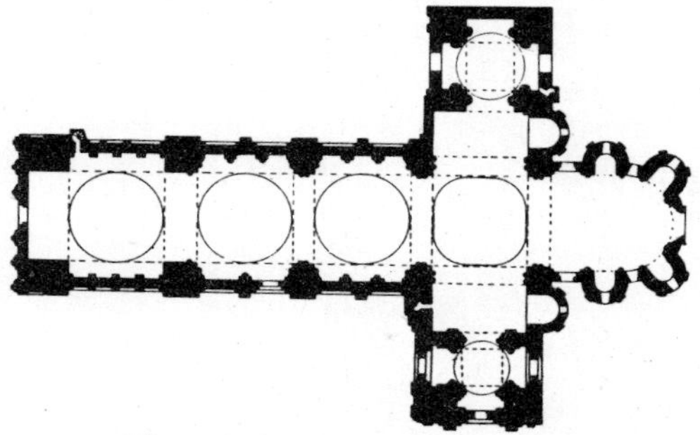

Plan of Angoulême Cathedral.
Scale 100 *ft. to* 1 *in.*

dows in the domes, which is not a matter of much importance since, with an aisleless plan, plenty of light can be obtained from the side walls.

There is no doubt that the aisleless plan can be employed on a large scale with excellent effects, both outside and in. That the naves in these examples are domed is, so to speak, an accident. They could just as well be vaulted, as in Angers Cathedral, which has a similar plan (see p. 246). The want of columns between the piers, which give scale in Roman and Byzantine buildings, is not felt so much as one might expect because their place is taken by arcading on the side walls, which produces much the same result. The chief objection, however, to the aisleless plan is the danger of the chancel's being unnecessarily wide. At Angoulême an attempt was made to solve this problem by narrowing the chancel so that it was only a trifle wider than the space between the piers of the nave, but at Fontevrault, which was built a little later, the arrangement is more ingenious. Here the square at the crossing is made narrower than the nave and is separated from it by an arch of fair proportions with narrow openings on either side. Eastwards is an apsidal-ended chancel encompassed by an ambulatory, out of which chapels open. The result is a complete chevet, joined to an aiseless nave, while any effect of incongruity, either outside or inside, is avoided by the projecting transepts.

The aisleless domed church, however, lacks the simplicity of the barrel-vaulted nave, which will be discussed later. The domed form is suited better to a centralised arrangement than to a Latin cross plan. In the examples we have mentioned, the disposition of domes of equal diameter along the axis of the nave inevitably produces a series of separate compartments without a dominating central motif. Whether the inspiration for these domed churches is to be found in Constantinople, in Venice, or even in the local remains of Roman domical buildings which might have survived up to the eleventh century, we shall never know. It is, however, certain that by the middle of the twelfth century no more domed churches were constructed in France, and that the Gothic technique of building, with its vertical aspiration, its ribbed vaults and traceried windows, had effectively taken their place.

CHAPTER VII

BYZANTINE ARCHITECTURE OF THE THIRD PERIOD

THE story of the culminating period of the Byzantine Empire, between its release from the Crusaders in 1261 and the fall of Constantinople to the Turks in 1453, makes sad reading. Its buildings cannot compare in size or magnificence with those of the earlier periods. They are, in fact, extraordinarily small, for they were no longer designed for the pomp and ceremony of a church militant, but erected for the private prayers and meditations of a people suffering almost constant war with the Mohammedans in the East. It must not be inferred, however, that because they are small they are architecturally insignificant. Indeed, they surpass in many respects the architecture that preceded them. They are simpler in design, and ornament is used very sparingly; they are invariably sited with great skill, either in quiet sequestered valleys or—dramatically—upon almost inaccessible cliffs; they possess a quiet charm and a classic simplicity that is all their own.

Apart from one church in Constantinople which, though of old foundation, was so thoroughly altered as to justify its inclusion here, nearly all the examples are to be found in Greece, a country which seems to have played a minor rôle until the last tragic phase of the Empire. The number of these lesser churches is surprisingly great, and it is to be regretted that a complete record of them does not yet exist. The better known are concentrated in two areas: on Mount Athos—a peninsula at the north-east of Greece where monastic communities were established from very early times—and at Mistra, a provincial capital in the Peloponnese, where the last of the Byzantine Emperors was crowned.

S. Saviour, Constantinople (Pl. 6). The Church of S. Saviour at Constantinople was founded by Justinian and took the form of a basilica. It was rebuilt in the eleventh century and, like many other churches in Constantinople, suffered greatly during the Fourth Crusade; it was not until fourteen years after the restoration of the imperial dynasty that steps were taken once more to rebuild the church. It was the first Christian sanctuary in Constantinople to fall into the hands of the Mohammedans in 1453, and was soon after converted into a mosque. In its present form the plan is, as one might expect, very irregular, and its chief attraction lies in the remarkable series of mosaics which still cover considerable areas of the interior.

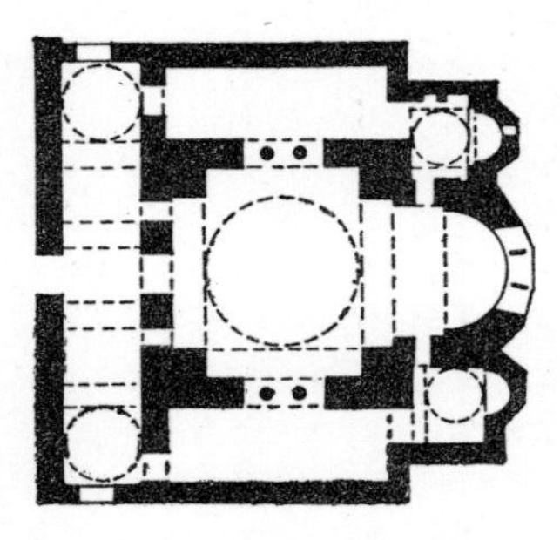

After Van Millingen.
Plan (restored) of S. Saviour, Constantinople.
Scale 50 ft. to 1 in.

These mosaics represent a remarkable flowering in the latter-day history of Byzantine art. They are characterised by great freedom from traditional forms, a more varied use of colour and a much more adventurous feeling for pictorial composition than was evident in earlier work, when the discipline of the Church was more rigidly enforced. It is interesting to note that the mosaics at S. Saviour are contemporary with Giotto's famous frescoes at Padua (1303–1306), and although there is nothing to suggest a connection between the two, their similarity is undoubtedly due to the new spirit of the age that was affecting life and thought East and West. In one way the fourteenth century was a time of freedom from control, and in another, it was a time of scarcity and unemployment. S. Saviour is the last effort, upon any scale, of Byzantine art in Constantinople. The city and empire at that time were suffering from the gradually increasing pressure of the Turkish invaders, and as a result many craftsmen were escaping to Italy, where they played their part in stimulating that great revival of the arts which we now call the Renaissance.

Mount Athos. On the peninsula of Mount Athos are preserved to this day not only many buildings, but also the spirit and habits of Byzantine religious life. Legend ascribes the foundation of Athos as a site for the ascetic life to the Virgin Mary, who is presumed to have landed at the Port of Clement, near the present monastery of Iveron; but the first historical records date from the ninth century. Throughout the Middle Ages it was regarded as a holy land, a residence for monks and hermits. In 1430, Athos, sharing the fate of Salonika, fell to the Turks, but was allowed to continue its monastic autonomy upon payment of tribute, so that

Turkish rule brought no vital changes to the religious constitution. There are now some twenty monasteries on Athos, inhabited by about five thousand monks drawn from Greece and the surrounding Slavonic countries. Nearly all the architecture dates from the fifteenth to the eighteenth century, and therefore extends by three centuries the period normally included in Byzantine studies.

Mount Athos affords unequalled opportunities for studying the planning and design of that conglomeration of buildings which constitutes a Byzantine monastery. The most notable feature, and the one which distinguishes it from its western counterparts, is the position of the church. Instead of occupying one side of a cloister, the Orthodox church is invariably situated centrally, and surrounded by a court. The arrangement of this court naturally varies according to the limitations of the site, but it is generally more or less rectangular, and accommodates the refectory, kitchen and stores, the library, infirmary and monastic cells. There are no windows on the outside of the lower floors, except where these were inavoidable, and a single strongly-defended gateway provides the only entrance. Finally, at some strategic point stands a tower, which was a part of the defences and a place of refuge in the event of attack by pirates. The churches stand in the middle of the courtyards and are of the cross-in-square type, but have certain additions by which they almost merit inclusion in a special class of their own. The transepts terminate in apses, instead of in the customary square ending, and these are reserved for the readers and chief dignitaries of the monastery;[1] the narthex is abnormally large, and in many cases gives access to side chapels which are miniature editions of the

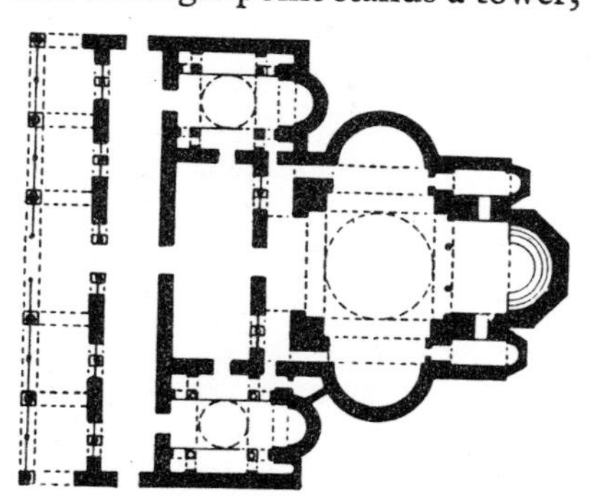

After Hasluck.

Church of the Monastery of Lavra, Mount Athos.

Scale 50 ft. to 1 in.

[1] This tri-apsidal treatment is, according to F. W. Hasluck (*Athos and its Monasteries*), presumed to have come from Armenian sources, but the Church of S. Elias in Salonika, twelfth century, and the ruins of S. Mary of the Mongols at Constantinople, thirteenth century, have similar arrangements and are therefore just as likely to have inspired this Athonite treatment.

original church; and additional domes are placed over the apses at the east, over the side chapels and frequently over each end of the narthex.

Inside, the churches are richly decorated with mural paintings, which follow the customary scheme in which every saint and martyr has his or her appropriate place. From the central dome there hangs by chains the corona, a circular gilt candelabrum which provides the most effective and dramatic lighting to the singular elongated figures that line the walls. Immediately beyond the crossing stretches the iconostasis, a carved and gilded wooden screen with doors, which forms a framework for two rows of icon pictures and which cuts off the chancel, or bema, from the nave. The bema inevitably has three apses, the central one containing the altar; the north flanking apse is used for preparing the Elements and the south as a treasury for the most sacred relics of the monastery.

The materials used in the construction of the churches and monastic buildings are generally rough rubble masonry. Occasionally tiles are inserted in the outer face, either to define the architectural lines or simply to provide decorative patterns; as a general rule, however, the churches are plastered and painted in horizontal bands of reddish brown and white, to imitate courses of tile and stone. The roofs and domes are leaded and of a very low pitch. In front of the church is the phiale, or sacred well, which usually has a dome carried on eight or more columns. From the water of this well the various rooms in the monastery are ceremonially blessed each month.

This, then, is the standard arrangement of buildings at Athos, but there are many variations in detail and in character. Each monastery has its own particular atmosphere. At Chilandari, which caters for Serbs and Bulgarians, the introduction of sculptured plaques, and the numerous carved doors, betray north Balkan influence. At Dochiariou, the church displays Moldavian features in the elongated proportions of the drums and in the use of buttresses; and at Russico one is presented with a scene that could only be paralleled in Holy Russia or in the stage settings of *Prince Igor* or *Boris Godunov*.

Churches in Greece. It is not possible to mention here more than a few of the lesser churches in Greece. Until a thorough survey is undertaken, one cannot even be sure that those mentioned are the most important. Probably no other country contains so many places of worship in proportion to its population. Many are far from villages or towns, and though often in ruins are still used for services on the name-day of the saint to which they are dedicated, and keep an ever-burning votary lamp. They are simple and unpretentious little buildings, constructed upon the cross-in-square plan, and either whitewashed or faced with roughly dressed stone, relieved by lines of brick or tile at each course, and crowned by dark red tiled roofs which, over the central dome, are either shaped to its curvature or conical.

The little whitewashed church of S. Sotiros, west of Athens, possesses all the features of the period. It stands on rising ground and is marked by four ancient cypress trees, one to each corner. The interior is fully frescoed, and the tiny dome is carried on four debased Ionic columns; such use of classical remains is very common, especially in the vicinity of Athens. Occasionally, one finds only two columns to support the dome on the western side, and two piers, which are an internal prolongation of the apse, on the eastern.

Omorphi Ecclesia ('Beautiful Church'), on the barren plain beyond Patisia, is one of the most charming of the many churches in the Attic countryside (Pl. 8). Its dome, enriched with angle columns, follows the Athenian style, and is carried on free-standing piers in place of columns on the west side, and on the two walls which divide the apsidal end on the east. Faded frescoes still adorn the interior, and a number of fragments of Byzantine sculpture, depicting peacocks and various animals entwined in a pattern of leaves, all in low relief, have been built into the walls.

Some two hundred miles to the north-west of Athens, in the heart of Greece, are the monasteries of Meteora, which owe their name (which means 'the monasteries in the air') to their remarkable position on the summits of gigantic rocks which rise like monstrous sugar-loaves up to 1800 feet from the Thessalian plain. These monasteries are among the most fantastic remains of Byzantine architecture. Once there were thirty, the majority being of fourteenth-century foundation. Of these, nearly half had disappeared before the middle of the sixteenth century, and today only six remain inhabited. The rest are, for the most part, in ruins, and no longer accessible. About a hundred years ago several of the monasteries could only be reached by means of a net and winch, controlled by the monks above, but more settled conditions in the early part of this century have led to the provision, in the surviving six monasteries, of a simpler, pedestrian approach. The churches, which are crowded into minute courtyards, are all tiny and of the cross-in-square plan. That of S. Stephen is adorned with frescoes, considerably disfigured by the Turks, and the Monastery of S. Baarlam has, in the narthex, a magnificent representation of the Last Trump.

The Church of the Holy Apostles, in Salonika, though only 55 feet by 60 feet externally, is one of the largest churches of the period. It was built in the fourteenth century and is the most elaborate example of the Byzantine use of decorative brickwork. There are five domes, one over the crossing and one over each of the angle spaces, and all are constructed of brick. The whole of the exterior is richly patterned. Bricks are arranged in herring-bone fashion, in squares and in diamonds (Pl. 6). The five domes rest on tall, elegant, octagonal drums, with brick columns at the corners, carrying complex arched cornices, contrived of bricks set angle-wise to give the effect of successive orders of dentils. In plan it resembles the Church of S. Theotokos Pammakaristos, at Constantinople (see p. 76), though in elevation every feature is taller in proportion.

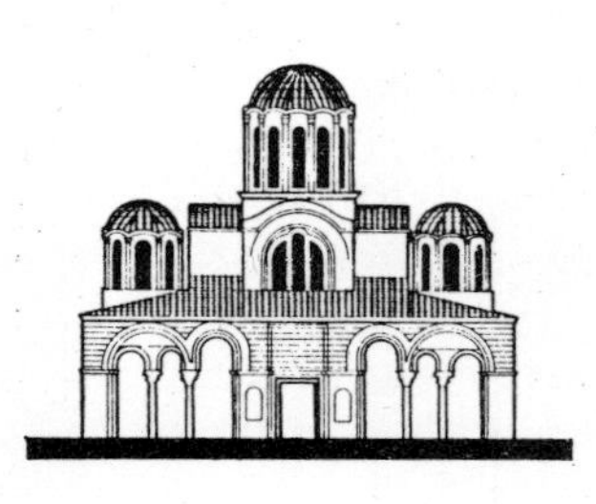

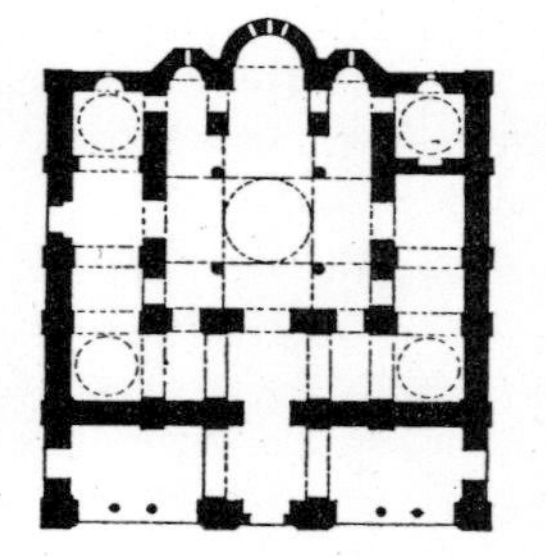

After Texier and Pullan.
Holy Apostles, Salonika.
Scale 50 ft. to 1 in.

In distinct contrast, the Church of S. Nicholas at Monamvasia, a promontory on the south-east coast of the Peloponnese, is strong, grey and forbidding, and constructed of limestone smeared with whitewash. The interior is plain and empty of any enrichment. The solitary dome is cemented over on the outside, as are the barrel vaults which cover the arms of the cross. Apart from the curious Renaissance doorway, a product of the Venetian occupation in the sixteenth century, there is no ornament outside of any kind. Instead, here is an architecture reduced to bare essentials, in harmony only with the barren character of that bleak and cragged coast.

Mistra. The city of Mistra, which lies on the foothills of

Mount Taygetus, some two-and-a-half miles from Sparta, is the most famous Byzantine centre in the Peloponnese, and probably the only purely Byzantine city in the world. For a brief period the district was held by the Crusaders, but in 1262 it was restored to the Empire, and Mistra became a despotate with the son of the Emperor reigning as Despot. For two hundred years Mistra prospered, and attained considerable eminence as a seat of Byzantine culture and learning; it was the last outpost of the Empire to fall to the Turks. For nine years after the capture of Constantinople, Mistra had maintained a precarious existence in the face of growing pressure from the Turkish armies. Then in 1462 the city, and the remainder of Greece, fell, so bringing to a close the Byzantine Empire and Greek dominion in Europe.

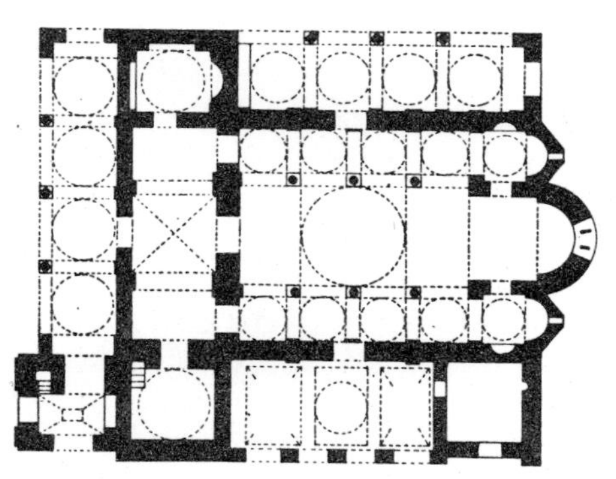

After Hamilton.

Pantanassa, Mistra.
Scale 50 ft. to 1 in.

Most of the churches in Mistra are built of rubble relieved by vertical and horizontal courses of brick, enriched by blank arcades and, inside, by some of the most beautiful frescoes in the world. Three of the churches, all of the fourteenth century, are of the two-column, cross-in-square plan, and three are domed basilicas with aisles. Of the latter the most important is the Pantanassa, which is now attached to a convent and has been partly restored. It has a bell tower with trefoil arches and an ovoid dome, similar in character to some of the earlier bell towers of Aquitaine and unlike any in the Byzantine world; there is a cloister walk, planned along the north and west sides of the church, which is entirely novel. Inside, the frescoes have broken away completely from the almost stereotyped forms of the earlier Byzantines. New subjects and new scenes are presented in a way that has no precedent. Gone is the staid tranquillity, and in its place emotional and pictorial values are dominant. In the field of art there is certainly evidence of that early Renaissance spirit which we have already noticed at S. Saviour in Constantinople; at Mistra it is coupled with new features in architecture, but in those last years of the Empire there was little opportunity to build upon any extensive scale, and whether the Greek spirit might once more have come into its own if Greece had been spared the intolerance of Ottoman tyranny, we can never tell. The evidence at Mistra, though slight, indicates a remarkable revival of Byzantine culture. There is evidence there of a Renaissance which might have surpassed anything that had gone before, and which is only now being appreciated.

Serbia. In the heart of the Balkans, south of Belgrade, there survive a number of small churches of great charm and quality, dating from the middle of the twelfth to the middle of the fifteenth century. They enshrine a remarkably complete series of Byzantine frescoes of exceptional beauty. The churches fall into four regional groups. The first and earliest is to be found in the district immediately east of old Montenegro, and its churches consist of a single nave, preceded by a narthex and surmounted by a cupola. The second developed in Macedonia, and followed the characteristic Greek cross-in-square pattern. Further north, around Skoplje, a variation called the Kosmet style is found, in which four lesser domes define the angles of the square, in the same way as at the Holy Apostles, Salonika. Finally, in the valley of the Morava, during the last tragic period of Serbian independence, there developed an especially interesting style akin to that of the churches in the monasteries of Mount Athos, with apses to the north, south and east. The architecture of Serbia is only now receiving the attention it deserves. The churches are minute in size, often with considerable rich brick ornamentation, and occasionally incorporating Lombardic features such as arched corbel tables under the eaves, pilaster strips and even ribbed vaults.

CHAPTER VIII

ROMANESQUE ARCHITECTURE

Historical Background

ON Christmas Day, A.D. 800, Charlemagne, King of the Franks, was crowned Emperor and Augustus in the Basilica of S. Peter, Rome. This event provides a convenient starting-point for the study of the revival of art and architecture in the West. There were three good reasons for the coronation. First, it was obvious that the Emperor at Constantinople was no longer able to defend or protect the western provinces of the old Roman Empire, even if he still styled himself Caesar Imperator. Second, there was strong dissatisfaction in the western Church with the Edict of the Eastern Emperor commanding the destruction of images (726), and the claim that the Patriarch of Constantinople was on an equal, if not superior, footing to the Pope of Rome. This discontent encouraged unity among the sects of the western Church; but unity could only be achieved if there were a powerful secular commander. Third, there was an urgent need for a leader to defend Christian faith and territory from the Saracens who, in the preceding century, had swept along the northern shores of Africa and crossed to Sicily, to Spain and far into France.

Under Charlemagne, the monarchy became the strongest instrument of government and conquest which Western Europe had witnessed since the great days of the Roman Empire. The whole system of public control was transformed and the foundations of the Feudal System laid; the Saracens were driven back into Spain, the Avars driven out of Hungary, and a Papal state was established which made permanent the rift between Rome and Constantinople. The Pope then excommunicated the Patriarch, and the Patriarch excommunicated the Pope. Art and architecture participated in a renaissance, inspired partly by Roman precedents and, in the first instance, still more by the Byzantine monuments that had been erected two centuries earlier by Justinian upon the soil of Italy.

After Charlemagne's death in 814, the Empire split up and new

Map showing Principal Centres of
Romanesque Building.

states were established in the West. But all was not lost. He had introduced ideas of civil government, he had created a powerful Church, and he had brought back to western Europe learning and civilisation. In no respect was that civilisation more fruitful than in the stimulus it gave to art, and especially to architecture. It is true that the number of buildings still standing which can be attributed with certainty to Charlemagne and his immediate successors is very small, and that the descriptions of the great abbeys that arose in the ninth century are much too vague to make accurate reconstruction possible. Nevertheless, the artistic energy of the new Empire and the countries which succeeded it was certainly concentrated upon the erection of churches and monasteries, and there is no reason to doubt the appropriateness of the title Romanesque to the style of their building, for it was the Roman, not the Byzantine, influence that was to prevail.

The fact that the architecture in Germany and France was largely inspired by Rome does not mean that it developed under Italian influence. One need not infer a regular progress of architecture northwards from Italy, for in the cities of Gaul there still existed many monuments of classical Roman architecture which could provide exemplars to Carolingian and later builders. The theory that the diffusion of Romanesque architecture in the eighth and ninth centuries was achieved by a group of Lombard masons called 'Comacini',[1] from the neighbourhood of Lake Como, is without historical basis. It probably originated in the resemblance of the word *comacinus* to Como, but *co-macinus* simply means 'a body of masons', whether at Como or anywhere else.

Between the eighth and tenth centuries the essential characteristics of the Romanesque style were determined, and the beginning of the eleventh century marked a new era of development. Christianity had taken deep root throughout western Europe, and a wave of church-building was passing over all lands. The great monastic Order of the Benedictines was at first mainly responsible for the prodigious activity in ecclesiastical matters and for many of the earlier phases of architectural development. In the previous century the monks of the Order had followed to some extent the building methods prevalent in Rome: the basilican plan, with its

[1] *Comacini* should not be confused with *Cosmati*, the name of a Roman family who produced distinctive mosaic and marble work, and who were responsible for the design of the cloisters of S. Paul Outside the Walls, Rome, and the Shrine of Edward the Confessor at Westminster. (See p. 188.)

nave and aisles, and roofs of timber, formed their model. But not for long. Before the eleventh century opened, a new movement had begun which, once fairly under way, developed with great rapidity and produced lasting results. It was largely inspired by *local* Roman remains and was only indirectly influenced by the art of Rome and Constantinople. From the north we note another influence, which manifested itself chiefly in a symbolic treatment of ornament—based, perhaps, originally on eastern traditions but rendered with a robustness foreign to the East. The carvings displayed a semi-barbaric symbolism and formed a striking contrast to the refined beauty and delicacy of Classical and Byzantine art. But these carvings, if sometimes rude and unskilled, had a powerful character of their own. Their crudity may be forgiven, because they indicated an infusion of vigorous new blood and heralded the overthrow of the Classical tradition and the approach of that great northern art which was to prevail up to the middle of the fourteenth century.

Structurally, the all-important feature was the reintroduction of the intersecting vault, with the result that the timber roof disappeared from the larger churches, or was used only as a cover to protect the vault beneath. The walls thickened; columns were replaced by piers, bulky in proportion since workmen feared the thrust of the vaults, and complex in plan because their functions were multiplied.

Italy. The Romanesque style did not appear in Italy until the close of the ninth century, and the number of buildings erected then was relatively few. This is not surprising when one considers the troubled state of the country. The Teutonic race of Langobards, or Lombards, which was conquered by Charlemagne in 774, was unskilled in building craft, and there is no evidence to show that its buildings possessed any of the features which afterwards were distinctive of Lombardic architecture. Many churches still existing which were formerly attributed to the Langobards of the seventh, eighth and ninth centuries, are now recognised as belonging entirely to the eleventh or twelfth century, although erected on the sites of earlier structures. This confusion arises partly because of the existence of documentary evidence which provides records of early establishments, and partly through 'wishful thinking' on the part of certain Italian scholars, who saw Italy as the cradle of civilisation. There is always the temptation to antedate a building, especially if documentary evidence is followed, since most churches are of old foundation and occupy sites previously built on.

Charlemagne's empire at the beginning of the ninth century included north Italy, France, the northern half of Spain and the greater portion of Germany and Austria. After his death and a century and more of confusion over the boundaries of the different kingdoms which arose from the ruins, Otto the Great consolidated the German Empire and in 951 became, through marriage, King of North Italy also. For the next two hundred years the German Emperors were all-powerful there. It follows, therefore, that most of the Romanesque churches in Lombardy were built under their rule, and consequently bear a close relationship to the contemporary architecture in the rest of the Empire. The old methods of building were not ignored, but were considerably modified. Some of the modifications introduced were improvements, designed to meet the exigencies of ritual requirements and to exploit new methods of construction; others were simply retrograde, especially in the matter of detail design, because of the inferior skill of the craftsmen, who could no longer draw upon the assistance of Greek skilled labour.

The new feeling which in the eleventh century made such headway in Lombardy and western Europe met with limited success elsewhere in Italy; earlier traditions still held their own. Venice was unaffected, partly because of its position as an Adriatic port having close commercial and artistic ties with the East, and partly because of its independence as a separate state. S. Mark's is a proof of how little it was influenced by western developments. In Tuscany, too, eastern influence was extremely strong, due to the fact that Pisa, which for two or three centuries was the most important town in the district, maintained, like Venice, a large trade with the East.[1] Florence scarcely existed, and Lucca and Pistoja followed the lead of Pisa. Farther south, in the Papal territory around Rome, the Early Christian basilican form remained supreme. The south of Italy was from 871 a Byzantine colony frequently harassed by Saracen raiders, until 1040, when the Normans took over control. Some of the architecture has already been described (pp. 90–94) and only a few examples can be

[1] As evidence of the close connection between the Eastern Empire and Pisa, it may be mentioned that when, towards the end of the eleventh century, the work of Pisa Cathedral was at a standstill for lack of funds, the Byzantine Emperor came to the rescue and found the money.

classified as Romanesque. Similar conditions occurred in Sicily, which from 535 to 827 was under Byzantine control and then fell to the Saracens. The Saracens' reign was, however, short-lived, for in 1060 the Normans crossed from south Italy.

The architectural result of these conflicts is a vast difference between the eleventh- and twelfth-century work of Northern Italy and that of the rest of the country. In the north the churches of that period are mostly fully-developed Romanesque, and possess all the traits customarily associated with work described under that head, such as ribbed and vaulted naves, clustered piers, and triforium galleries; whereas farther south, when these features do occur, they are found in conjunction with others which belong strictly to another and earlier art movement. The hyphened heading, Byzantine-Romanesque, has been coined for the work and possesses the advantage of suggesting the main sources from which it was derived; but it is confusing, for in some cases the Byzantine influence is paramount, in others the Romanesque. It has been considered better, therefore, to group under one heading —Byzantine—those which are domed and have structures that are essentially eastern in character, and under another—Romanesque —those in which the long nave and basilican plan predominate, even if the superficial decoration is Byzantine.

France. In France the churches exhibit almost as much variety as their contemporaries in Italy, notwithstanding that the influence which caused the difference in the latter country hardly existed in the former. The Saracens had been driven out of France long before, and although here and there a detail may suggest Saracenic origin, the resemblance in most cases is probably accidental. The Byzantine Emperors had no footing in France, and it is very doubtful if Byzantine craftsmen ever entered the country; and yet, in central France—in Aquitaine—there is a number of domed churches which can only be classified as Byzantine and which have already been described (pp. 94–98). Of Classical influences, however, there are innumerable traces in the south, where Roman buildings were plentiful; the number of these buildings still existing is probably only a small fraction of those standing in the eleventh century. The detail of the south is almost entirely based on Roman models. In the north, remains of ancient works were few and unimportant, and the people were of a different race; the language spoken was different. Moreover, the King of France, in early days, could claim complete control over but a small portion of what is now France. Burgundy, at the beginning of the eleventh century, was part of the German Empire; the Dukes of Normandy and Brittany were to all intents and purposes their own masters; in both south and north were other dukes and counts who virtually ruled their large domains as they pleased. They acknowledged the King in Paris as their suzerain, but suzerainty in feudal days was a very doubtful force. In the latter half of the twelfth century more than half of France belonged to, or was dependent on, the Kings of England; no wonder, therefore, that, apart from differences of race and language and the presence or absence of Classical remains, the architecture of the south differed much from that of the north.

Spain. Spain exercised little influence on the early development of Romanesque architecture, because the whole of the country, with the exception of the mountainous districts near the Pyrenees and the north-west part along the Bay of Biscay, was in the hands of the Moors until the eleventh century was far advanced. The triumph of the Christians began with the recovery of Toledo in 1085, and this was followed by other successes, until the whole of the northern half of the country was in their possession. Seville was not captured until 1248, nor the Moors' last stronghold, Granada, until 1492. Street, in his *Gothic Architecture in Spain*, mentions two churches in Barcelona which were probably built in the tenth century, and some eight or ten which belong to the eleventh, but most Spanish churches are later.

The introduction of French culture and art was the most important formative influence. Towards the end of the eleventh and the beginning of the twelfth century there was a steady influx of French Crusaders, eager to displace the Moslem population. The result was that the Romanesque architecture of northern Spain closely resembled the Romanesque of southern France, with the superficial addition of a proportion of Moslem detail, executed by Moslem craftsmen who remained in the reconquered districts.

Britain. In her development of Romanesque architecture, Britain was at the beginning singularly detached from the rest of Europe. Britain was never a part of Charlemagne's domain, and in the midst of all the lawlessness of the Dark Ages the Church was the only possible source of art and civilisation. But when Rome recalled her legions in the first half of the fifth century, the country fell into the hands of the Saxons and the people returned to paganism, so that any churches that may have been built were destroyed. In Ireland Christianity continued after the Romans left England and, from the evidence of manuscripts, flourished exceedingly. Architecturally, however, there is little to be seen. In the sixth century the Irish Church, as a proselytising force, was second to none, and the fame of its teachers extended over the greater part of north-western Europe. S. Columba converted northern and western Scotland. His near-namesake, S. Columban, settled in Burgundy, and when driven from there passed with S. Gall and other monks into Switzerland. The number of churches abroad dedicated to S. Columba, S. Chad and S. Gall, and the numerous old Irish manuscripts which have been discovered in Switzerland and Germany, show how widespread was Irish influence. The second conversion of England to Christianity dates from the mission which Gregory the Great, Bishop of Rome, sent to this country in 596. In the following year Augustine, Mellitus, Paulinus and some forty other monks of the Benedictine Order landed in the Isle of Thanet. Their success was immediate. In a few years the whole of England was once more Christian. The Roman monks and their adherents early came into collision with the followers of S. Columba. The great point of difference between them, the keeping of Easter, was settled in Rome's favour by King Oswy of Northumbria at the Synod held at Whitby in 664, and after that the power of the Papal Church increased, and that of Ireland declined. Christianity, however, was not to prevail unmolested in this country for long, for towards the end of the eighth century the Danes began a series of raids which culminated in the submission of the Saxons to Sweyn in 1013. The Saxon chronicles state that the Danes 'everywhere plundered and burnt as their custom is', and the last foray of Sweyn's seems to have been unusually sweeping in this respect. Not many churches escaped the fire, and of those that were fortunate many were pulled down fifty years or so later by the Normans, in order to be rebuilt on a larger scale and in a more sumptuous fashion. Probably many of the churches built under Sweyn's son, Canute, after his baptism, were demolished for the same reason.

There is, therefore, little still standing that was built before England came under the influence of the Normans; and of the architecture which we call Anglo-Saxon nearly all was built after A.D. 1000. Nevertheless, the few examples which have survived have particularly interesting characteristics of their own. In the field of sculpture, indeed, they surpassed anything brought by the Normans. Norman influence was evident sixteen years before Hastings, when Edward the Confessor, with the aid of Norman craftsmen, began his Abbey at Westminster. After 1066 the story of Romanesque architecture in England is linked with parallel developments in Normandy and, through Normandy, with the great architecture of Lombardy. There can be little doubt that the Normans obtained their inspiration originally from Lombardy; although they soon introduced special traits which differentiated their work from contemporary buildings in Italy, Germany, and other parts of France. They certainly did not bring the germ of their architecture with them from the north, and they can hardly have obtained it from the neighbouring royal domain of France which, in the first half of the eleventh century, had, to a great extent, lost the pre-eminent position in the arts which it enjoyed at the time of Charlemagne. The nationality of the two prelates who exercised much influence over William I and his successor supplies the clue to its origin. Both were Italians: Lanfranc came from Pavia; Anselm was a native of Aosta.

End of the Period. Until the middle of the twelfth century the development of the new ideas proceeded slowly and methodically. Men were in no haste to throw over the old traditions; in fact, in the greater part of Italy they never entirely abandoned them. Rome, both through its early churches and its still earlier imperial monuments, was still the quarry for ideas as much as it was a quarry for building materials. But now a less conservative tendency manifested itself, due largely to the increasing interest taken by the people in ecclesiastical matters, and the growing power of the masonic guilds, which coincided with the gradual weakening of the hitherto overwhelming pre-eminence of the monastic Orders. A new era dawned. New forms, new ideas, took the place of the old, and in 1140, in the Abbey of S. Denis near Paris, a new and revolutionary style was born which, though owing much to the Romanesque, was sufficiently distinct in its character to deserve a title of its own—Gothic. This date, though convenient, must not be regarded as a terminus to one phase of architectural development. The building of the choir of S. Denis is merely a great junction to which many lines converge, and then branch off again to different countries with regional characteristics. It is only a point of convenience at which this particular volume of the story of architectural development may conclude.

Arrangement. The architectural historian is confronted with many difficulties if he attempts to present a consecutive narrative of the development of Romanesque architecture in western Europe. On the one hand there was the undoubted unity of aim which was inspired by a united Church; but on the other there was the independence of each national group, with its own tradition, its own climate and its own particular kind of building materials, all of which were seriously to affect modes of construction and of detail design. In England alone is one able to follow, in a logical, chronological sequence, the development of Romanesque architecture, after paying only slight attention to the initial stimulus given by the Normans. But in France there are two stories: the southern, with its long connection with Roman building technique, and the northern, with its experimental striving towards an original style. In Italy there were four formative forces: Roman, Byzantine, Saracenic and Lombardic, which are mixed in varying proportions in different areas, and which make it impossible for the student to identify the architecture as one unified style.

A further difficulty is that one is continually tempted to make assumptions which are not always borne out by facts. The chief of these assumptions is that variations in structure always followed a logical order, and that the later mode was inevitably an improvement on the earlier. Another is that early work, particularly in sculpture and decoration, is always crude, and that later work is refined. But most important of all, and the pitfall which the student of Romanesque and Gothic must avoid, is the assumption that no designer ever thought of anything new for himself, but was forced by some inflexible law to derive everything from someone else's previous achievements.

In an endeavour to avoid, if not to surmount, these difficulties, it is proposed, in the chapters which follow, first to consider the planning requirements of the church in different areas; second, to analyse the kinds of structure that developed from the plan; and third, to study the detail design, the ornament and the decoration which played so important a part in the total aesthetic effect of the Romanesque style. After this we shall consider the story of each country in turn—Italy, Germany, Spain, France, Normandy and England—prefacing each with notes on the important architectural characteristics, and following with descriptions of the most important examples.

CHAPTER IX

ROMANESQUE ARCHITECTURE

Planning

MOST of the very early Romanesque churches in western Europe seem to have followed the typical Early Christian basilican plan. The majority have disappeared. They have either been razed to the ground, like the church at Silchester, or else have been so altered and added to that their original designs are difficult to make out. They were built during the period of migration which we call the Dark Ages, and were severely simple. From those that remain it appears that the most usual plan was a nave with single aisles and only one apse at the east end. A few were tri-apsidal, and according to Viollet-le-Duc the original church of S. Denis, near Paris, had an unbroken transept dividing the apses from the nave and aisles in the same way as at S. Peter's and S. Paul Outside the Walls at Rome.

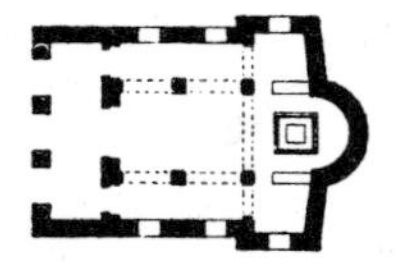

Church at Silchester. *Scale* 50 *ft. to* 1 *in.*

Basse Œuvre, Beauvais. The church of Basse Œuvre (sixth or seventh century), three bays of which alone remain, gives a fair idea of the simplicity of these early examples. It provides a link between the Early Christian basilican form and the true Romanesque. In this church the arcades are low, and in place of columns there are piers which support semicircular arches. The space between the arcade and the clerestory, which is considerable, is a plain surface, which may originally have been painted. In these early churches, unlike the later Romanesque

Sectional view of Church of Basse Œuvre, Beauvais.
Scale at section 50 *ft. to* 1 *in.*

examples, this space is very rarely arcaded[1] or decorated, for neither funds nor workmen were forthcoming to treat the wall surfaces with marble or mosaic in the Early Christian manner. The walls carry timber trusses with a boarded ceiling. In the Basse Œuvre more deliberate design is visible outside. The arches on the side windows are of rough red tiles alternating with stone voussoirs; the west window has a brick archivolt of great delicacy, the pattern being a most unusual one, and the western wall is faced with small squared stones (about 6 inches square), which are laid with care.

Types of Plan. From the ninth century onwards the planning of the greater churches in western Europe exhibited great advances over the simple arrangements of the early churches. Most of them developed the basilican plan, with its long aisled nave, by a considerable extension of the presbytery to the east and the addition of transepts, which resulted in a cruciform shape. There were also others which were circular in plan, and are of great interest because they show unmistakable evidence of an eastern influence which was absent in churches built after the close of the Romanesque period. They are, in fact, connecting links between the East and the West, between the civilisation of the Byzantine world and the new religious and artistic movement which at the beginning of the ninth century was in its infancy.

THE CRUCIFORM PLAN

S. Gall. A most interesting documentary record of a great monastic establishment is provided in the manuscript plan which was discovered in the library of S. Gall in Switzerland, and which was originally presented to the Abbot of that monastery early in the ninth century. This plan is, in effect, a 'project' for what was then considered to be a perfect monastery. It shows a group of buildings occupying an area of about 500 feet by 425 feet. On the the north side are the Abbot's lodging, the guest house, the school and the doctor's quarters, together with the herbarium which supplied the dispensary and the kitchen. Next, on the east, is the infirmary and beyond, the cemetery. The south side provides the essential accommodation for the monks: the cloisters, library,

[1] In the monastic church of Montier-en-Der (*c.* 998) there are galleries over the aisles, and consequently triforiums to the nave, but this is exceptional.

refectory, dormitory, wine cellars and ancillary buildings. To the west are the farm yards, including stables for horses, sheep pens and cattle byres, all arranged with considerable skill. The church, which forms the core of the plan, is divided by two rows of

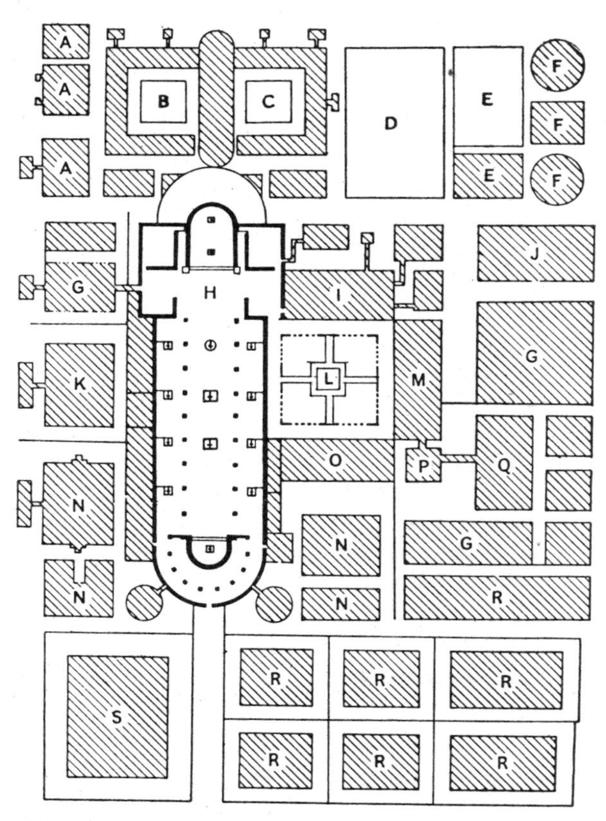

Plan of a ninth-century monastic establishment after the manuscript plan of S. Gall.

KEY

A. Doctor's quarters.
B. Infirmary.
C. House of Novices.
D. Cemetery.
E. Gardeners' quarters.
F. Poultry houses.
G. Workshops.
H. Church.
I. Calefactory, with dormitory over.
J. Threshing floor.
K. School house.
L. Cloisters.
M. Refectory.
N. Guest houses.
O. Cellars.
P. Kitchen.
Q. Bakehouse and Brew-house.
R. Farm buildings.
S. Unnamed: Abbot's Lodging?

columns into a nave and aisles. There are two apses, one at each end, which accommodate altars, and a number of additional altars arranged down the aisles and along the centre of the nave. The double apsidal ending is one of the most characteristic features of German churches, but was not developed in France and England. While the undoubted examples of Carolingian architecture are very few, and the recorded descriptions generally too vague to enable reasonable assessment to be made, this plan for S. Gall provides proof of the degree of refinement and completeness which had already been reached in the monastic system.

Causes of Changes. The advances in planning, and the modifications which were introduced, are traceable to various causes. The most important of these are: (1) the need for additional altars, occasioned chiefly by the large increase in the number of clergy and monks; (2) the insistence on more marked separation between clergy and laity within the church; (3) relic worship, which encouraged pilgrimages and necessitated planning for the circulation of crowds; (4) alterations in rules relating to baptism and burial.

Additional Altars. The plan of S. Gall did not show the increase in size of the eastern arm which was the most remarkable architectural development in the following centuries; but it would be satisfactory so long as the nave in addition to the choir was given up exclusively to the monks. However, this arrangement presented many difficulties if the church of the monastery was also the church of the people, in which their representative, the Bishop, had his chair, as at Canterbury, Durham, Norwich, Winchester, etc.; or if the Church was a cathedral pure and simple, unattached to a monastery and served by secular canons, as were York, Beverley, Lincoln, etc., and so many of the examples in France. It also required modification in the case of Cistercian monasteries, in which accommodation had to be provided for the numerous lay brethren who worked in the fields belonging to each monastery and who were little more than agricultural labourers.[1]

In the case of a large monastic establishment, a considerable number of altars in the church was essential. The one altar (or even the three which are occasionally found at the eastern end of an Early Christian church) was insufficient. At first the practice

[1] At Fountains Abbey, a Cistercian monastery, the nave was for the lay brethren, and their altar was placed at its east end. The aisles of the nave were screened off for the use of the monks.

was, as shown in the plan of S. Gall, to place additional altars in the nave. In the Abbey Church of S. Albans, now the cathedral, each pier of the nave had an altar on its western face.

Separation of Clergy. The monks did not wish to close the churches to the people from whom they derived so much of their income, yet they desired privacy. To obtain this they removed the altars from the nave and erected them farther east, while providing one altar at the eastern end of the nave for the use of the laity. From the eleventh century onwards the separation of clergy and laity was complete, and a whole section to the east (which was, in effect, a continuation of the nave) was screened off and reserved exclusively for the clergy, except on days of festival when the entire church was open to all. The arrangement of S. Albans is typical. Here the choir extends three bays into the nave and three bays beyond the crossing. To the east is the high altar, and beyond this, separated by a lofty screen, are further chapels. To the west of the choir is the altar for the laity, with seats for the officiating clergy. In England, in most cases, the laity seem to have had access to additional altars which were placed in the transepts. When the choir was entirely east of the crossing, as in all the later cathedrals, the transepts naturally appertained to the nave. Even when the choir extended westward of the crossing into the nave, as at S. Alban's, effective separation from the transepts was easily obtained by means of choir stalls or screens. The extension westward of the choir was more marked in cathedrals to which monasteries were attached, or in abbey churches which were not cathedrals. In Westminster Abbey the choir still occupies three bays of the nave, in Norwich Cathedral two bays, in Gloucester and Winchester Cathedrals one bay.

Eastern Extension. Two plans of eastern extension were followed in the latter half of the eleventh century. The earlier and simpler plan consisted merely in lengthening the chancel by the addition of two bays, or more, between the transepts and the eastern apses. The aisles were lengthened as well, although sometimes, as in the Abbaye-aux-Dames, Caen, they were completely cut off from the chancel by walls. S. Georges, Boscherville, and the Church of Cérisy-la-Forêt, Normandy, are typical examples of the simple elongation of the chancel. In both, the aisles finish square, while the chancel of each has an apse. The transepts stand out beyond the aisles, and have apses or altars on the east walls, showing that additional altars were even then considered necessary. This was also the original plan of the Abbaye-aux-Hommes, Caen (*c.* 1066) and of Canterbury Cathedral (*c.* 1070). The chief drawback to the above plan was that circulation around the east end was difficult; the aisles formed culs-de-sac. This was a very serious objection in churches where pilgrimages to shrines and relics were frequent, and where pilgrims came in vast numbers.

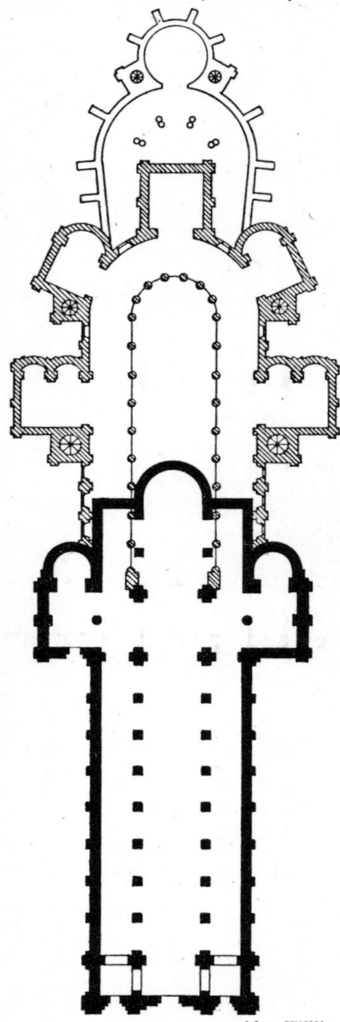

After Willis.

Canterbury Cathedral. Plan illustrating eastern extension. In black, cathedral at the time of Lanfranc, 1070–1077; shaded, 1090–1110; in outline, 1179–1184.
Scale 100 *ft. to* 1 *in.*

Eastern Ambulatory. The later and more complicated plan, which may have been adopted in a few instances in the tenth century but did not become general for nearly a hundred years, solved the circulation difficulty by providing an ambulatory behind the central apse. The apses to the aisles were swept away, and the aisles continued behind the High Altar. It is impossible to say in which church this plan was first adopted, or even in which country it was first conceived. An eastern ambulatory, with a gallery over, occurs in the Church of S. Stephano, Verona, which Cattaneo, with some hesitation, ascribes to the tenth century. In France it seems to have been introduced early in the following century, but in England not until 1089, Gloucester Cathedral being probably the first example.[1] The eastern ambulatory plan was

[1] Simpson considered that the difficulty of circulation had been overcome in some of the early circular churches, but unless the altar was placed within the inner circle the problem of circulation still remained.

especially favoured in those churches whose possession of the bodies of saints and martyrs or other valuable relics attracted large crowds, as at S. Martin, Tours, S. Denis, near Paris, S. Sernin, Toulouse, and Canterbury Cathedral after the murder of Thomas à Becket. The crypt of the original cathedral at Chartres, which still exists, was built early in the eleventh century and has an ambulatory which, it is almost certain, was continued above. The east end of Romsey Abbey Church (*c.* 1120) shows an equally

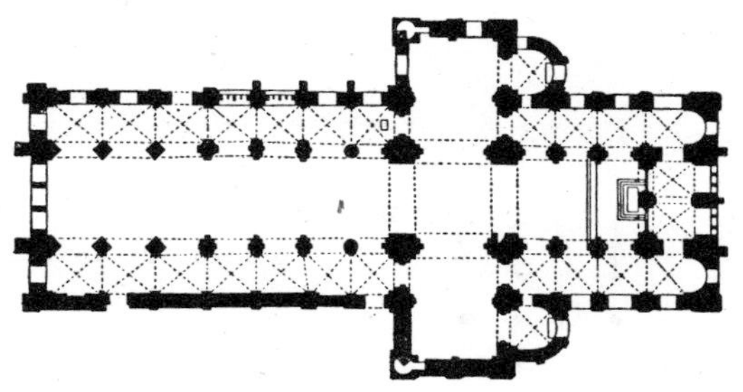

Romsey Abbey Church.
Scale 100 *ft. to* 1 *in.*

suitable though slightly different plan for providing the necessary circulation. This is not strictly speaking an ambulatory, but the aisles are continued east of the chancel, and open into a passage behind the high altar. The ending is thus square, an important detail which will be referred to later (p. 229).

The Chevet. In some of the earliest examples the outside wall of the ambulatory forms an unbroken semicircle, as at Morienval

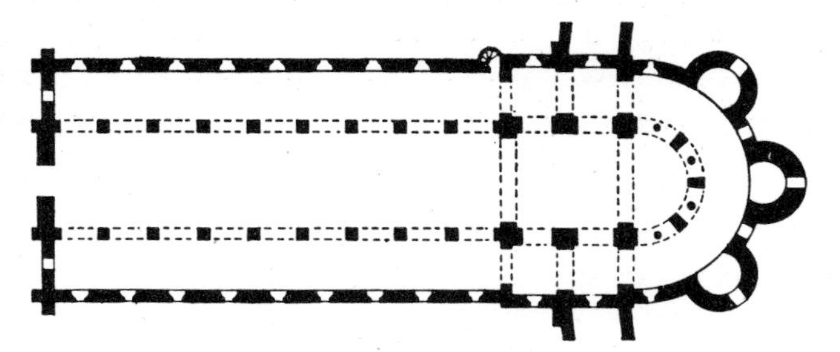

Church at Vignory.
Scale 50 *ft. to* 1 *in.*

(Oise) and S. Saturnin (Auvergne), but in most churches apses project beyond the curving wall and contain altars. These apsidal chapels at first were small, and almost without exception semi-circular in plan. Between them, as a rule, were windows. In most early examples there were only three chapels, as at Vignory (Haute-Marne), *c.* 1030, although sometimes there were five, as at S. Sernin, Toulouse, and occasionally four, as at Notre-Dame du Port, Clermont-Ferrand. This ambulatory with chapels—the characteristic ending of nearly all the great churches of northern France—is called the 'chevet'. It will be recollected that the Early Christian termination was a simple large niche; this ending was maintained in Romanesque churches in Italy, Germany, and in those parts of the south of France where the Roman tradition was strongest. But in the north of France the apse was defined by

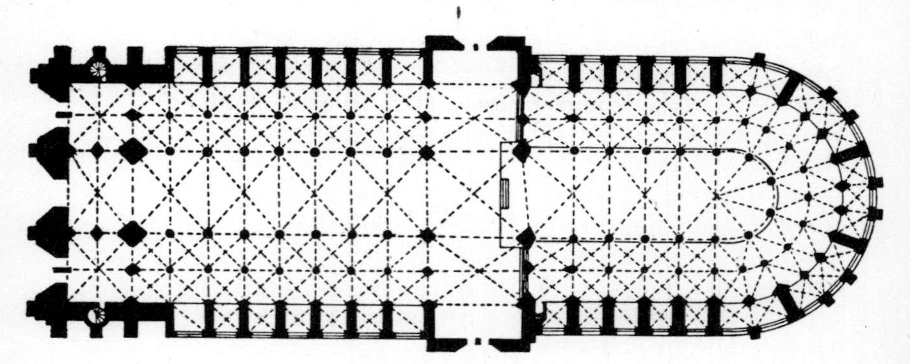

Notre-Dame, Paris.
Scale 100 *ft. to* 1 *in.*

a range of columns with the aisle, from which opened a number of chapels, curving round it. Sometimes double aisles were carried round the apsidal ending, and the number and size of chapels increased, which gave the east end a complexity absent from the simple apse of the early basilicas. In Notre-Dame, Paris, the chevet is of a simple kind, but in Le Mans Cathedral (1230) there are as many as thirteen chapels surrounding the choir, seven at the end and the remainder at the sides; between these are windows, probably because the projection of the chapels is considerable and the windows in them could not give sufficient light to the ambulatory.

The chevet plan in its simple form was fairly general in English cathedrals built in Romanesque times, when French influence was paramount, but afterwards it gave place to a square termination.

The eastern arm in England was considerably longer than in most contemporary foreign examples, showing that a desire for length existed here from quite early days. Thus the bays between the crossing and apse number four at Norwich, Durham and Bury St. Edmund's (*c.* 1089–96); in Canterbury Cathedral, when it was remodelled in 1110, this number was doubled.

Nave Arcade. In some of the early Romanesque churches piers were combined with columns, a feature already mentioned in connection with the Early Christian churches of S. Maria in Cosmedin and S. Clemente, Rome (pp. 17 and 28). In Münster Cathedral and S. Michael, Hildesheim (*c.* 1020), piers took the place of columns every third bay; at Drübeck (*c.* 1000) and elsewhere, columns and piers alternated.[1] All these churches were timber roofed, were built, in fact, before the general introduction of vaulting; so the alternation of large and small supports does not appear to have anything to do with vaulting requirements. At S. Miniato, Florence (1013), the piers which were introduced every third bay did, however, carry transverse arches.

Aisleless plans. Very different from the many-aisled churches of northern France are the churches entirely without aisles of the south. It is difficult to believe that they belong to the same country, to the same style of building and to the same period. The aisleless plan of southern France owes its origin to Roman rather than Early Christian tradition.[2] The Cathedral at Albi (*c.* 1282), which is typical, is the direct descendant of the Basilica of Constantine. Both buildings have the wide, centrally vaulted space, internal buttresses taking the thrusts of the vault, and side recesses. They differ only in the number and size of these recesses. In the basilica there are only three; in the cathedral there are twelve, exclusive of those round the apse. The reasons for the difference are that the mediaeval builders rejoiced in

[1] A detail of some interest in these churches, and others contemporary or of slightly later date in Germany, is that the columns are generally monolithic and, following classical precedent, diminish in diameter from base to capital, with an entasis.

[2] Simpson considered that the aisleless plan had many advantages, and deplored 'the fetish of the aisled plan' which still held the field early in the twentieth century. 'In mediaeval days the aisled plan had its circumambulatory advantages . . . but for modern congregational purposes aisles of any width are an anachronism. No one can seriously maintain that columns and piers are not obstructions to the service of the present time, but in barely one modern church out of ten are they dispensed with.'

the reduplication of parts (which the Romans, except in the Colosseum, aqueducts and other similarly designed buildings, avoided), and were afraid, perhaps, of the dangers attending the construction of great squares of vaulting a few inches only in thickness.

Cistercian Influence. Until the end of the eleventh century the Benedictine Order was all-powerful in determining matters of church planning and ritual, but in 1098 the Cistercian, a rival Order, was founded. This Order was inaugurated in protest against the extravagance of both Benedictine living and Benedictine building. The Abbey Church of Vézelay, which appears plain by comparison with later Gothic churches, was declared by the most famous member of the Order, S. Bernard of Clairvaux, to be unnecessarily elaborate and over-enriched. 'I say naught,' he wrote, 'of the vast height of your churches, their immoderate length, their superfluous breadth, the costly polishings, the curious carvings and paintings which attract the worshipper's gaze and hinder his attention. . . . So many and so marvellous are the varieties of divers shapes on every hand, that we are more tempted to read in the marble than in our books, and to spend the whole day in wondering at these things rather than in meditating the law of God. For God's sake, if men are not ashamed of these things, why at least do they not shrink from the expense?'[1]

S. Bernard, the Puritan of the Middle Ages as he might be called, laid down stringent rules for his followers. 'A church,' he declared, 'shall be of the greatest simplicity, and sculpture and painting shall be excluded—the glass shall be of white colour, and free from crosses and ornaments.' He further stated that 'no towers or belfries of wood or stone of any notable height shall be erected,' and he seems to have disliked triforiums, for they are generally absent from Cistercian churches. Inasmuch as an apsidal eastern ending was universal in Benedictine churches, he declared for a square ending. An example of this is shown in the extremely interesting sketchbook of Villard de Honnecourt, a

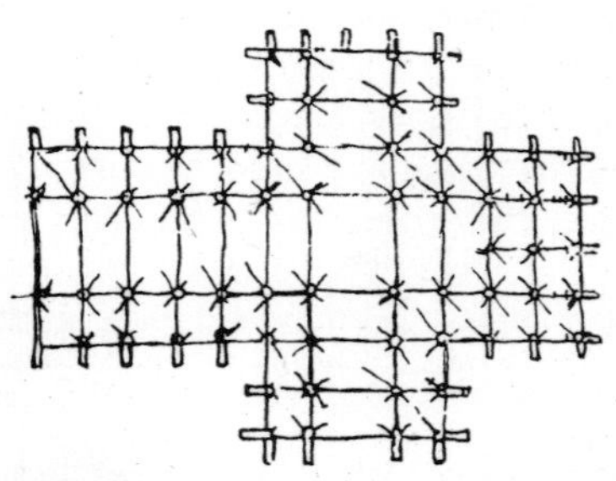

Plan from V. de Honnecourt's Sketch-book.

[1] *Apologia ad Guillelmum,* trans. G. G. Coulton.

thirteenth-century French architect; under it the artist has written, 'Vesci une glize desquarie ki fu esgardee a faire en lordene d'Cistiaux.'[1]

To what extent S. Bernard's mandate influenced the development of church planning is difficult to state with certainty. The effect of it has been exaggerated by some writers. The builders of the great French cathedrals and large parish churches paid little attention to it and, until the Renaissance upset their ideas and destroyed their traditions, continued to develop the chevet form. But in churches built for the Cistercians in other countries, S. Bernard's instructions in the main were followed. The plans of Chiaravalle, near Milan, Las Huelgas, outside Burgos in Spain, Maulbronn in Germany and Furness and Buildwas in England, show a remarkable uniformity. They are not, however, new plans, but reversions to an old one. They follow that early basilican plan which had a transept at the extreme east end, with chapels extending beyond it, the only difference being that the chapels are more numerous than was thought necessary before, and are rectangular.

It is a mistake to suppose that the marked feature of English cathedrals and churches—their eastern rectangularity—is due to Cistercian influence. The square east end was an English tradition. It occurred in the Abbey Church of Romsey, which was Benedictine in foundation (see p. 124). It is found in pre-Norman churches at Bradford-on-Avon and Dover Castle; in churches in Ireland and Scotland of an early date; in the eleventh-century cathedral of Rochester; and in countless eleventh- and early twelfth-century parish churches in England, such as Old Shoreham, Dareth, Barfreston and Patrixbourne, Adel, etc., built long before S. Bernard became a power. Nor is the square east end found only in Britain; there are examples in Italy, France, Germany and Belgium, built before the beginning of the twelfth century. All that the Cistercians did was to revert to the simplicity of the Early Christian plan, but they did not in fact adhere to such simplicity for long.

Baptism. Two important rites of the Christian religion, baptism and burial, had some influence on church planning. In the days of the early Church, when pagans were being converted in large numbers and adult baptism was general, a separate baptistery

[1] 'Here is a square church which was designed for the Cistercian Order.'

was a necessity, for the unbaptised were not admitted into the church itself. But early in the eleventh century, as infant baptism became more customary and parish priests were permitted to baptise, fonts were introduced into the parish churches. In some parts of Italy separate baptisteries continued to be built well into the twelfth century, as at Parma, Pisa, Novara and Asti; but outside Italy, with the possible exception of S. Jean, Poitiers, no building exists in western Europe which can be stated definitely to have been built as a baptistery, and the original purpose of even the Poitiers example is uncertain.

It might be expected that a special setting for so important a rite as baptism would have been made in churches after the introduction of the font, and that a portion of each building would have been designed for the rite. But in no country was this done, probably because, as any priest could perform the rite in any church, the ceremony had lost, to some extent, its previous great importance.[1] In English cathedrals the customary position of the font is near the western door, on the south side,[2] but its original position in every case may have been different. In parish churches the font is generally at the west end of the aisle, near the south door, and this is undoubtedly its original position as a rule, although in churches with western towers it not infrequently occupies the space under the tower, or immediately to the east of it.

Burial. In the early days of Christianity the sanitary laws of the Romans still prevailed, and bodies were buried in the catacombs or in graveyards outside the city. However, the objection to cremation, the insistence on burial in consecrated ground, the wish of the deceased or of his relatives to secure the most sacred spot, and above all, the desire to pay special honour to those who had devoted their lives to the advancement of religion or had lost them in its defence, brought about a change. It was strongly resisted at first, but in 563 the Council of Braga gave permission for burial in churchyards, 'in case of necessity', but on no account within the walls of the church. In 813 the Council at Mayence

[1] It has been suggested that the western apse in some of the German examples was designed as a baptistery, but this is unlikely (see pp. 195–6).

[2] In Winchester and Chester Cathedrals it is on the north; in Ely it occupies a good position in the south transept at the west end, and in Peterborough it is placed in a similar position and has a bay to itself, but it is unlikely that the somewhat unusual western planning of these last two cathedrals was due to baptismal requirements.

decided that 'no one shall be buried in a church but bishops, abbots, or worthy priests, or faithful laymen,'[1] a fairly comprehensive and elastic list; another Council, held at Meaux, left it to the bishop and presbyter to settle who should be accorded the honour. Once the custom was sanctioned it spread rapidly, and considerable areas were provided for the disposal of the dead.

The early burials were in small eastern crypts, not much more than passages, as in S. Apollinare in Classe, Ravenna,[2] Torcello Cathedral, and S. Ambrogio, Milan, altars being placed above the bodies. But the size of the crypt rapidly increased until, in many churches of the eleventh and twelfth centuries, it occupied the whole area below the chancel, which was raised several feet above the floor of the nave. The best known raised chancels are in S. Zeno, Verona, and S. Miniato, Florence (p. 186). It is impossible to overrate the fine effect produced in these two churches by this plan. In many of the early examples, of which the Ravenna church may be regarded as typical, although the chancel is raised the crypt is not visible from the nave; but in the two churches of Florence and Verona just mentioned, the front of the crypt is open and arcaded, and the vista from the nave down to the vaulted crypt and along the length of the chancel above is one of the most effective features to be found in Romanesque church architecture. Raised chancels were contrary to the rule of the Byzantine Church, and consequently in those parts of western Europe which came under its influence, notably southern Italy, the crypt is entirely sunk or the nave floor raised to the level of the chancel. In Trani Cathedral, an example of the latter arrangement, the crypt extends under nearly the whole area of the chancel. In more northern Europe, in Germany, France and England, chancels raised over crypts are far from uncommon. But the west ends of the crypts are, almost without exception, closed. That all were so originally is somewhat doubtful. It is possible that alterations and subsequent additions have destroyed the original design.

The Monastery. The greater and more important churches formed the nucleus of conventual establishments, or monasteries, under the control of an abbot (in the case of priories, under a

[1] A. Ashpital, *R.I.B.A. Journal*, 1860–61.

[2] As S. Apollinare is stated to have been finished in 549, the Council of Braga's ruling appears to have been a protest against an existing custom.

prior).[1] When the monastic church was used as a cathedral it was called a conventual cathedral, the bishop, or archbishop, being the superior of the monastery and spiritual ruler of that part of the country which was called his diocese.

The general disposition of monastic buildings in all Benedictine and Cistercian settlements was remarkably similar, such variations as there were being largely the result of limitations imposed by the site. The most important buildings were, naturally, those devoted

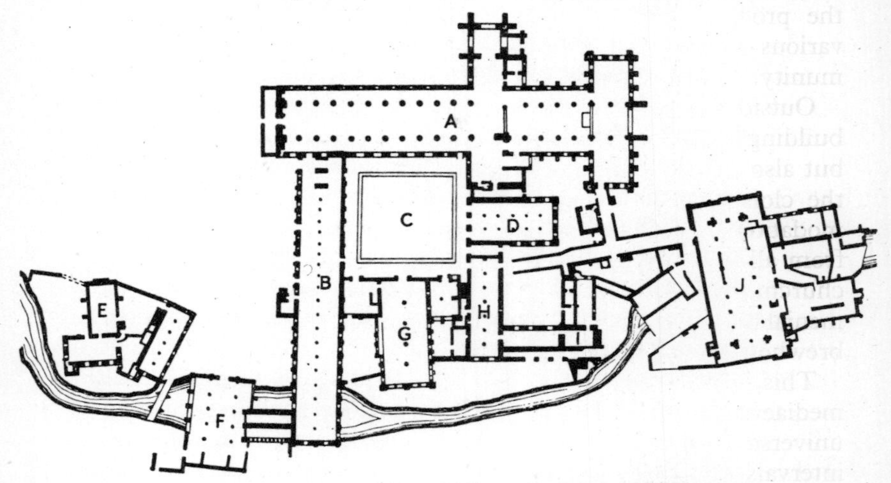

Ground plan of Fountains Abbey, Yorkshire (Cistercian).
Scale 200 ft. to 1 in.

KEY

A.	Church.	F.	Infirmary?
B.	Cellars. (Guest rooms over.)	G.	Refectory.
C.	Cloister.	H.	Calefactory.
D.	Chapter House.	I.	Brewhouse.
E.	Guest houses.	J.	Abbot's house.

to the monastic life. These included the cloisters, which provided a link, a covered way, between the living quarters of the monks and the church itself. The cloisters were generally square in plan and placed for warmth on the south side of the nave. The Chapter House—a place of assembly where the monks would gather to discuss the business of the monastery—was approached from the east side of the cloister.

[1] It is a mistake to call a settlement for monks a monastery and a settlement for nuns a convent. A convent simply means a religious association, whether of monks, friars or nuns; a monastery means the actual group of buildings, whether for monks or nuns.

In Cistercian monasteries the Chapter House was invariably rectangular in shape. The area on either side of the approach was called the undercroft, and was divided into various rooms, the most important being the sacristy, or treasury, in which holy vessels were stored. The upper storey was used as the dorter, or dormitory. The side of the cloisters farthest from the church, generally the southern side, was occupied by the frater, or refectory, with the kitchens lying to the west. The western side was the province of the cellarer, who was chiefly concerned with various secular activities and acted as estate agent for the community. The rooms above were generally used for guests.

Outside the cloister, to the west, the most important group of buildings was the infirmary, which catered, not only for the sick, but also for the aged and infirm. On the east, and linking with the cloisters, lay the abbot's lodgings, which provided accommodation for the more distinguished guests. At some distance from all these buildings, and generally on the north side of the church, provision was made for the lay servants in the so-called menial buildings, which included the stables, granaries, bakehouse, brewhouse, laundry, etc.

This, then, constituted the principal accommodation of the mediaeval monastery. The whole was arranged to an almost universal plan, and was surrounded by strong walls, punctuated at intervals by watch-towers. Within the grounds there were the cemetery, the herbarium, the fish pool and the orchards, and outside, the wide arable fields. The church was undoubtedly the most important and dominant architectural feature, but the ancillary buildings are not without interest. They were built in the same materials, involving similar but slighter constructional skill and incorporating, especially in the cloisters and Chapter Houses, equally delightful detail.

The Builders. The theory that the monks built their own churches and that they were active artists, masons and designers is now no longer held.[1] Texier considered that 'until the thirteenth century most churches were built by monks; their own hands executed everything,' but the evidence to support this statement is lacking. While there may occasionally have been a cleric with architectural ability, just as there might have been a monk skilled in botany or mathematics, and while Benedict's rule provided that

[1] This subject has been thoroughly investigated by R. E. Swartwout in *The Monastic Craftsman*, 1932.

craftsmen might pursue their crafts with due humility if the abbot permitted, the religious duties imposed upon all must have left little time for serious practice of architecture. There is no doubt that the monks may have assisted from time to time in the construction of the monasteries, as they did recently in the building of Buckfast Abbey, but they were not the designers. The cause of the myth is no doubt the constant use of the word *fecit* or *construxit* applied to the heads of monasteries in so many mediaeval chronicles. But these words mean little more than 'ordered and paid for', or 'caused to be built'.[1]

The monasteries of western Europe were designed by lay architects, who were called by various titles—master mason, *magister*, or *ingeniator*—and the names of nearly a thousand have been preserved. They were much more actively concerned with the scene of operations than are our architects today. With the architect was an overseer, whose duties were largely financial and who represented the interests of the employers. Further, there is no reason to assume that the builders were particularly pious men. They must have been highly skilled, but records indicate that they were not so very different from the tradesmen of today. There is something singularly up-to-date in the following criticism of masons made by John Wyclif (*c.* 1360): 'They conspire together that no man of their craft shall take less for a day than they have agreed among themselves, although he should by good conscience take much less, and that none of them shall do steady true work which might hinder the earnings of other men of their craft.'[2]

CENTRALLY PLANNED CHURCHES

We were fortunate in being able to cite the S. Gall manuscript to illustrate the changes which had taken place in the development of the basilican plan up to the time of Charlemagne. We are equally lucky in having, in the cathedral at Aix-la-Chapelle (*c.* 780), an authentic example of a circular church of the same period (Pl. 12). This was built as his tomb house by Charlemagne, and here he was found enshrined, seated on a throne, robed in imperial purple, when the tomb was opened in 1165. The building has a marked

[1] Even as far back as the thirteenth century, Matthew Paris expressly warns us that for a building to be attributed to a particular Abbot only means that he arranged for it to be built and provided the funds.

[2] Wyclif, *Select English Works*, Ed. T. Arnold.

Byzantine feeling, though later additions mask the original plan. It consists of an octagon surrounded by a vaulted aisle, enclosed within a multangular outer wall. On one side is a porch, flanked by turret staircases; on the other was probably a small chancel. The likeness between the plan of this church and that of San Vitale, Ravenna (cf. p. 65), is unmistakable, although Aix-la-Chapelle lacks the columned niches between the piers surrounding the central space which gives San Vitale its distinctive beauty.

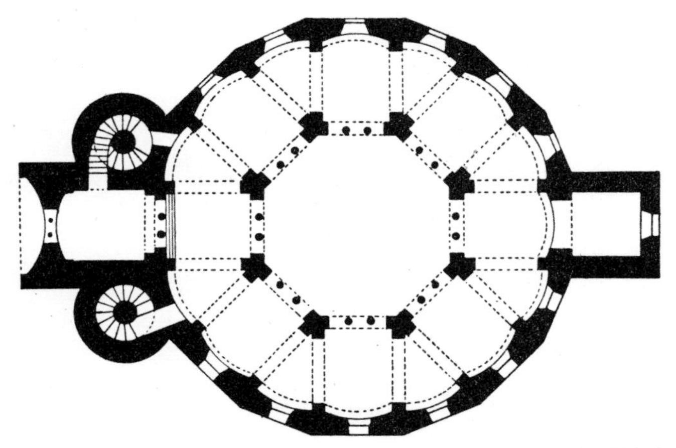

After Hubsch.

Cathedral of Aix-la-Chapelle. Original plan at first floor.
Scale 50 *ft. to* 1 *in.*

At Ottmarsheim, also in Germany, is a church similar in size and plan, although two centuries later in date than Charlemagne's church. The outside wall is octagonal, not multangular, but otherwise the differences are slight. Both churches have galleries which are arcaded on the front. Churches of this type are also found in Italy, at Bologna and Brescia. The example at Brescia is the more important; here the central part is domed, the surrounding aisle being circular and vaulted. The vault is not a continuous barrel vault, as in Roman circular buildings, such as the Tomb of Costanza (p. 44), but is an intersecting vault divided into square and triangular bays by transverse arches which cross from the piers to the aisle wall. This type of vaulting suggests that the church does not date from the time of Charlemagne, as was formerly supposed; the outside, too, with its arched corbel courses, pilaster strips and openings under the eaves below the low-pitched timber

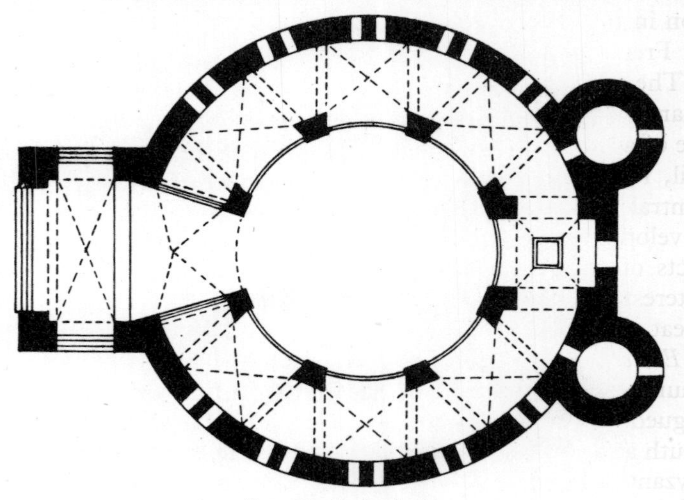

Brescia Cathedral.
Scale 50 ft. to 1 in.

roof, provides further evidence that the church belongs to the eleventh or twelfth century.

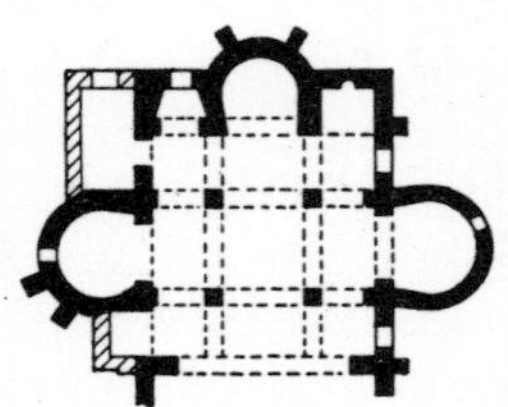

Church of Germigny-les-Prés.
Scale 50 ft. to 1 in.

Cross-in-Square Plan. The curious Church of Germigny-les-Prés (Loiret), which is said to have been built at the beginning of the ninth century, is, in some respects, more interesting than the circular buildings. In plan it consists of a square which, in orthodox Byzantine fashion, encloses a Greek cross, the cruciform portion being defined by four piers. Apses, which in plan resemble horseshoes, project from the sides. Above the crossing rises a moderately lofty square tower, with a dome which is almost certainly a recent innovation. The arms of the cross are covered by high barrel vaults and the apses by semi-domes at a lower level. In plan the church, save for its side apses, is like S. Theodore, Constantinople (p. 76) and numerous small churches in Greece. Further remarkable evidence of Byzantine influence is afforded by the remains of mosaic decoration in the eastern apse, which Viollet-le-Duc considered unique on French soil.

The Church of S. Croix, Montmajour (*c.* 1016) and that of S. Martin de Londres, both in southern France, are of a similar type. Their plans are quatrefoil, formed by four apses around a domed central square. This type of plan was never developed in western Europe until the architects of the Renaissance, with their renewed interest in centralised planning, realised its great possibilities.[1]

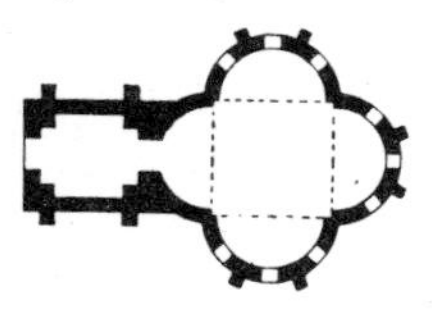

S. Croix, Montmajour.
Scale 50 ft. to 1 in.

Eastern Influence. To what extent these centrally planned churches were the result of eastern influence is a point that may be argued. It is well known that during the Romanesque period the south and south-west of France had commercial relations with the Byzantine Empire. The remarkable group of domed churches around Perigueux, which have already been described under Byzantine work (pp. 94–98), is evidence of the power of Byzantine influence. The fact that, until 1076, Christian pilgrims were freely permitted to enter Jerusalem on payment of a small legal toll, is even more important. For there can be no doubt that many of the small circular churches were inspired by the Church of the Holy Sepulchre in Jerusalem. *M.* Anthyme S. Paul states [2] that between the years 990 and 1000 pilgrimages to Palestine were general, and that one Foulgues Nerra, who died at Metz in 1040, had visited Jerusalem four times. The church as it then existed was therefore well known, but what was its plan? Constantine's church, the first to be built there, was basilican. He built it to the east of, and detached from, a great apse, about 120 feet in diameter, which he placed around the spot where he believed the Tomb to be. His work was destroyed; but about 1040 his namesake, Constantine Monarchus, Emperor of the Eastern Empire, built a circular church around the Tomb, of which apparently only the aisle was covered, the central part being open to the sky. When the Crusaders reached Jerusalem in 1099, they at once began the rebuilding of the church; but instead of following the Eastern

[1] There is a very interesting reference in William of Malmesbury: *Gesta Pont.*, 199, to King Alfred, who 'made a church, small indeed in area . . . contrived in a new manner of building. For four piers embedded in the ground carry the whole erection, with four chancels of elliptic plan round the edge.'

[2] In his *Histoire Monumentale de la France.*

Emperor's plan of a detached church, they built their chancel on to the circular church. The result was a western circular nave—the building of Constantine Monomachus—and an eastern oblong chancel. There can be little doubt that the church as rebuilt supplied the plan for many 'Templar' churches throughout western Europe, such as S. Giovanni al Sepolcro at Brindisi, S. Tomaso, near Bergamo, the Rotunda at Constance,[1] the church at Charroux, in Poitou, and the Temple in Paris which was destroyed at the Revolution.[2] In England there were fifteen examples, but only two survive intact, at Northampton and Cambridge; a third, the Temple Church in London, was severely bombed in the last war.

The small Church of S. Tomaso may be taken as typical. It has a circular nave, about 15 feet in diameter, covered by a dome, and an oblong bema, or chancel, which ends with an apse. In the centre eight columns support a vaulted gallery which forms a triforium.

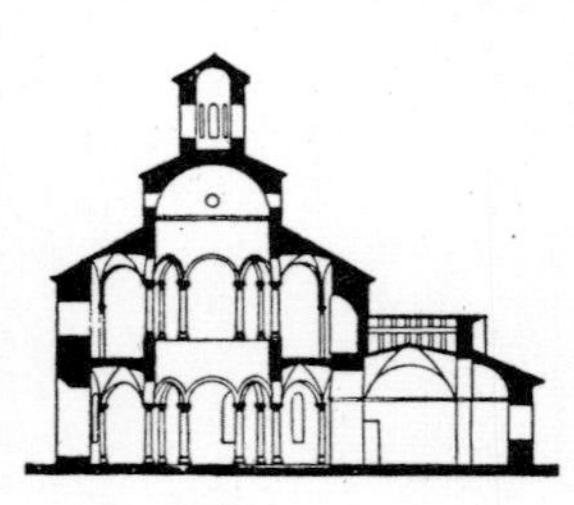

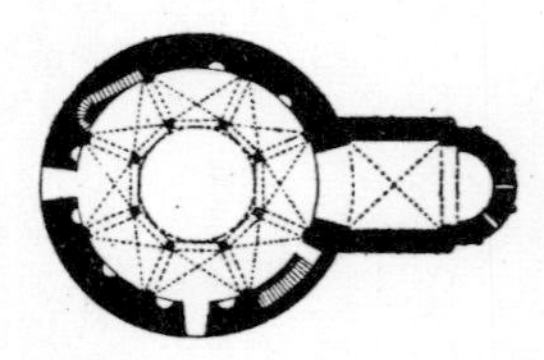

S. Tomaso, Bergamo.
Scale 50 ft. to 1 in.

Conclusion. The circular and centralised type of plan did not persist beyond the Romanesque period. The development of the western monastic system made such plans unsuitable. Romanesque architecture had to fulfil the needs of a growing society, which the finite circular form, however attractive it might be architecturally, could not do. It was therefore the basilican plan that prevailed, a plan which could, by multiplication of bays, allow for indefinite expansion in length.

[1] Built by Bishop Conrad, '*sepulchrum Domini in similitudinè alias Jerusalimitani*'.

[2] Although the Templars may have taken the plan from Jerusalem, it had been employed before, and probably had a Byzantine origin.

CHAPTER X

ROMANESQUE ARCHITECTURE

Structure

THE *Arch and the Vault.* The significant features of Romanesque construction are the arch and the vault.[1] Without the arch, the wide openings between columns and piers could not have been bridged, and without the vault the large floor spaces, necessary for congregational and ritual requirements, could not have been covered in a sound and satisfactory manner. Timber roofs might, it is true, have been employed, as in the Early Christian churches—and were, to some extent, especially in England and Italy—but the desire for security from fire, for permanence and monumental effect, led to the adoption of the stone vault. The use of the dome, which was the alternative, did not spread beyond the orbit of Byzantine influence, and in south-western France, where a tradition of domical construction had been developed, it was abandoned before the close of the Romanesque period in favour of vault construction.

The vault was no invention of the Romanesque period. Of the two forms, the barrel vault and the intersecting vault, the former was well known to the Egyptians and the Assyrians, and both were extensively used by the Romans. But although the forms remained much the same, the methods of construction adopted by the Romanesque builders—especially in the intersecting vault—are in many respects different from those of earlier work.

Barrel Vaults. Some Romanesque barrel vaults, like those of the Romans, are solid, the outer covering being bedded on top of the vault itself. In the majority of cases, however, they are only a foot or so thick, and a protecting timber roof is superimposed in the same way as on intersecting vaults. One practical disadvantage of a barrel vault over an aisled church is that, being

[1] The lintel occurs occasionally over small windows and doorways, especially in domestic work, and it spans the larger doorways in many churches. Generally, however, it carries only a light panel of stone (the tympanum), the main weight of the walls being supported by surrounding arches.

continuous, it presses equally on voids and solids, on arches as well as on piers. In the words of Sir George Gilbert Scott, it entails 'an illogical arrangement of divided substructure and continuous superstructure.' This disadvantage, so far as it affects internal appearance, is partly overcome in many twelfth-century churches, especially in Burgundy and Auvergne, by the strengthening of the barrel vault at intervals with transverse arches which spring from the piers of the arcade. These transverse arches do not carry the vault as they did in the Roman building known as the Baths of Diana at Nîmes, because they are too far apart. A second and more important disadvantage is that good clerestory lighting is impossible, since any side windows have to be kept below the springing.[1] Barrel vaults were never popular in England in Romanesque times. The best early example is to be found in S. John's Chapel in the Tower of London, where the vault springs above the galleries and terminates in a semi-circular apse (see p. 266).

Advantages of the Intersecting Vault. The intersecting vault has two important advantages over the barrel vault. First, it concentrates the thrust and weight of the vault on the points best capable of receiving them, namely the piers; and second, it permits clerestory windows at the sides as high as the apex of the vault. Both these advantages were known to and thoroughly appreciated by the Romans.

Development of the Vault: Transverse Arches. The earliest Romanesque intersecting vaults, like those of the Romans, were continuous, as in the crypt of Rochester Cathedral. The first modification made by the eleventh-century builders was to divide the vault into square bays by transverse arches. These arches sprang from pilasters, or attached columns, projecting from the face of the wall or pier, and as their span was less than that of the vault, they appeared below it. At the same time, longitudinal arches (or wall ribs) were introduced so that the infilling of each bay (or severy, to use the more architectural term), rested on four arches, thus concentrating it more efficiently on the piers.

Diagonal Ribs. The next development was the most revolutionary of all. This was the introduction of diagonal ribs at the lines of intersection, or 'groin' lines, of the vault. The vault then

[1] Simpson regarded this as a blessing in disguise, because he thought the principal light to a church should come from the west end, and that obtrusive side lighting was a nuisance. But this argument is only valid if the nave is exceptionally short.

became a ribbed vault, as distinguished from a groined or intersecting vault, and each bay was now composed of (1) a constructional framework of transverse arches, longitudinal or wall arches,[1] and diagonal ribs; and (2) the infilling, or web, which rested on the frame. The latter, as it had only its own weight to carry, could be merely a few inches thick and, in effect, was quite independent of the walls. The principle of a combination of thrusts concentrated at given points was now complete, and the stage was set for the later developments of Gothic architecture.

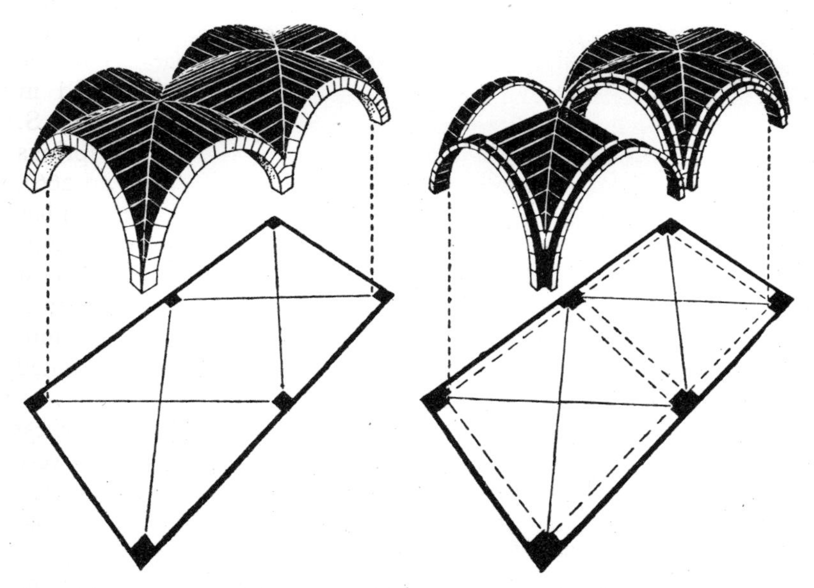

(Left) Intersecting vault. (Right) Intersecting vault with transverse and wall ribs.

Early Ribbed Vaults. Diagonal ribs first appeared in churches towards the end of the eleventh century, but they did not become general for some fifty years. Most Romanesque vaults of the first quarter of the twelfth century are without them, and in Burgundy, because of the conservative instincts of the monastic Orders which were especially powerful there, they were often omitted in later work. There can be no doubt that the rib considerably simplified the building of vaults of wide span, particularly by reducing the

[1] In many early vaults in England and France, the wall ribs were omitted, since the great thickness of the side walls rendered them unnecessary.

amount of timber centering required, and the Romanesque builders deserve great praise for realising its possibilities. But did these builders, strictly speaking, originate diagonal ribs? Did they not merely reintroduce them in a modified form? In Roman intersecting vaults there were diagonal ribs of brickwork; but these did not project below the surface of the vault and, being covered with concrete, they lost their independent functions and became simply reinforcement at the weakest point of the vault. Nevertheless, the Romans used them for much the same reason as they were used later, merely, as permanent centres to carry the infilling.[1] It is more than possible that by the eleventh century the old methods had been entirely forgotten, but even admitting this, the Romanesque builders cannot be credited with an entirely new invention. The real novelty was that the Romanesque builders did not hide or disguise the reinforcement of the groin, but exposed the ribs as essential elements of the structure with aesthetic significance. The structural value of the ribs has been so often emphasised that their aesthetic merit is sometimes forgotten. It is on the ribs that the eye rests and not on the infilling, the form of which is to a great extent lost through poor lighting.

Which country deserves the credit for being the first to use visible ribs below the groins cannot be decided with certainty. All countries were engaged in trying to find a satisfactory solution to the same difficulty. In France, ribbed vaults appeared simultaneously in different parts of the country at the beginning of the twelfth century; at Bordeaux and Poitiers in the south, at Quimperlé (Britanny) in the north, around Beauvais and in the valleys of the Seine, Marne, Oise, etc. At Morienval (Oise), a narrow ambulatory round the eastern apse is covered by ribbed vaults, and the date of these is said to be 1120. In the district around Beauvais and Soissons many churches of about this date have aisles vaulted with diagonal ribs.

S. Ambrogio, Milan (Pl. 10). The claim of priority for Italy rests with S. Ambrogio, Milan, the wide nave of which has ribbed vaults. The east end of this church is ninth century. The nave, according to Cattaneo, was built 'in the second half of the eleventh century.' If this approximate date is correct, one of the widest of Romanesque vaults—its width is 44 feet—and also one of the most effective, was

[1] In Roman intersecting vaults, such as those of the Basilica of Constantine, etc., the weight of the vault was concentrated over the piers in much the same way as in Romanesque construction.

built twenty years or more before the similar vaults of France. It is difficult to believe this, although it may be true. Cattaneo continues: 'In 1129 the second belfry was erected, and in 1196 they repaired the damage done to the edifice by the fall of an arch in the principal nave.' This sentence mentions two dates when building operations were in progress. The building of the nave may have preceded that of the campanile by only a few years, which would give *c.* 1120 for the nave vault. But 'the fall of an arch', if it were a transverse arch, means the collapse of two bays; and there are only three vaulted bays to the nave of S. Ambrogio. Cattaneo's own statement, therefore, shows that part of the nave vault must have been rebuilt after 1196; perhaps the whole of it was. On the other hand, the angle shafts which carry the diagonal ribs are so important that they must be part and parcel of the original design. They would never have been made so large if they had been intended merely to carry groin lines. One may, therefore, fairly assume that diagonal ribs were intended from the first, and the real question is, was the nave built forty or fifty years before the tower—the date of which is known to be 1129—or at about the same time? This kind of vault was not so difficult to build as were many later ones in England and France, because, although its span is considerable, it springs low down, only a few feet above the crown of the arches of the main arcades.

Angle Shafts and Ribbed Vaulting. Angle shafts, on a smaller

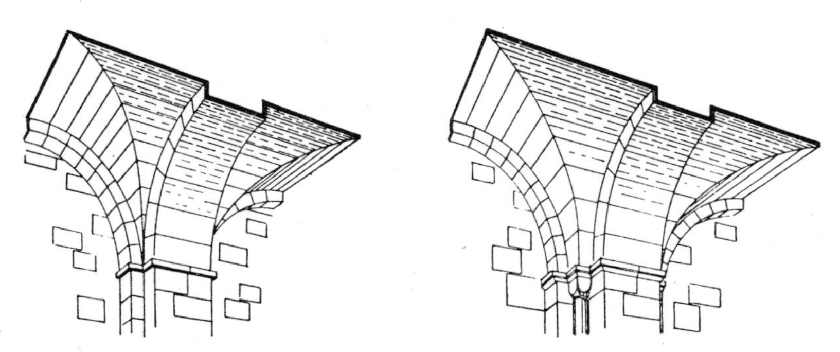

Diagrams illustrating (left) springing of groined vault with no angle shaft; (right) the same, but with introduction of angle shaft.

scale than those in S. Ambrogio, are not conclusive evidence that the vaults over had diagonal ribs. There are angle shafts to the vault under the gallery of the north transept, Winchester, but no diagonal ribs. Angle shafts were introduced before diagonal ribs were thought of, because the groin lines of the vault otherwise had to start from the inner angle of the pier carrying the transverse arch, which did not provide a satisfactory springing.

Durham Cathedral. For England, a strong claim can be made for priority, but even that cannot be entirely substantiated. In Durham Cathedral, the small vaults over the aisles of the choir are ribbed vaults, which were completed by 1096. These were certainly the earliest in this country. Now the most curious feature of the Durham vaults is that the ribs do not appear to have been built independently of the web, or infilling, and the infilling is no lighter than in an ordinary groined vault; so one must inevitably deduce that while the rib may have strengthened to some extent the weakest line of the vault, it was introduced primarily for aesthetic reasons. 'It represents the ultimate fulfilment of that tendency towards articulation which had driven Romanesque architects forward for over a hundred years.'[1] Naturally, the question of priority regarding diagonal ribs has aroused considerable controversy. For it was the introduction of the rib that led the way to the solution of the problem of covering large spans with stone and that encouraged, more than did any other feature, the subsequent developments of Gothic architecture.

Early Difficulties. While diagonal ribs were a great advance, they introduced a difficulty which had not existed before. In a square vault without ribs, the arches of which are semi-circular, the groins are semi-elliptical and therefore weak in form. This weakness does not matter in Roman vaults, since the groin lines appear unconstructional and are simply the meeting lines of barrel vaults at right angles. But when diagonal ribs are added, the whole structure is changed, for the ribs have to carry the weight of the infilling and must, therefore, be strong. The Romanesque builders tried making the ribs elliptical or segmental, as in Durham Cathedral, or else semi-circular. The latter form was strong, but when the other arches of the vaults were semi-circular also, and sprang from the same level, the result was practically a dome and should have been built as such.[2] The domical form was avoided in some cases by the stilting of the transverse and longitudinal

[1] N. Pevsner, *An Outline of European Architecture*, 1948.

[2] *M.* Corroyer, in his *Gothic Architecture*, says that in the Church of S. Avit Senieur, in southern France, it *is* a dome, the stones being laid in rings, and the ribs acting merely as stiffeners.

arches, so that their crowns should be at the same level as the apex of the diagonal ribs.

Most early vaults were over aisles; their spans were consequently small and the builders could, to some extent, 'cook' the curves without producing weak or ugly lines. Exact setting out of these vaults was rendered difficult by the fact that although many side vaults were approximately square, few were exactly so and some were unmistakably oblong. The problem was complicated further in the case of vaulting over the curving ambulatory,

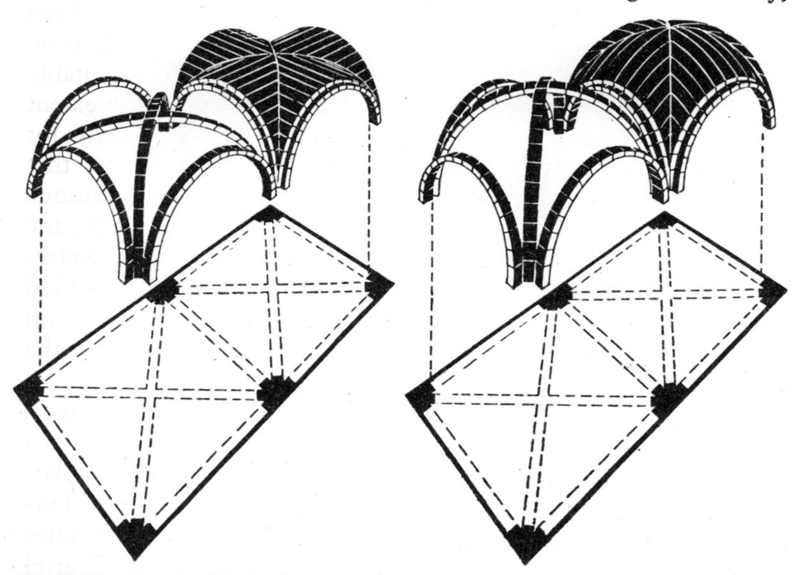

(Left) Vault with elliptical diagonal ribs and with semi-circular transverse and wall ribs; (right) domical vault having all ribs semi-circular.

where only the two transverse arches could be of similar span. This generally involved excessive stilting of the arch between the nave and the aisle. These difficulties were never properly solved in Romanesque times. It was not until the pointed arch was adopted in vaulting that longitudinal, transverse and diagonal arches could be built, all rising to the same height no matter how wide or varied the spans might be.

Vaulting of Oblong Spaces. It will be appreciated that the early Romanesque vaults could be most nearly successful only when applied over square bays. Over the nave of Vézelay Abbey Church and the choir of S. Georges, Boscherville, Normandy (*c.*

1120) there are oblong bays, with the result that the wall ribs have to be stilted considerably, and the transverse arches slightly, in order to reach the same height as the apex of the diagonal ribs. This is not altogether satisfactory, since the weight of the vault bears too much on the transverse arches and too little on the wall ribs. It may be asked, why should not all vaults, except in the special problem of the ambulatory, be square? The answer is that in the majority of churches the nave is about double the width of each aisle and, consequently, if a bay of the aisle be square the

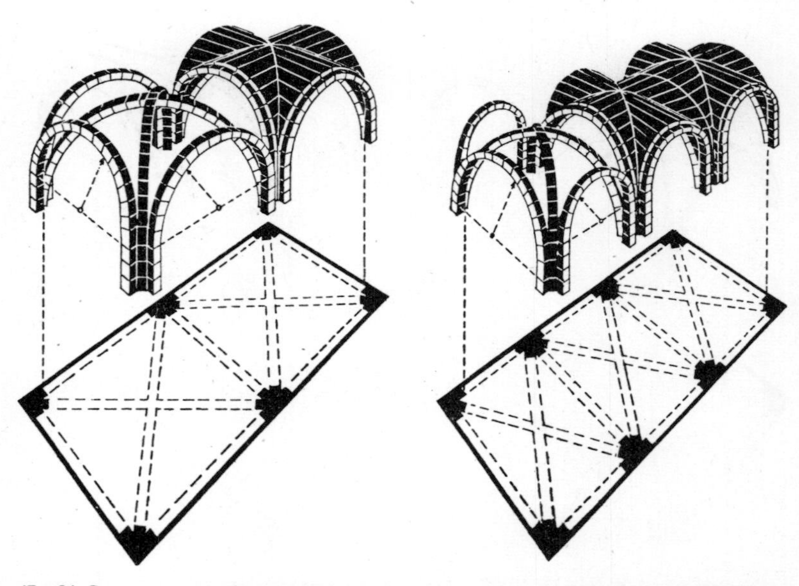

(Left) Square vault with semi-circular diagonal ribs and with stilted transverse and wall ribs; (right) Oblong vault with semi-circular diagonal ribs, slightly stilted transverse ribs and greatly stilted wall ribs.

corresponding bay of the nave must be oblong. Before the pointed arch became general, the oblong form was avoided, as in S. Ambrogio, Milan and in many early French and German churches vaulted with semi-circular transverse arches, by one bay of the nave vault being made to correspond to two bays of the aisle on either side; all bays being thus approximately square. But the objection to this plan is the immensity of each bay of the central vault and, consequently, of the span of its diagonal ribs.

Sexpartite Vaults. As a corrective to this excessive extent, the French designed what is known as the sexpartite (or six-part) vault. All early ribbed vaults are quadripartite (or four-part); that is to say, each bay is divided into four compartments by the diagonal ribs. In the sexpartite vault an intermediate transverse arch is introduced, which cuts the diagonal ribs at their intersection and thus supports them. This arch, in the early essays, was built under the web, which was formed independently of it. Examples are in the nave of the Abbaye-aux-Dames, Caen, and the church of Bernières-sur-Mer, both in Normandy. The next step was to let these intermediate arches take their share in

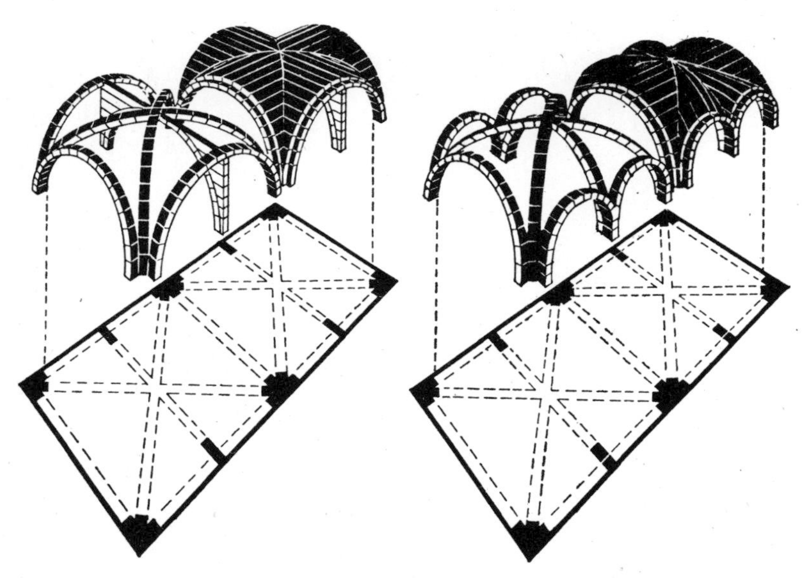

(Left) Quasi-sexpartite vault, having intermediate diaphragm arch; (right) True sexpartite vault, with slightly stilted wall ribs.

supporting the web. The result was the true sexpartite vault, *i.e.* a vault divided into six compartments. It was a great favourite in France for thirty or forty years, but it was abandoned early in the thirteenth century. Aesthetically it is unsatisfactory, since it results in twisted arched forms in the web where it joins the wall face. Nearly all these sexpartite vaults are much scooped, and the small intermediate side arches have to be stilted considerably; in the Church of La Trinité, Angers, the intermediate arches are stilted as much as 8 feet. In England there are few examples of the sexpartite form. The choir of Canterbury Cathedral (the work of William of Sens, a Burgundian), and the south transept of Lincoln Cathedral, however, are vaulted in this manner.[1]

S. Philibert, Tournus (Pl. 21). Probably the most curious solution to the problem of covering oblong bays, while providing good side lighting and avoiding the stilting of transverse or longitudinal arches, is found in the Church of S. Philibert, Tournus, the nave of which was finished about 1019. This has transverse arches which support barrel vaults running transversely from north to south at a higher level. The structural advantages of this system are many. Each vault forms an abutment to its neighbours, and it is only at the ends that precautions have to be taken to resist the thrust. At the west end of this church there was no difficulty, since the narthex was two storeys in height and there was a thick wall to receive the vault. The choir at the east end was built about a century later, and therefore the original method of resistance is uncertain. At the crossing there is now a dome, over which is a tall tower whose weight is more than sufficient to counteract the thrust of the last barrel vault.

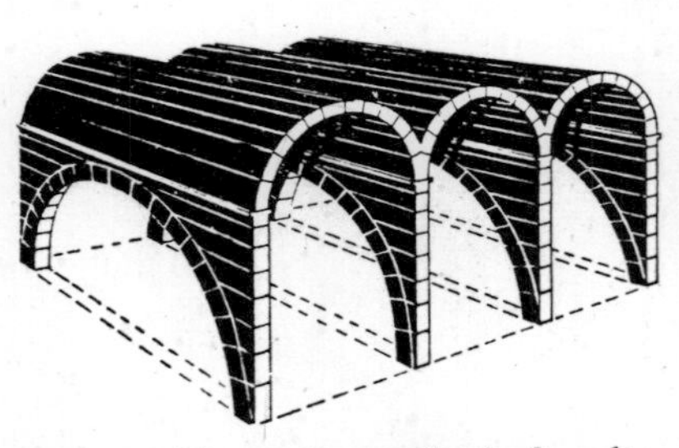

Diagram illustrating method of vaulting over oblong bays, as adopted at S. Philibert, Tournus, by means of transverse semi-circular arches carrying barrel vaults which run transversely from north to south.

It is a little strange that the method of vaulting in the nave of S. Philibert was not more generally followed elsewhere. It provides most effective indirect lighting, for the high clerestory windows are almost invisible from the nave. The barrel vaults hardly show, because one's view is interrupted by the lower transverse arches. The same method was adopted in only a few later examples, and these over aisles, not over naves. It was applied over the galleries of Notre-Dame in Paris, but these were swept away during alterations which were made some fifty years after the church was first built. In England we have a similar example

[1] In early sexpartite-vaulted churches, the columns along the nave are alternately large and small—which is logical—but in some of the later examples (Notre-Dame, Laon Cathedral, etc.) the columns are of the same size. At Noyon, columns alternate with larger piers.

over the aisles of Fountains Abbey, Yorkshire (*c.* 1150); although the vaults are now destroyed, their haunches remain and the original design is clear. S. Philibert is the earliest example in Europe, but this mode of vaulting appears to have been not uncommon in Persia.[1]

Sections of Churches. The form of vault adopted largely dictated the sectional outline. While some churches are aisleless and others have nave and aisles of equal height, the majority of cathedrals and large continental churches have more or less lofty

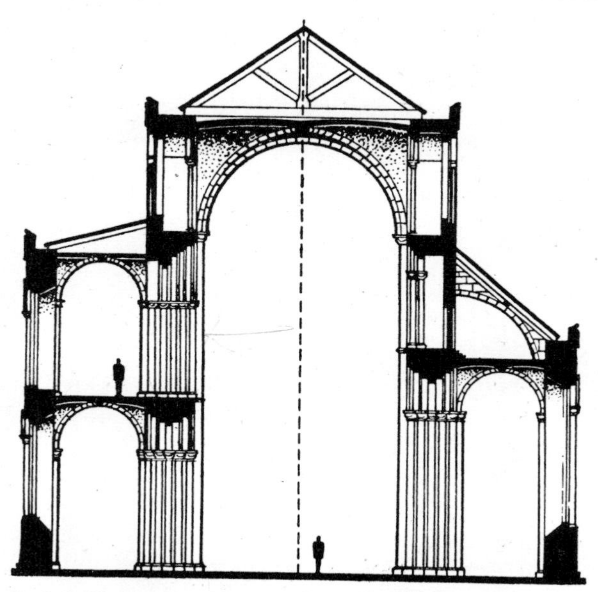

Left half shows section through Romanesque cathedral having triforium gallery; right half shows section through Romanesque cathedral having triforium passageway and lean-to roof over aisle.

naves with lower side aisles. The nave wall is customarily divided into arcade, triforium, and clerestory. In some churches, however, the clerestories are omitted, as in the South of France, where a simple barrel vault was adopted; in others, where the aisles are high, as in many German examples, the triforium is omitted. Generally, however, the arcades divide the nave from the aisles,

[1] In the Tag Eïvan, which is ascribed by *M.* Dieulafoy to the sixth century, barrel vaults are carried on very wide transverse arches in the same manner.

and the triforium masks the lean-to roofs which cover the vaults over the aisles; the clerestory windows light the nave and rise above the aisle roof, reaching nearly to the apex of the vault, or to the underside of the wall plate when the church has a timber roof. In most Romanesque churches the triforium or middle storey consists either of a spacious gallery or of a mere passageway in the thickness of the wall, just sufficient in width to allow of free circulation all round the church. In both, arcading comes in front on the face of the nave wall, and in the latter case there are a few openings behind to provide access to the lean-to roof, which otherwise would be cut off entirely from the church. The triforium gallery, which could, through its arched roof, provide the necessary abutment to a vaulted nave, is one of the features of Romanesque design which distinguishes it from Early Christian architecture. In the Early Christian basilicas, the area of wall between the arcade and the clerestory is, with rare exceptions, unpierced and unarcaded, and forms a broad band which is generally decorated with mosaics, as in S. Apollinare Nuovo (see p. 30), with paintings or, more commonly, with marble panelling. In northern countries there do not appear to have been craftsmen capable of carrying out similar methods of decoration, but masons were plentiful and, moreover, had command of the building operations. Hence arose the custom of treating this space in masonic fashion, and not with applied decoration.

The majority of Romanesque churches in England and France have galleries as wide as the aisles below, and often quite as lofty. The reasons for these galleries, and for some large churches having them and others of equal importance being without them, are not quite clear. All large Byzantine churches had galleries, but in Rome only two basilicas, S. Lorenzo and S. Agnese, are galleried; for centuries they were omitted entirely in Italy. Their reintroduction in the West dates from the outburst of church building which began soon after A.D. 1000. In Byzantine churches the galleries were for women; but the separation of the sexes was not insisted upon so strongly in the West. In the monastic churches they were probably provided for the laity, since the monks at first monopolised the whole of the area below, and in cathedral churches they were possibly required to accommodate the crowds which, on days of high festival, overflowed from the nave.[1] In the two

[1] The galleries of Notre-Dame, Paris, are crowded now on Easter Day during High Mass.

largest Romanesque churches at Caen, one, l'Abbaye-aux-Hommes, has them; the other, l'Abbaye-aux-Dames, has none. In Gloucester Cathedral there are galleries over the aisles of the choir, but in the nave merely a low passageway with insignificant arcading in front.[1] The Germans seem to have had a rooted objection to triforiums in any form, and in both their early and late work the spaces between the windows and the arcades are often left absolutely plain.

The design of the arcading at triforium level is not necessarily affected whether there is a spacious gallery or merely a passageway. The effect produced, however, is different, because galleries always have windows in their outside walls and are consequently light, whereas in the other case the background is dark. Each country possesses its own characteristics in triforium design, and in each these change considerably from century to century.

There are some churches abroad which have spacious triforium galleries but no clerestories. In northern Italy there are several, of which S. Ambrogio, Milan, is the most remarkable. This is a rib-vaulted church, but most of the examples are to be found in southern France, notably in Auvergne, and these are barrel-vaulted. In all such cases the upper windows were omitted, because the vault allowed little room for them.

Materials. Stone was the favourite material of the Romanesque builders, although marble, brick and, in certain parts of England, flint, were all used for walls. In Italy walls were often faced with marble as an applied veneer, but some were constructed in marble throughout. In southern France there are many fine churches built entirely of brick, and brick was the material generally employed in northern Germany, Holland and Belgium, because of the scarcity of stone. In England the art of brick-making, which had flourished during the Roman occupation, had died out and was not re-introduced until the fourteenth century.[2] Churches with walls built and faced with flint are most common in Sussex, the churches at Old and New Shoreham being excellent examples. In the eleventh century the craft of the mason was more advanced in some countries than in others. Italy naturally came first, since she had

[1] Amongst other Romanesque churches with spacious galleries are S. Ambrogio, Milan, S. Michele, Pavia, S. Remi, Rheims, and the cathedrals of Ely, S. Albans, Peterborough, etc.

[2] The tower and other eleventh-century parts of S. Albans Cathedral are built chiefly of old Roman bricks taken from the neighbouring ruins of Verulamium.

behind her a long tradition of masonry construction. England was perhaps the country most behindhand, although in some of the pre-Norman work there is finished execution and delicacy of detail which was not equalled for fifty years after the Norman Conquest. In little Odda's Chapel, near S. Mary's, Deerhurst, in Gloucestershire, built in 1056, the few mouldings that remain have much more refinement than any work immediately following can show.

Many of the stone walls of the second half of the eleventh century in England were built of rubble entirely; only the quoins, buttresses, and jambs and arches of doors and windows being of ashlar. The walls were consequently excessively thick. The outer and inner faces were plastered and generally painted. Restorers have swept away the plaster from the outside—and curiously enough, often from the inside as well, leaving rough, uncoursed stonework that was never intended to show—and it is now difficult to find an English church stuccoed as it was when it was first built. While the contrast between a stuccoed wall and its stone dressings is very effective, there is an objection to the outer skin: although a preservative at first, it soon decays, and when it does the final result is patchy restoration or damp walls. This disadvantage led to the gradual disuse of random rubble, which required outside cementing, and the substitution, in buildings in which ashlar facing throughout was not possible, of rubble in regular courses. Most cathedrals were faced with ashlar both inside and out, the core alone being of rubble, but the workmanship was rough and the mortar joints wide until the beginning of the twelfth century.

Buttresses. We have already seen, in the construction of the aisle vaults at Durham, how the rib was introduced to satisfy an aesthetic need rather than a structural necessity. The same may be said of the buttress. The Norman churches were built with walls of considerable thickness, well able to withstand the load and thrust of vaults. Internally the bays were marked by the piers from which the transverse arches sprang, and it must have been felt that some similar articulation was desirable outside. Each bay, therefore, is defined by buttresses which are little more than pilasters, uncommonly wide but of very little depth. They rise as a rule from a plinth to a projecting parapet, without a break, and stop flush with the face of the latter. They are often absolutely plain, although sometimes an attached shaft is worked on each angle. Where there is no parapet the buttress finishes on top with a plain slope or set-off.

There is a marked difference between this method and that adopted in Italy and southern France. In Italy the builders were content, where there were no vaults, to dispense with the buttress altogether, or to follow the Roman precedent and strengthen the inside of the wall. In southern France the feeling was the same. The function of the buttress is to counteract the thrusts of arches; whether it is placed inside or outside the building is immaterial, so far as mere stability is concerned. In southern France, stained glass was not used, and wall painting was the principal means of decoration. Deep internal buttresses provided greater wall area for this kind of treatment and, at the same time, the side lights were almost entirely concealed from view in the nave—a desirable feature in a country of exceptionally bright sunlight.

Romanesque buttress.

Pointed Arch. Until the middle of the twelfth century the semi-circular form of arch was usual; but it was not universal. So much has been written about the semi-circular arch as the distinctive mark of Romanesque architecture and the pointed arch as the exclusive property of Gothic, that it should be remembered that the pointed form was known and used by the Egyptians, Assyrians, pre-Hellenic Greeks and Etruscans, more than a thousand years before the Christian era; and by the Copts of Egypt and their conquerors, the Saracens, some centuries before the pointed arch appeared in the West. It was first employed in Romanesque architecture in the barrel-vaulted buildings of the South of France, certainly before the end of the eleventh century and possibly earlier still. There they adopted the old Roman tradition of the solid vault, with its extrados made up to form two sloping sides, on top of which the outer covering of slates or tiles could be laid direct without the intervening timber roof which was customary farther north. It is true that many of the eleventh-century churches had semi-circular arch sections, but the builders soon perceived the advantages of the pointed form. Not only is it stronger and easier to build, but it exercises less thrust and the mass of solid material above the apex is considerably reduced. The nave of S. Nazaire, Carcassonne (*c.* 1096), which has a pointed barrel vault over the nave and semi-circular vaults over the aisles, provides an excellent example of the early use of this pointed form. Elsewhere in western Europe the date of the introduction of the pointed arch varies considerably. In northern France it first appears between 1100 and 1120. In England it was not used before 1140, the approximate date of Fountains, Malmesbury and Buildwas abbey churches. It occurs 'accidentally', so to speak, in arcading of interlacing semi-circular arches, as early as the first half of the eleventh century; but it is a fallacy to suppose that the builders obtained the suggestion of the form from these arcades. Even if the pointed arch had not been used long before this interlacing arcading was introduced, the fact remains that the builders would be unlikely to abandon the semi-circular form, which had behind it centuries of tradition, merely for a hint conveyed by an accident in decoration. The pointed form was above all a logical structural expedient. In Sicily, and in portions of southern Italy, its introduction was early owing to Saracenic influence;[1] in Germany it was late, for the conservative Teuton clung to his fine round-arched Romanesque until the end of the twelfth century. In the greater part of Italy the pointed arch did not appear until later still; in fact it never entirely superseded the classic form. In the little Loggia del Bigallo, Florence (*c.* 1360), and in many contemporary Italian buildings, all arches are semi-circular. The pointed arch in Romanesque work is certainly a rarity, and its widespread adoption is rightly associated with Gothic rather than Romanesque architecture.

After Fergusson.

Section through Church of S. Nazaire, Carcassonne, showing pointed barrel-vaulted nave and semi-circular barrel-vaulted aisles. The outer aisles (hatched) were added in the 14th century.

Scale 50 ft. to 1 in.

[1] It is impossible to say how early it appeared in Sicily; but it was certainly in common use there before the Normans appeared in 1060, otherwise they would not have adopted it so universally in their churches in the island.

Construction of Arches. The method of construction adopted by the Romanesque builders differed in many respects from Roman precedents. In Roman stone arches, big voussoirs were the rule, and in most cases these extended the full depth of the wall. The soffit was flush, or else relieved by sunk moulded panels. The Romanesque builder preferred smaller stones, which did not, as a rule, bond more than a few inches into the wall, the intervening space being filled with rubble. This answered fairly well at first, since the wall above was either merely faced with ashlar, the core being of rubble, or else was rubble throughout; but it was soon discarded in favour of a series of voussoirs, on different planes, or in what is commonly called different 'orders'.

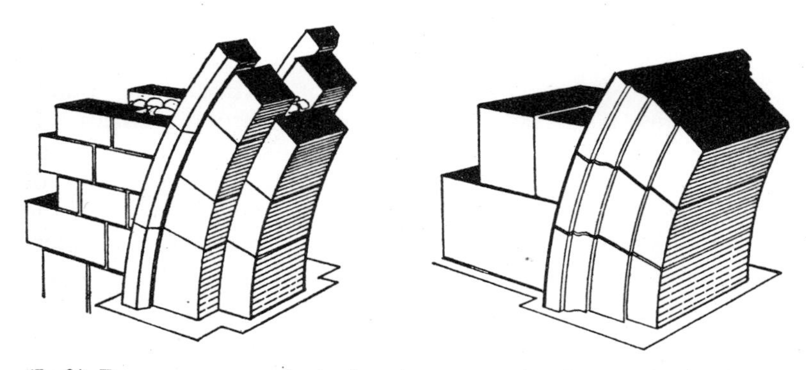

(Left) Romanesque method of arch construction in two 'orders' with label and with rubble infilling; (right) Roman method of arch construction, having voussoirs extending the full depth of wall.

In this system of subordination, the bottom ring of voussoirs, or inner order, was built first, and formed the central part of the soffit. It was not the full width of the wall above; not more than half its width, on an average. It carried the core of the wall; and, in addition, the outer rings, or orders. These partially rested on it and partially projected on either side, until the last, and outer, rings or orders were placed at a distance equal to the total thickness of the wall. One advantage of this method of building was that it diminished the amount of centering required, since when the first order had set it acted as a centre and support for the rings above it. The 'springer', or bottom stone of the arch, was, except in very large churches, in one piece of stone, which reached from side to side and from front to back, often with two or more orders worked on it. This stone afforded a solid bed from which the smaller stones of the different rings could spring, and at the same time slightly diminished the span and consequently the thrust of the arch. A large stone was possible here because there was no difficulty in hoisting it into position and setting it.

In most English cathedrals the arches of the arcades are built in three or four rings, and the Romanesque doorway of Malmesbury Abbey Church has as many as nine. The builders in Italy and the South of France were slow to realise the advantages of subordination and, in consequence, for some centuries they continued to make their arches with flush soffits, or, in technical language, of one order only. Even when they used two orders, the lower one was by far the more important, the upper one projecting merely a few inches in front, as at S. Zeno, Verona, and S. Ambrogio, Milan.

Columns and Piers. The method of arch construction by means of the subordination of orders, together with the introduction of

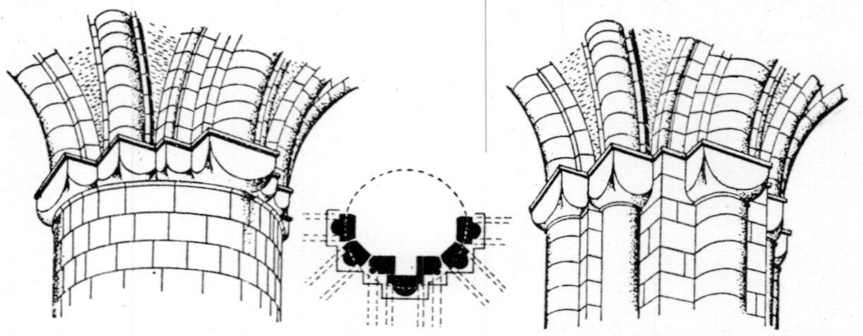

(Left) Shows difficulty of relating arch ribs to circular column below; (right) Shows solution achieved by means of clustered piers.

ribbed vaulting, called for radical changes in the plans of pier or column supports. In Italy and southern France, where principles of subordination were not followed, many columns retained, to a considerable extent, classical proportions, and not only tapered but had an entasis. In England and Normandy, however, the columns were only faced with ashlar, their cores being of rubble; hence their excessive girth, apparent strength and real weakness. They had no fixed proportions, such as were usually followed in classical work.[1] Further, these circular columns provided a most un-

[1] The columns in Tewkesbury Abbey Church and Gloucester Cathedral, for instance, are about double the height of those at Hereford; and yet the diameters are practically the same.

satisfactory seating for the various arches and ribs which they had to support. A rectangular pier was better, a cruciform pier better still, and a subordinated, or clustered, pier the ultimate solution. Piers were, of course, no novelty in the eleventh century. They had been used long before, in the sixth-century churches in Syria, and in association with columns in S. Clemente and S. Maria in Cosmedin, Rome. In other Italian churches they had been employed throughout, partly because the supply of antique marble columns, which for centuries after the fall of the Roman Empire had been so plentiful, had begun to fail, and partly because a simple pier could be built with unskilled labour at much less cost than a column. These early piers were all rectangular and unmoulded. The first alteration in their form was made in the ninth or tenth century, when aisles were divided longitudinally into bays by transverse arches. To carry these arches a 'nib', or pilaster, was added to the back of each pier, a corresponding pilaster projecting from the wall on the other side of the aisle. The pier thus became T-shaped.[1] The next step was to make it cruciform in

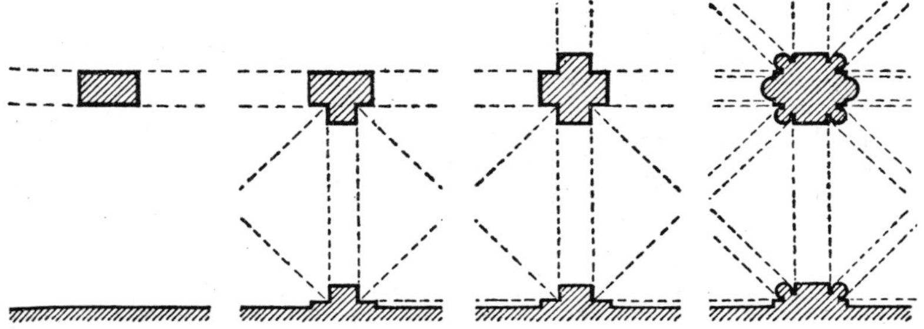

Development of the pier: reading from left to right—plain, T-shaped, cruciform and clustered piers.

plan, so that arches thrown across the nave as well as the aisles could have something substantial to spring from. By this method a shaft was attached to the aisle side of the pier to support the side vaulting, while another, on the nave side, was carried up the wall to the under side of the vaulting ribs, or, when the church was not vaulted, to a point below the tie beam of the roof.[2] The cruciform

[1] T-shaped piers were used in Syria, in the sixth century, at Roueiha (see p. 40), for much the same reason as for their adoption in later Romanesque churches.

[2] In S. Albans Cathedral, the piers of the north side of the nave are amongst the plainest of piers which are not simply rectangular. They have no attached shafts, but the angles are rebated to agree with the orders of the arch above.

pier was satisfactory until the introduction of the diagonal rib, which could not easily be accommodated in the angle between the adjoining 'nibs'. To get over the difficulty, and to reconcile all parts, the subordinated, or clustered, pier was devised. It was so planned that each order of an arch and each diagonal rib had its corresponding member in the pier below. In effect, it was the result of adding to the pier, or column, shafts which corresponded with the orders of arches and with the vaulting ribs of the nave and aisle, so that they appeared as a group of columns with each column in the group supporting its own order or rib. This is the clustered pier, a feature which, together with many others, was to contribute greatly towards the development of the fully articulated Gothic style.

It is not claimed that the English were the pioneers in the pier development described above. The clustered pier found its way into England from Normandy, where it occurred, fully developed, in the Abbaye-aux-Hommes, Caen, begun in 1066; an earlier example than any we can boast. Elsewhere on the Continent there are many examples of it in eleventh-century work. In the nave of S. Ambrogio, Milan, the large piers are clustered, the small, cruciform. On the other hand, in the fine Romanesque work in Germany, the piers are extremely simple, and while columns are general, clustered piers are rare. Even in the large Rhenish churches—Speyer (Spires, or Speier), Worms, Mayence (Mainz) —the columns are plain rectangles, or T-shaped, or cruciform.

CHAPTER XI

ROMANESQUE ARCHITECTURE

Detail and Decoration

THIS chapter is, in an important sense, a continuation of the previous one; for the outstanding feature of much Romanesque architecture is the integration of the detail and decoration within the structure. Ornament is seldom merely applied decoration; more often it is a means of emphasising the underlying method of construction. We have already noticed how the rib and the buttress, though introduced at first to satisfy an aesthetic desire to articulate the structure, were closely related to the whole constructional system. In the same way, the form of carving of a column capital was dictated by the problem of relating the column to the rectangular mass which it supported. The orders of the arches, however decorative in themselves, were primarily devices to facilitate construction. Even when decoration was applied, as for example in wall painting, its use was not purely decorative but, like the mosaics of the Byzantines, instructive in illustrating the story of the Bible. The same applies to figure sculpture. Almost all the arrangements of the church were adapted to provide instruction; they were visual aids towards the understanding of the Christian faith. The church was the medium through which the people, in an illiterate age, learned the history of the world and of heaven and hell. Sculpture, music and painting in Romanesque times were to be found only in the churches and cathedrals.

The interiors of these sacred buildings not only had greater significance for the people of the time than they have for us today, but they were also very different in appearance. There was much more colour. The windows, small though they were, permitted light to illuminate the bright decoration; the mouldings of the arches were picked out in paint and often with gilding; the sculptured figures were richly coloured. Today the cathedrals, with their mellow interiors and weathered walls, can give little idea of the bright and sharp qualities of their original state.

Methods of Decoration. Decoration can be introduced into a church in three ways: (1) by the application to the wall surfaces of colour by means of marble veneers, mosaic or paint; (2) by the employment of different materials used structurally; and (3) by the enrichment of the structure by means of mouldings, carving, arcading, etc.

APPLICATION OF COLOUR

Marble Veneers. The old Roman system of covering walls with a thin veneer of marble, which was practised so successfully by the Byzantines, was followed in the two main centres of Tuscany—Pisa and Florence. In Pisa, the casing of white marble is enriched by dark, narrow bands along the triforium and by simple geometric patterns of marble tesserae set in the blind arcades outside. At S. Miniato, Florence, where there is no triforium, the walls above the arcades are divided into various patterns by a simple arrangement of strips of dark marble on a light ground.[1]

Mosaic. Mosaic work, like marble panelling, is limited in Romanesque architecture to Italy.[2] Whether it originated there or in the East is a disputed point; for it seems likely that the art of glass mosaic, which reached perfection in Constantinople in the sixth century, was almost entirely the product of Greek craftsmanship. Examples of this work are found in Italy down to the twelfth century, but almost exclusively in those areas which came under Byzantine influence—in Venice and in Sicily, which have already been mentioned. By the end of the Romanesque period, mosaic art had died in the West. One reason why it was abandoned is that Romanesque architecture did not lend itself as well to this kind of applied decoration as did the Byzantine or Early Christian churches. The triumphal arches in the last, with their fine expanse of wall over, did not occur, and the open triforium galleries at the sides occupied the space over the arcades formerly available for mosaic decoration. The compartments of the vault might have provided good surfaces for mosaic treatment, as had the domed surfaces of the Byzantine churches, but this possibility never seems to have occurred to the Romanesque builders. The art was almost moribund in the West by the time the ribbed vault was in general use, and applied decoration was limited to paint.

[1] The same type of decoration is employed on the west front, but this last is presumed to have been rebuilt in the fourteenth century.

[2] The only exception farther west is the remnant of mosaic in the apse of S. Germigny-les-Prés (Loiret).

Paint. Painting in tempera or in fresco was practised from the first centuries of Christianity, but the surviving examples are few. Many have been destroyed, many covered by later paintings or by plaster or whitewash.[1] So far as can be judged from somewhat scanty remains, such pictures came only at intervals, or in bands. The walling in between, above and below was coloured a plain tint, and double lines of red or yellow formed frames to the pictures. As a mural painter, the Romanesque designer was far inferior to his colleague in the Eastern Empire. The Romanesque workman was a builder, and more concerned with construction than with painted decoration. The most important use of colour in decoration was to emphasise the structure; the arch mouldings, the ribs of the vault and the column capitals were often painted. It was in these places that the brightest and gayest colours would be used.

EMPLOYMENT OF DIFFERENT MATERIALS

In north Italy, brick and marble, or brick and stone, were interchanged with the happiest results. Farther south, brick was abandoned, and marbles of different colours were used alternately. Sometimes shafts of columns in lighter marble were built against a darker background, so giving added emphasis to the structure. Elsewhere marbles might be used purely decoratively, simply producing patterns on the wall. In France, especially in the district of Auvergne, red and white volcanic stones were used to produce a diaper motif.[2] In Germany and northern France, materials of different colours were seldom used. In England, also, stone facings were generally of one colour, although in parts of the country where red stone and yellow exist side by side, often in the same quarry, one might be used for arches and piers and the other for walls.

ENRICHMENT OF THE STRUCTURE

The structure of Romanesque building was enriched in four ways: (1) by mouldings, which were used to form string courses and

[1] The paintings on the western sides of the piers of S. Albans Cathedral are fair examples of later Romanesque work (see Pl. 17).

[2] A similar treatment occurs in Chichester Cathedral in the tympanums over the openings of the triforium gallery, some of which are filled with lozenge-shaped stones in different colours.

column bases and to define arch forms; (2) by carved ornamentation, which was often incorporated within the system of mouldings; (3) by means of wall arcading and fenestration; and (4) by figure and foliage sculpture, which is found in column capitals, in niches, and especially in the tympanums over important doorways.

Mouldings. Mouldings in Roman arches were worked on the voussoirs and invariably projected in front of the wall to form an archivolt. In Romanesque arches the mouldings were recessed, being worked on the faces and soffits of squared stones. It is true that over the arch there was often a projecting hood moulding or 'label'; but this, except in the smallest examples, was never worked on the voussoirs of the arch itself but on separate stones in long lengths above them. Labels were introduced above arches to throw the rain to the sides and prevent it from running down and injuring the mouldings. There is, therefore, an excellent reason for labels on the outside of the building. Inside, they were also useful when the walling was of rubble, plastered over, since they formed a break between the plaster and the stones of the arch.

Unmoulded arches are rare in England in churches built after the Norman Conquest, but examples occur on the north side of the nave of S. Albans Cathedral. In Italy and southern France they were the rule during the eleventh and twelfth centuries, but the label over was moulded although the voussoirs were plain. Mouldings on the structural parts of buildings are a useful index to the changes in architecture, and through them the date of any work can often be determined when other evidence is conflicting and unreliable.

The scale and contours of mouldings underwent considerable change as the style progressed from Romanesque to Gothic. As a general rule, mouldings followed in section the shape of the arch. Thus, when the arch was semi-circular, mouldings were segments of circles. The most characteristic feature of early Romanesque mouldings was the 'torus', or three-quarter round—sometimes called the 'bowtell'—which was often used in combination with the 'cavetto', or hollow. In many English Romanesque cathedrals, the lowest order in the nave arcades often consists of a single semi-circular moulding, which, as can be seen at Durham, produces a remarkably fine effect.

In France, the mouldings during the Romanesque period were simpler and fewer than in England, the deep hollows and bold rounds being found only in Normandy,[1] where Caen stone provided an ideal medium. Even there, however, the mouldings were generally fewer. In Italy, less attention was paid to mouldings. The Italian workmen did not develop the mason's craft to the same extent as did the builders in England and France. When they wanted relief from simplicity, they preferred to rely on the flat coloured decoration obtained by different marbles, which has already been described. In this they were only following the traditions which had existed in the country for centuries. Even when mouldings were used, these were generally slight, and there

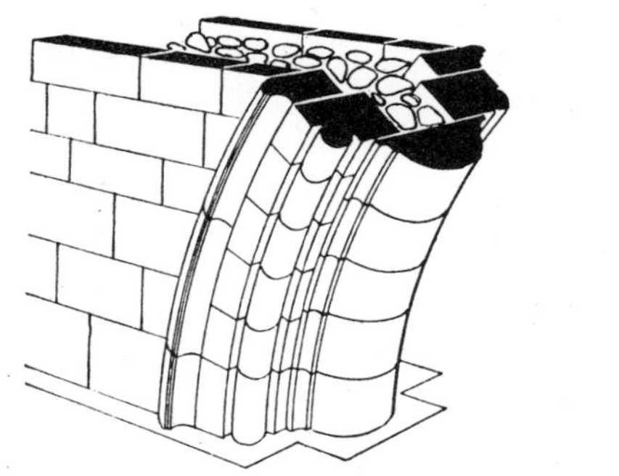

(Left) Typical English arch of two orders with label, having characteristic half-round inner order; (right) Typical northern French arch of two orders with three-quarter-round or 'bowtell' mouldings.

is little difference discernible between early and late examples. The absence of mouldings, however, is due not only to traditions of craftsmanship, but to the materials used and to combinations of materials. Marble possesses, through its figuring, a decorative quality rarely found in stone; and in arches built of alternate voussoirs of marble and brick, as are many in northern Italy, mouldings are unnecessary, and in fact would largely destroy the colour scheme. The same reasons cannot be said to apply in Germany, but there, too, arch mouldings are rarely found. Instead, the Germans seem to have relied upon simplicity and strength, which are more in keeping with the solid and bold construction of their buildings.

Horizontal Lines. Plinths, string courses and parapets give a horizontal emphasis to Romanesque design. In all but the smallest

[1] In one example, the ruined church of the Abbaye d'Ardennes, near Caen, the details are practically identical with contemporary examples in England.

buildings, some kind of plinth was introduced. This generally consisted of one or more chamfered or moulded projections a few feet from the ground, which provided a visible footing from which the main wall would start.

Projecting string courses were placed immediately below windows on the outside and often on the inside as well. Normally they stopped against the buttresses or the internal piers. Another projecting course would be placed along the springing line of the window arch; this would coincide with the abacus of a capital and provide a seating for the arch label moulding.[1] The most marked horizontal emphasis was given by means of the parapet, which in nearly all cases projected in front of the wall below, and was carried on corbels which, more often than not, were carved as grotesque heads. The parapet itself was quite plain, and the reasons for its projection were to provide more space behind for the gutter and flashings and also to protect, like the string courses below, the main surface of the wall.

Wall Arcading. The wall surfaces, both inside and out, were often decorated by arcading, a device which was common in Early Christian work and did not disappear until the large Gothic traceried windows swallowed up the wall space and left no surface to decorate. In general design and in detail, arcading followed the same evolution as the structural parts of buildings, the arches and shafts being moulded and carved in the same way. Throughout the eleventh and twelfth centuries, intersecting arches were common (Pl. 18). In the north these were always semi-circular, but in southern Italy and in Sicily they were pointed.

Windows. Windows in Byzantine and Early Christian churches were, as a rule, numerous and large; but in Romanesque churches, especially in the earlier examples, they were few in number and generally small.[2] The change occurred in Italy in the ninth century, when the prevalent Eastern custom of filling windows with pierced slabs was discontinued. These slabs obstructed a considerable amount of light; when they were abandoned, one

[1] The mouldings of strings are much the same as the labels over openings, and consisted in Romanesque times of little more than a fillet and a chamfer.

[2] In the large churches of England and northern France, where more light was required, they were larger than in the south. In many English cathedrals, such windows have, at a subsequent period, been divided into two by a central mullion, and tracery has been inserted in their heads, as at Peterborough Cathedral.

reason for large windows disappeared. There was no longer any need for a great deal of light, since the old method of decorating walls with mosaics had fallen into general disuse and fresco painting had hardly taken its place; and further, as the builders required far stronger abutments for their vaults than had been necessary in the days of timber roofs, fewer and smaller windows were more practical.

Many of the Romanesque windows must have been 'wind-eyes', and protection from the prevailing wind was achieved by the insertion of timber frames sheeted with linen or vellum. In the wealthier establishments glass may have been substituted, but it was expensive and therefore rare; it has nearly all been lost, because early glass was likewise fitted into removable wooden frames.

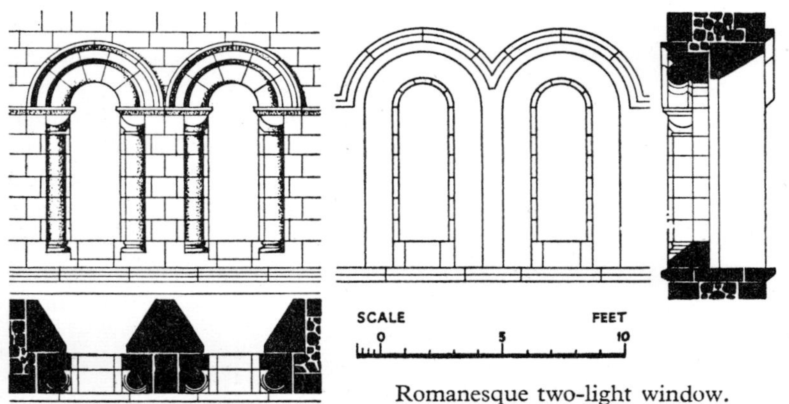

Romanesque two-light window.
(Left) Outside elevation; (right) Inside elevation.

In 675, Benedict Biscop, Abbot of Wearmouth, was obliged to obtain glassworkers from France, and in 758 Cuthbert, Abbot of Jarrow, appealed to the Bishop of Mayence to send him artisans to manufacture 'windows and vessels of glass because the English were ignorant and helpless'. Except for these references, there is at present no evidence of glass having been made in England between the Roman period and the thirteenth century. Few remains of Romanesque glass exist[1]; such decoration as there was seems to have been based on scroll and leaf patterns, and did not include figure or pictorial compositions of any kind.

[1] The restored windows of S. Denis, Paris, have remnants of glass belonging to the year 1108.

Romanesque windows were seldom more than twice their width in height and were generally placed singly; but in domestic work, in church belfries, and in the east ends of churches especially, two or more were often grouped together. When in groups, the lights were divided from one another by either walling or shafts. In the former case they appeared from the outside as though they were separate windows, connected only by a hood moulding and not always by that; whereas from the inside, owing to the wide splaying of the jambs, they united to form one window. The outer jambs were sometimes plain, or merely chamfered, but more often they were enriched by shafts from which sprang arches concentric with the window head. In walls arcaded on the outside, it was the general practice to pierce some of the bays of the arcading for light, and this continued to be the custom so long as the walls remained arcaded.

Division by shafts was usual in Italy, Germany and southern France. The shafts were often placed in the centre of the wall, in which case their capitals had considerable projection in front and at the back but very little at the sides, like many Byzantine examples of earlier and contemporary date (see p. 57). In English work before 1066, the central position for the shaft was generally adopted; but after that date (in northern France as well as in England) shafts were nearer the outside face of the wall, so as to leave more room for splayed jambs on the inside.

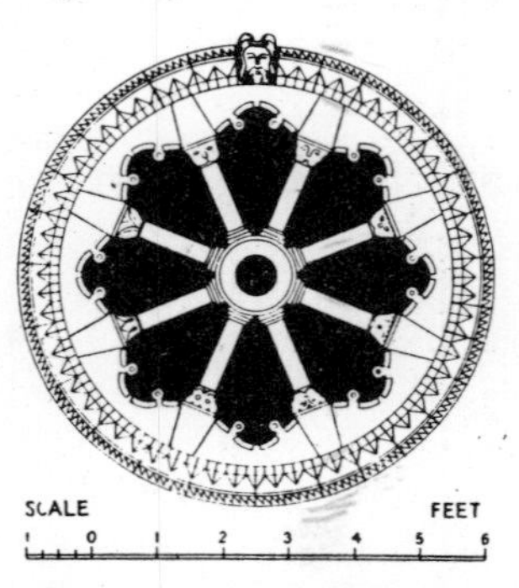

Romanesque wheel window; Patrixbourne, Kent.

Circular windows are common features of Romanesque architecture. Documentary evidence shows that they existed in the transepts of the Carolingian Church of S. Riquier (Somme), which was begun in 780, and later they occurred in churches throughout western Europe. In England they are to be seen in several pre-Conquest churches.[1] The early examples were not as a rule large, and generally consisted of simple round openings with characteristic surrounding mouldings; but at Peterborough Cathedral, Barfreston and Patrixbourne, in Kent, the

[1] At Avebury, Bosham, Bibury, and Barton-on-Humber, and in the towers of Dunham Magna and S. Benet, Cambridge.

openings were considerable and were divided by shafts which radiated from the centre. A similar treatment is found at S. Zeno Maggiore, Verona, and S. Etienne, Beauvais, both of the twelfth century. These are known as 'wheel' windows, and were the forerunners of the large 'rose' windows which form such an effective feature of later Gothic architecture.

Carved Ornament. In Romanesque architecture, ornament is not something which is added or applied to a structure, like mural painting, but is rather the modification or enrichment of structural forms. The Romanesque designers, especially in England and France, enriched the mouldings on arches, on ribs and on string courses. This ornamentation is largely geometrical, simple and easy of execution. The chevron, or zig-zag, the billet and the nail-head are the most common types. It is a kind of ornament which gives an almost barbaric richness to particular parts of the building, in contrast to the abstract severity of most of the architecture, but it is more the work of the craftsman than of the artist. In England, the columns which support the nave arcade are often richly ornamented by flutings which are vertical, spiral or zig-zag, or else form lozenges. They were cut in the stones after the columns were built. All these patterns occur in Durham Cathedral and in Waltham Abbey Church. In Italy and Sicily the small shafts which surround the cloister garths are similarly ornamented, and the flutes or grooves are filled with an inlay of glass mosaic.[1] The arch mouldings in Italy and Germany have very little of this purely geometrical decoration. In its place there are rich interlacing foliage patterns, often with beasts, birds or human figures disposed within, which betray Byzantine inspiration and, in Italy, Greek craftsmanship.

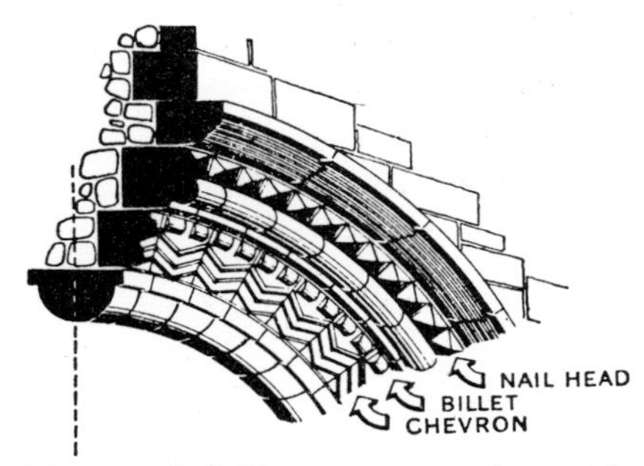

Characteristic Romanesque arch moulding enrichments.

Capitals. Where piers are plain and rectangular, capitals may be dispensed with, since the pier is generally the same width as the

[1] A similar treatment was applied to the grooved shafts round the cloister at Chester Cathedral.

arch and wall above; a moulding is usually set at the springing line, and this is partly ornamental and partly a seating for the timber centering of the arches. In many early churches, a simple abacus is all that parts pier and arch. When, however, a round column has to support a wall at the springing of an arch which is wider in all directions than the column, then some form of spreading capital is necessary.

In many of the Byzantine churches of the sixth century, and in some of the early basilicas, in which antique columns and capitals were largely re-used, the difficulty of starting an arch from the top of a column led to the introduction of a 'dosseret', or shaped block between the arch and the capital proper (see p. 56). The dosseret is confined almost entirely to Byzantine churches, and to early churches in Italy in which Byzantine workmen were employed, or in which local masons copied eastern methods. In more northern Romanesque work, it is discarded entirely, the arch starting directly from the top of the capital. In the Romanesque capital, the portion below the abacus is generally convex. It will be seen that the problem to be solved was one of uniting the square seating of the arch with the circular plan of the column. This was achieved by taking a square block of stone or marble and rounding off the lower parts so that it should sit satisfactorily on the column below. The result was a capital of convex outline. If a concave form were required, rather more stone would have to be cut away in the lower part, the result resembling the classical Corinthian capital. The convex capital is found in all countries, but each has several varieties. In Normandy, England and Germany it is generally somewhat clumsy in form—the term often applied to it being the 'cushion' capital—but in Italy and southern France the surface is often enriched with great delicacy and profusion of ornament. It was a common practice to paint the surfaces of the capitals that were plain, or alternatively to carve the blank faces into two or three cushions, producing a scalloped effect.

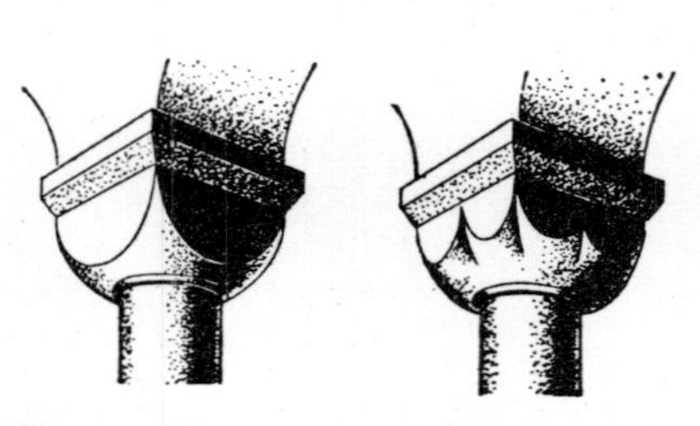

Types of Romanesque capitals. (Left) Cushion capital; (right) Scalloped capital.

Most of the capitals with a concave curve below the abacus are more or less imitations of Roman Corinthian, the measure of correctness depending on the strength of classical traditions in the locality. Thus in Italy and southern France, the Romanesque capitals are distinguished from the antique only by a certain coarseness of workmanship; whereas farther north the differences in form are so great that it is sometimes difficult to trace any resemblance. In work in central France, even as late as the thirteenth century, the capitals are modified Corinthian, but other leaves than the acanthus are carved, and the shape and mouldings of the abacus are very different from those in Roman examples.

Sculpture. Throughout the Romanesque period and the Gothic period which followed, sculpture was limited to conventional symbols and to figure representation which was strictly confined to the service of the church. It provided the people with pictorial representations that were easy to understand. The treatment of these sculptured pictures, though often crude, was on the whole strong and vivid. The wicked were shown descending to hell, the righteous carried up to heaven, in costumes which the people saw every day in the streets; the angels above, the devils below, and the Saviour in judgment between, provided the characteristic theme of the tympanums over the main doorways to the churches.

Byzantine art dominated the whole western world at this time. This was probably due to the iconoclastic controversy in the East, which forbade figure sculpture and threatened the livelihood of Byzantine artists so that they had to seek refuge in the West. In Italy, much of the work was pure Byzantine and executed by these refugees. The real home of Romanesque sculpture was, however, beyond the Alps, in Germany, England and France, where native sculptors probably had to rely on Byzantine miniatures and ivories for inspiration. Byzantine influence was ever present, but the quality of the sculpture varied in different areas. A. W. Clapham[1] recognises three main types in England, in which Anglian, Scandinavian and German influences predominate. The Anglian tradition is typified by its representations of the Crucifixion, of which the Romsey rood is the finest; the Scandinavian by its low reliefs and its curious intertwining foliage; and the German, or Ottonian, by the strong Byzantine element, which is seen at its best in the York Madonna, a relief carving in the local Tadcaster stone.

In France, the principal schools are in the district around Toulouse, in Burgundy and in Provence. Of these by far the

[1] *Romanesque Architecture in Western Europe*, Oxford, 1936.

most fascinating is the Burgundian school, of which magnificent examples exist in the representations of the Last Judgment over the west doorway of Autun Cathedral and of the Pentecost over the west doorway of the nave of Vézelay Abbey Church. Both belong to the first half of the twelfth century, and one of their chief peculiarities is the smallness of the heads of the figures; in other Romanesque work the heads are unnaturally large. The drapery in both cases is highly formalised and bears a close resemblance to that of the archaic Greek sculpture of the seventh and sixth centuries B.C. Viollet-le-Duc's theory, however, is that the special characteristics of this school of sculpture are taken from Byzantine Greek paintings, which the work undoubtedly resembles. On the other hand, it is not impossible that craftsmen from the East were employed in France. To what extent Byzantine Greeks penetrated into France in Romanesque times is a point that has never been decided. The remarkable development of a pseudo-Byzantine architecture in the district around Perigueux has already been mentioned (pp. 93–96). The Abbots of Cluny, in Burgundy, certainly had close relations with the East, and not only sent missions to Antioch and other parts of Syria, but also imported works of art—silk hangings, carved ivories, paintings, etc. It is quite possible that the missionary monks persuaded workmen to return with them. This Burgundian school spread as far as Chartres and Le Mans; the figures flanking the west doorways of the former and the south porch of the latter are almost identical in treatment with those of Vermenton Church, Burgundy (*c.* 1130). The figures themselves stand under canopies and on high bases, with their haloed heads projecting forward, while behind each rises a short portion of a cylindrical shaft which is crowned by a capital. This was the customary design towards the end of the Romanesque period, and the example at Chartres has never been surpassed. The employment of figures as an integral part of architecture in this way must have involved the closest co-operation between sculptors and masons, and it is doubtful whether such a happy combination of sculpture and architecture has at any time been equalled.

TOWERS

Towers have been included in this chapter rather than under the heading of structure, because Romanesque towers were largely developed to satisfy aesthetic needs. It is true that they had a function: to carry bells; but, as a single tower would be sufficient for the purpose, this cannot justify the multiplication of towers which is so common in the cathedrals of France, Germany and England; and in Italy the bell towers, or campanili, were commonly quite detached and so had no direct influence upon the general development of the structure of the churches.

Until recently it was thought that the campanili in Verona, Ravenna and Milan were as old as the sixth century, but we now know that none is older than the ninth, that the Ravenna examples belong to the tenth and that the three examples in Verona are all of the eleventh century. This does not mean that towers did not exist before the ninth century; indeed, a mosaic of the fifth century in the Church of S. Maria Maggiore, Rome, shows two churches near which are round towers. What is now certain, however, is that between the ninth and the eleventh century most of the surviving Romanesque towers were built, and that towers became indispensable units in the composition of Romanesque cathedrals throughout western Europe, providing opportunities for the greatest skill in detail design and in proportioning.

There were many alternative positions for towers. A single tower could be placed over the crossing, at the west end, central with the nave, or at the east end; or it could be detached entirely from the church to which it belonged. Towers could be arranged in pairs at the west end, at the ends of the transepts, or at the eastern ends of the aisles; or single towers could be planned in combination with pairs to form a pyramidal composition. All these arrangements are to be found in surviving examples.

Single Towers. A central tower over the crossing in a cruciform church gave the roofs of the nave, choir and transepts something to stop against. In a church without transepts it allowed the roofs over the western and eastern ends to be at different levels without an ugly break. There was therefore a sound aesthetic reason for central towers. In England and Normandy they were the rule in cathedrals and in the larger monastic churches, though those in Normandy were less dominating than in England. The Germans, on the other hand, seldom built them, preferring octagonal cupolas over the crossings, as did the designers in northern Italy. A possible objection to a central tower is that it requires, to support it, piers considerably larger than are needed elsewhere. In a cruciform church, however, with transepts as high as the nave and choir, even when there is no central tower the piers at the crossing still have to be stronger than other piers, in order to resist the thrusts of the arches of the arcades.

Before the Conquest, some central towers had been built over crossings in England, and after it very few large churches were designed without them. Among Romanesque examples, the finest are those of S. Albans Cathedral, built with Roman bricks from the ruins of Verulamium; Tewkesbury Abbey, exceedingly massive and bold; and Norwich Cathedral, more slender and crowned by a later spire.

A single tower at the west end is an old tradition in England. The number of Anglo-Saxon examples still remaining is proof that before the Conquest this position was general, which is all the more interesting since single western towers are rare in early work abroad. The Italian basilican church had a narthex, never a tower, at the west end. Byzantine churches had no towers at all. In Normandy, in the eleventh century, where low towers over crossings were the rule, it was exceptional to build them at the west end except in pairs. In the centuries immediately following S. Augustine's mission to England, a tower was not only a belfry but also a place of refuge for both people and priests. In most villages the church occupied the most central or the highest point, and it was therefore only natural that the stronghold should be attached to it; and although there was no particular reason for choosing a western position, this was at least as convenient as any other and had aesthetic advantages as well. Whatever was the reason the English so early adopted single western towers, they never tired of them. Ely is the only *cathedral* with one tower at the west end, but there are thousands of parish churches, of all dates and in all parts of the country, with this feature. In fact, it remained the custom long after the mediaeval period had passed.

In Italy single towers were invariably placed to one side of the church and were often quite detached, so that they appear, as it were, as afterthoughts. They were generally later in date than the main buildings, and fear of earthquakes may account to some extent for their isolation. A central tower over the crossing is almost unknown, but many churches had an octagonal lantern at that point, a feature which was ultimately developed at the Cistercian Abbey of Chiaravalle, near Milan, into a lofty, many-staged tower terminating in a spire.[1]

[1] A similar termination of about the same date (12th-13th century) is to be seen at S. Sernin, Toulouse.

A round detached tower is among the most curious of all the architectural features of Romanesque times. This form appears to have been adopted first in Ravenna in the tenth century, and shortly afterwards (although the date is uncertain) in Ireland and Scotland, and culminated in the unique leaning tower of Pisa.

James Fergusson, writing in 1867, mentioned that 118 round towers were still to be found in Ireland, of which 20 were perfect, or nearly so; and two fine examples still exist at Abernethy and Brechin, in central Scotland. In nine cases out of ten these towers were planned, like those at Ravenna, quite apart from the church with which they were associated. The doorways were invariably more than 7 feet above the ground, which suggests that they were primarily towers of refuge; and the openings in the upper storeys were all small and crude in detail. The towers varied in height from 60 to 130 feet, and were constructed of carefully dressed stone, tapering upwards and culminating in a steep, conical stone roof. Whatever may have been their origin, there can be no doubt that they were in some way associated with the church, as bell towers, strongholds, storehouses or marks of dignity. The adoption of a circular form was especially strange in areas of good building stone. It is true that in some districts of England, round towers were built in later Romanesque times; but these were strictly confined to Sussex and some of the eastern counties, where flint was the building material and masons would wish to avoid the problem of quoins.

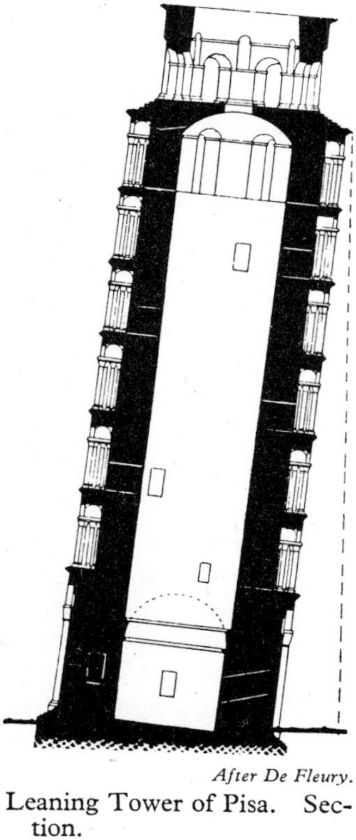

After De Fleury.

Leaning Tower of Pisa. Section.

Scale 50 ft. to 1 in.

The most extraordinary of all Italian towers is the leaning tower of Pisa, which inclines 13 feet out of the perpendicular. The generally accepted theory regarding its non-verticality is that this was the result of bad foundations. The building was begun in 1174, and when it was only 35 feet above the ground the extent of settlement was noticed. Only slight additions were made to try to obtain a horizontal bed for the stone courses, but these do not appear to have been very successful, since after the completion of the third gallery above the ground storey, work was abandoned until 1350, when the three remaining storeys were added and the upper belfry stage set back in the inner wall. It is not the inclination of the tower that renders it unique, for there are many leaning towers in Italy, but its design. Its ground storey has a blind arcade, like that of the cathedral, and above this rise six tiers of arcaded galleries, surmounted by a belfry of smaller diameter. The whole, though late in date, is designed to harmonise closely with the earlier cathedral, and especially with the treatment of the apse.

There may be said to be three distinct schools of tower design in Italy, excluding the round towers of Pisa and Ravenna: (1) Venetian, (2) Lombardic, and (3) Roman. Each possesses distinctive characteristics. Towers of the Venetian type are frankly belfries, with open loggias at the top which form the bell chambers. Except for small slits which light the staircases, they are without openings. At the angles, and in between, are slight pilasters which start from the base and run up the face without a break to support arches immediately under the bell loft. There are no horizontal divisions at all. Since the collapse in 1902 of the great campanile at Venice,[1] the finest surviving example is at Torcello (Pl. 11).

The Lombardic towers differ chiefly from the Venetian in that each storey has windows, and is marked by a horizontal string course carried on small round arches, which stop against wide stiles or pilasters at the angles and divide the wall into panels. The windows increase in size from narrow slits immediately above the ground to very wide openings at the belfry level.

Roman towers are without pilasters, but solidity of appearance is given by the windows being kept well in the centre of each face. The storeys are marked by cornices, which are carried all round, and take the place of the Lombardic string courses. There are some thirty-six surviving campanili in Rome and its immediate neighbourhood, and nearly all were erected between the eleventh and thirteenth centuries. There is generally a blind storey at the base equal to the height of the church, and the number of storeys

[1] This campanile was built in 888, and rebuilt in 1908.

over varies in number up to seven, each side being lit by openings of two or more lights, with round arches and dividing shafts placed centrally in the wall.

The type of tower first followed in other countries was the Lombardic, but more pronounced buttressing soon led to its modification. Campanile towers, pure and simple, are rare outside Italy. At Vienne and at Puissalicon, near Béziers, both in Provence, the detached and storeyed type of Lombardic tower is found, and the cathedral of Uzès has a remarkable circular bell tower with traces of Lombardic ornament. At Yatton Keynell, Wiltshire, there is a graceful tower with sloping sides, almost Venetian in character. Most western Romanesque towers, however, are closely related to the fabric of the church and have wide buttresses or piers of slight projection at the angles.

In France, the characteristic form of Romanesque tower is that in which the lower part is square and the upper part round or octagonal. This feature was adopted in the transeptal towers of the Abbey church at Cluny; it is seen at its best when treated as a lantern over the crossing and crowned by a steep pyramidal or conical stone roof, as at the Abbaye-aux-Hommes, Caen.

Many towers of Romanesque times still survive in England and Normandy, and show considerable variety in arcading and enrichment. It is, however, by their sheer bulk and height that they impress most. They represent considerable structural achievements. The building of western towers, in which the walling rests directly on the ground, is straightforward, but the raising of a tower two or three hundred feet above the ground upon four legs thirty or forty feet apart, at the crossing of a cathedral, is astounding. It is true that the piers are exceptionally large, but then the walls which they carry are exceptionally thick. The foundations were often negligible, with the result that some towers collapsed soon after they were built, as at Winchester, and that many, like those of S. Albans, Hereford and Rochester, had to be drastically strengthened and underpinned and in some cases completely rebuilt. Nevertheless, those that have survived provide tangible proof of the astonishing aspirations of the Romanesque designers.

The termination of a tower with a spire is a feature peculiar to western Christianity, and one which was developed with the greatest skill in Gothic times. Many of the existing Romanesque towers are now without spires, but it seems probable that timber structures of some sort were intended in most cases. These were mostly square in plan, like those at Tournai Cathedral, or octagonal, like that at the Abbaye-aux-Hommes, Caen. A most interesting termination is to be found in the 'helm-roof' at Sompting, Sussex, which alone of Saxon churches has retained the original termination of its tower. This consists of a steeply pitched gable on each face, from the apex of which rise the ridges of a pyramidal roof (Pl. 13). A similar treatment is to be found in the Rhineland churches of Laach, Lièges and Cologne.

Pairs of Towers. The most effective and suitable position for a pair of towers is at the west end. They frame the principal doorway and the central part of the front and, in addition, they mask the aisles at the sides; to conceal the aisles seems to have been one of the chief aims of the Romanesque builders in northern France and in England. Only one of the towers would carry the bells. In most Romanesque churches in Normandy and England, these western towers were planned, but it often happened that their erection was postponed while work proceeded farther east, so that when at length the task was resumed, either the towers were built in the style of the moment, which would be Gothic, or they were abandoned altogether.

Towers over the transepts are far from common, although they have certain structural advantages when used in conjunction with a central tower, by providing a terminal load to withstand its lateral thrust. Towers rise over the transepts in a few examples in southern France, and in England, Exeter Cathedral alone has towers in this position—the only remaining portions of Romanesque work.

Pairs of towers at the east end are even rarer, except in Germany, and there they are turrets rather than towers. At S. Abbodonio, Como, in Italy, and Morienval in France, the two towers rise above the aisle roofs at the junction of the nave and choir, and at Tournai towers crowned by steeply pitched roofs are situated on either side of the apsidal end, with most striking effect.[1]

The smaller height of the cathedrals of England rendered the building of a central tower easier, and the combination of this with a pair of towers at the west end was one of England's most important contributions. The central tower invariably dominates the composition, in contrast with the French examples, where so

[1] At Hereford, two towers were designed, and probably built, at the eastern ends of the side aisles.

often a mere lantern is all that shows above the roof. The character of the western towers had been first determined in Normandy, but it was in England, as can be seen at Durham and Tewkesbury, that the great dominating central tower was developed with the most superb results. Many other English cathedrals have this characteristic composition, the central towers standing on Romanesque piers, as at Canterbury and York; but these were built, or re-built, in Gothic times and therefore do not come within the scope of this volume.

CHAPTER XII

ROMANESQUE IN ITALY

THE chaotic state of affairs throughout Italy from the ninth to the twelfth centuries was naturally reflected in the arts of the country. The history of the period is a continuous account of internal troubles and external wars; of conflicts between Pope and Emperor; of state fighting against state; of the efforts of the Eastern Emperors to retain their footing in Italy, and of the determination of the Saracens and the Normans to wrest the land from them, or from anybody else who happened to be in possession.

Out of this confusion there developed an architecture that was not national but regional. In the north, with Milan as its centre, there developed the Lombard style. A hundred miles south, in Tuscany, with centres at Pisa and Florence, a distinctly different architecture evolved. Around Rome, on the other hand, the Papal State held firmly to its classical traditions and contributed remarkably little to Romanesque development, although what building there was had its own local character. Farther south, in Apulia and Sicily, the influence of Saracen, Byzantine and Norman resulted in a hybrid architecture in which different methods of construction and decoration mingled together in a most unusual way.

LOMBARDY

Milan was the centre of architectural advance in northern Italy, and it was there, and in the neighbouring towns, that Italian Romanesque architecture was first fully developed. The new style involved a complete break from the Early Christian basilica by the substitution of piers for the column arcade and the general use of the stone vault instead of the timber ceiling. The first step, involving a T-shaped pier which would carry vaults over the aisles, appears to have been taken in the tenth-century Church of S. Eustorgio, Milan. Then, probably towards the end of that century, the cruciform pier, by means of which support could be provided for arches spanning the nave, was adopted in the Church of SS. Felice and Fortunato, Vicenza. It is likely that in the first instance these arches were simply diaphragm arches, but before long, vaults were introduced over the aisles; according to Kingsley Porter,[1] the first completely vaulted church in Lombardy was built at Mazzone, *c.* 1030. The most revolutionary step, however, in which the diagonal rib and the clustered pier were combined, was possibly taken in the little church of Sannazzaro, not far from Milan, which is presumed to have been founded in 1040, and may therefore have been completed before the middle of the eleventh century. This structural revolution was accompanied by many other innovations. As a general rule, the churches were of only two storeys: that is, a main arcade with either a clerestory or a triforium. Transepts were developed in many examples, and it became usual to cover the crossing with an octagonal dome, the transition from the square to the octagon being achieved by squinch arches at the angles. The cupolas thus developed were, with few exceptions, covered by low-pitched roofs. Similar features are to be found in Germany, southern Italy and southern France. In most cases they were surrounded by windows which, as in S. Ambrogio, Milan, admitted a flood of light near the east end of the church.

The west façade was invariably treated as a flat, low-pitched gable end, which extended across the whole building and concealed the division of nave and aisles; this did not, therefore, always line up with the roofs behind. The plain façade was relieved by doorways which were often elaborate, having not only the series of recessed orders typical of so much Romanesque work, but in addition a projecting porch supported on detached columns. This feature is common in many churches in Italy and is not limited to Lombardy. Sometimes it is two storeys high, as in the cathedrals of Verona and Piacenza, but is more often of one storey only, as, for example, at S. Zeno, Verona. The porches are vaulted, and possess as a rule two peculiarities: one is that the vault, being carried on detached columns placed well away from the wall, could not possibly stand if it were not for iron ties which prevent it from spreading; and the second is that the columns rest on the backs of animals, generally crouching lions. Where this device originated is not known; it can be seen in Carolingian manuscripts, and must have come from the East, though it is unknown

[1] *Lombard Architecture*, London, 1917.

in Byzantine work. According to Clapham,[1] the earliest example appears at the Cathedral of Aceranza, in southern Italy, which he dates at 1080. Windows in southern Italy are sometimes treated in a similar way. At the sill level of the east window of Bari Cathedral, for instance, carved elephants project boldly to carry shafts which support a rich archivolt. On the south transept there are two more examples, and in other churches at Bari, Trani, etc., further instances are to be found.

The external treatment of the apsidal ends provides an especially interesting example of rational construction; for the wall above the springing of the semi-dome had only to withstand the thrust of the covering timber roof, which was negligible when compared with that exerted by the semi-dome on the wall below, so that no great strength was required in the upper part. It was therefore possible to treat it as an open arcaded gallery. The openings were simple at first, as in the apses of S. Ambrogio and S. Vicenzo-in-Prato, Milan, and soon the motif was used on the west front as well, as at S. Michele, Pavia, where it ascends and descends under the eaves of the gable.

At S. Michele the openings around the apse are grouped in pairs. In some other examples they form a continuous gallery, the openings being separated from one another by marble shafts. Germany copied the feature from Italy, and in the south of France the design is frequently met with. In Tuscany it was elaborated and duplicated to such an extent that the arcaded gallery front is one of the most distinctive characteristics of this region. The same treatment is generally found in the central cupolas which, being relatively low in profile, are not so striking as our English central towers; but in Germany, where they often group with other towers and turrets, they can be very effective.

S. Ambrogio, Milan (Pl. 10). The date of the building of S. Ambrogio has probably been the subject of more controversy than that of any other building in the country. According to Cattaneo,[2] the east end dates from the time of Archbishop Angilbertus (824–859), but Clapham claims that it belongs to the tenth century. Rivoira[3] places the main building at not before the end of the tenth century, Kingsley Porter and Cattaneo at the last half of the eleventh

[1] *Romanesque Architecture in Western Europe*, Oxford, 1936.
[2] R. Cattaneo, *Architecture in Italy from the VIth to the XIth Centuries*, 1896.
[3] G. T. Rivoira, *Lombardic Architecture*, 1910.

century, while Clapham maintains that 'the only direct evidence of its date points to the first third of the twelfth century.'[1] Whether or not the structure can claim to be the prototype of others, it is nevertheless remarkable in that it combines in a magnificent way those features which distinguish Lombardic architecture. The plan is basilican, but with this difference: that in place of the continuous colonnade we now have a plan of few and large piers with smaller supports between, an arrangement which made it possible to have vaults over both nave and aisles, all approximately square, one bay of the nave corresponding to two

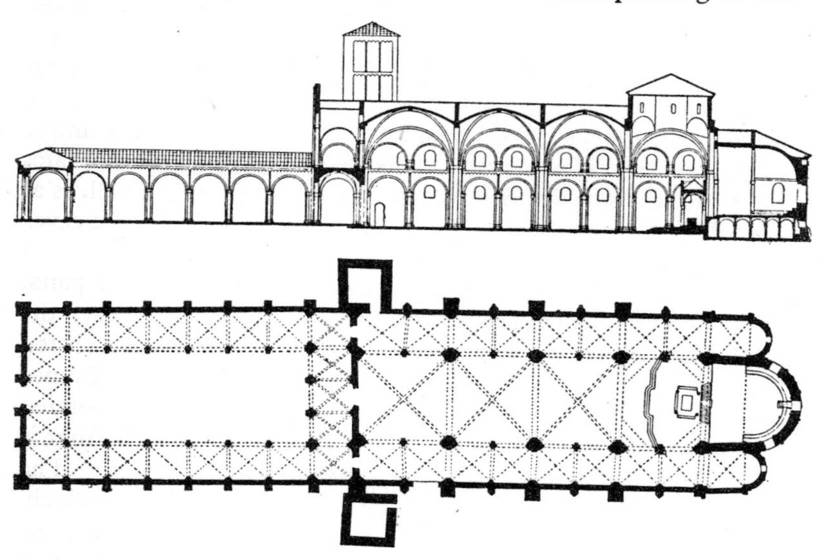

After Dartein.

S. Ambrogio, Milan.
Scale 100 *ft. to* 1 *in.*

bays of the aisles. In no other way could the wide vault of the nave and the narrower vault over the aisles have been satisfactorily supported. The nave bays in consequence are few and wide. Here is the chief reason for the differences in proportion and appearance between the Early Christian basilica and the Romanesque church. In the latter, massive supports which could maintain the weight and thrust of the vaults were essential. In the former, all that had to be carried was the dead load of clerestory wall and timber roof. In S. Ambrogio, there are three great piers

[1] *Op. cit.*, p. 35.

some 40 feet apart on either side of the nave, from which the longitudinal, transverse and diagonal ribs spring. The height from the floor to the crown of the diagonal ribs is just over 60 feet, the crown of the supporting arches being 10 feet less because the vaults are domical. This is no great height considering the width, if comparison be made with later Romanesque and Gothic churches, but the proportions, curiously enough, are almost exactly those of the Basilica of Constantine, which was 83 feet wide and 120 feet high. The piers and transverse arches are of stone, the diagonal and longitudinal arches of brick with pieces of stone set irregularly. These may be part of the original design or may be due to subsequent alterations. The charm of the church lies in a large measure in its lighting. This is ample, although the source is not always evident. The flood of light on the altar and its baldachino is obtained from a high ring of windows in the octagonal cupola above. The few aisle windows are generally concealed by the piers, and the windows at the back of the triforium, which assist in lighting the vaults, are, of course, invisible from the nave. The west windows are large, but they are shadowed by the gallery outside. Altogether, the effect produced by an apparent absence of windows is surprisingly good.

S. Ambrogio differs from other contemporary churches in Lombardy in having no transepts and in the possession of a cloistered atrium at the western end, one side of which forms a narthex flanked by towers. Over the narthex is a gallery with three large openings in front, spanned by a low-pitched gable in a similar manner to that adopted in some Syrian churches (see p. 39).

S. Zeno, Verona. The Church of S. Zeno, Verona, built in the first half of the twelfth century, has almost all the characteristics of a vaulted church: sturdy clustered piers alternating with lighter columns and, on the outside, more strongly-marked buttresses than are customary in Italy; and yet, apparently, it was never vaulted. Transverse diaphragm arches, however, were evidently thrown across the nave from each of the big piers, starting from capitals halfway up the walls. One of these arches still remains towards the west end; the others were removed when the church was heightened and the choir remodelled early in the fourteenth century. To this later period belongs the present timber ceiling of the nave. S. Zeno has a clerestory but no triforium, in which respect it differs from S. Ambrogio and other churches in Lombardy. The west front is distinguished by its large wheel window, its pilaster strip decoration, its magnificent projecting porch and its tall, detached campanile, enriched with alternate courses of brick and marble and culminating in an open-arcaded bell chamber and a steeply-pitched roof (Pl. 11).

S. Michele, Pavia. S. Michele, Pavia, is in many ways the most interesting of all the Lombard churches. It was built at either the end of the eleventh or the beginning of the twelfth century and possesses nearly all the features which we associate with Gothic architecture. Its plan is cruciform; it has ribbed vaults, clustered piers, and deep buttresses which are incorporated within the church in the French manner. All that the church lacks are window tracery and the pointed arch. When it was first built it had two nearly square quadripartite ribbed vaults over the nave; the existing oblong compartments are much later. There is a raised choir over a vaulted crypt, and the eastern bay immediately preceding the apse is of domical form, being constructed of semi-circular ribs over an oblong plan. The typically Lombardic western front consists of a wide, flat gable, relieved only by the stepped arcade under the eaves and the deeply recessed porches, richly carved with scroll and interlacing patterns.

The plan is astonishingly irregular. The lines of the nave are not at right angles to the western façade, nor even parallel with each other, with the result that the breadth of the nave varies over 3 feet from one end to the other. Nor are the bays of the nave, strictly speaking, square, but irregular oblongs, the dimension along the axis of the church being considerably greater than the width. The crossing is not square and the dome above is consequently an irregular octagon with no two sides equal.

TUSCANY

The contrast between the architecture of Tuscany and that of Lombardy is considerable, and may be attributed partly to the greater wealth and commercial importance of Tuscan cities and partly to the presence of local marbles; in Lombardy the main building material was brick, which had encouraged great ingenuity in construction, but in Tuscany the various marbles provided opportunities for more skilful craftsmanship. There are two important schools in Tuscany, centred in the city states of Pisa and Florence. Pisa, then a port, was a great sea power by the beginning of the tenth century, and its cathedral, consecrated in 1118,

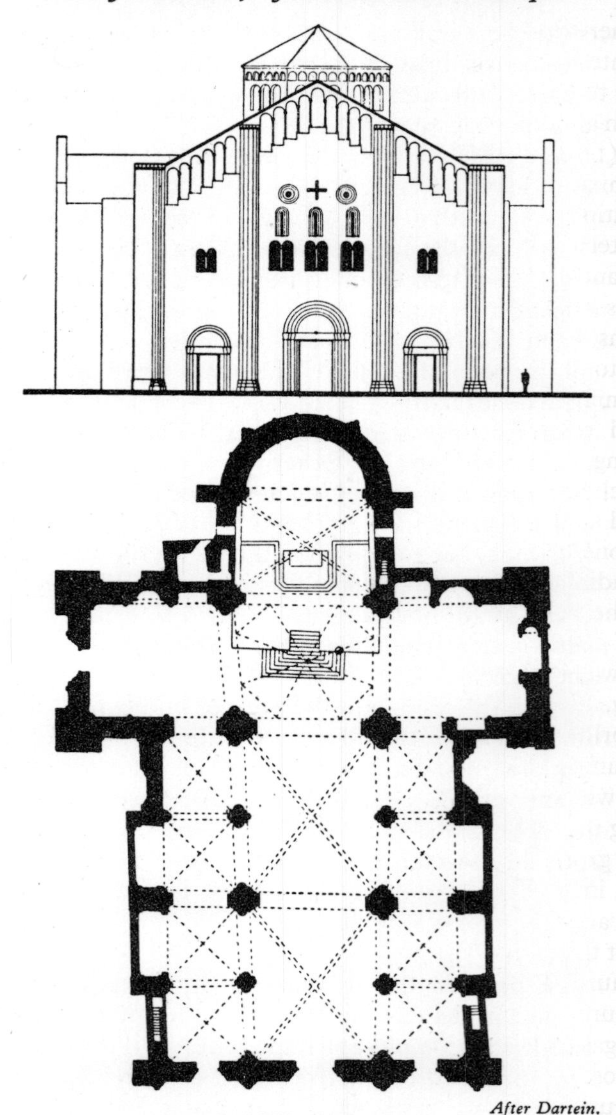

S. Michele, Pavia.
Scale 50 ft. to 1 in.

presents us with a fully-developed style without any precedents. The churches of Lucca and Arezzo, and those in the dependency of Sardinia, followed the lead of Pisa. The school of Florence, on the other hand, which is exemplified in the Church of S. Miniato al Monte, and in the Badia at Fiesole, seems to have adhered more closely to classical and Early Christian forms.

Pisan architecture differs from that of Lombardy in the following ways: (1) The adoption of marble casing throughout in preference to a mixture of brick and marble. This is sometimes used in alternating bands of light and dark—a method first adopted at Pisa and afterwards carried to extremes in the mediaeval cathedrals of Siena and Orvieto—or else in the facing of the carcase with thin veneers of different coloured marbles to form simple geometrical patterns. (2) The treatment of the western front so that it conforms to the section of the building, by having a high central gable to terminate the nave and lean-to gables at the ends of the aisles, instead of a single façade gable. (3) The widespread use of arcading. The whole of the ground storey is generally arcaded, the arches springing from pilasters of slight projection, which are carried across doorways and have above them open galleries set in tiers, one above the other, in contrast to the single ascending and descending gallery of the Lombards. (4) The use of a timber roof over the nave in preference to a ribbed vault. This allowed the use of columns rather than piers along the nave arcade, because there was less weight to be carried.

Pisa. One of the most delightful architectural compositions in the world is that formed by the cathedral, baptistery, leaning tower, and Campo Santo at Pisa. All but the last, a cloistered rectangular court which was begun about the end of the thirteenth century, belong to the Romanesque period. The most important building in the group is the cathedral, which was begun in 1063 and consecrated in 1118. It consists of a nave and choir, both with double aisles, and wide, projecting transepts each with single aisles and an apse at the end. The aisles throughout are vaulted, but the rest of the church is covered by timber roofs. Over the aisles there is a triforium (an unusual feature in Tuscany), which forms a high, wide gallery round the church. The transepts are cut off from the crossing by the continuation of the arcades of the nave and the triforium galleries. The plan indicates that not only were transepts an innovation little understood at Pisa when the church was built, but that the architect wished to adhere to the basilican plan of continuous arcades.[1] The result is excellent; there is no feeling

[1] A similar plan, in which the transepts are divorced from the nave, was followed at S. Demetrius, Salonika (p. 34).

of weakness, such as is often apparent in mediaeval churches when the arches of the crossing are far higher than those at either side; and in few churches in Europe are there such fine perspective effects as can be obtained here, looking along the transepts across the church.

According to Vasari [1], the architect was Boschetto, a Greek, but there is little that is Byzantine about the plan, and only incidental features suggest eastern influence. In its purity of line, its subtlety of proportions, there is, however, something almost classical that is not evident in other works of the time. As in Greek temples, many devices have been introduced to ensure the desired optical

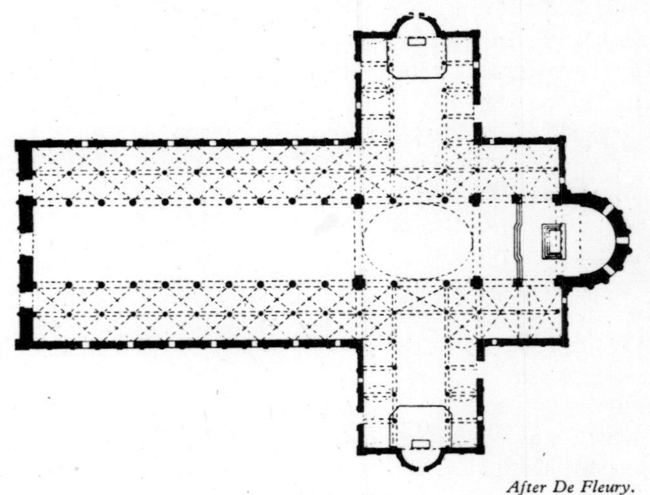

After De Fleury.

Pisa Cathedral.
Scale 100 *ft. to* 1 *in.*

correction and to provide subtle variety to the façade. Along the flanks, the lines of the string courses are not straight, but rise and fall, so regularly that it is difficult to believe that these curves are unintentional. The horizontal lines of the arcading on the western front curve downwards towards either end just enough to ensure that when viewed from the centre they appear perfectly horizontal. The arcades, which are ranged one above the other to form a proto-façade, appear at first sight to be all the same but in fact vary considerably (Pl. 9). 'Now,' said Ruskin, 'I call *that* Living Architecture. There is sensation in every inch of it, and an

[1] *Lives of the most famous Architects, Painters and Sculptors.*

Pisa Cathedral, west front

Plate 9

S. Miniato, Florence

S. Ambrogio, Milan; exterior

Plate 10

S. Ambrogio, Milan; interior

Campanile, Torcello

Leaning Tower, Pisa

Plate 11

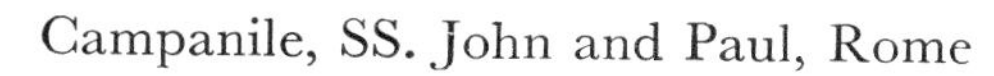

Campanile, SS. John and Paul, Rome

S. Zeno Maggiore, Verona; porch

Worms Cathedral; view from south

Worms Cathedral; nave

Plate 12

Monreale Cathedral; apsidal end

Aix-la-Chapelle Cathedral; interior

accommodation to every architectural necessity with a determined variation in arrangement which is exactly like the related proportions and provisions in the structure of organic form.'[1]

The least satisfactory features of the exterior design are at the crossing. Because the transepts, with their single aisles, are narrower than the nave, the roofs come at a lower level and cut into, and abut awkwardly against, the central octagon. Nor is the oval-shaped dome a beautiful object. The best part is certainly the west end, which has considerable dignity. Its lines, moreover, are truthful, inasmuch as they agree with the section of the church behind, an accordance which is unusual in many Italian western façades.

The baptistery, which is situated some 200 feet from the west end and on the main axis of the cathedral, is a very strange creation, built on a circular plan and covered by a steep cone which penetrates a surrounding hemispherical dome. Externally it is decorated with the same arcading as that of the cathedral, but was later furnished with Gothic pinnacles and enriched with sculptures by Niccolo Pisano.

The campanile, or leaning tower, is placed to one side of the eastern end of the cathedral and has already been described (pp. 171–2). According to Lethaby, 'it may be said to have been designed by rolling up the west front of the cathedral.'[2] Altogether, these three Romanesque buildings—the cathedral, the baptistery and the leaning tower—constitute a most remarkable architectural group.

The Italians seem to have been quickly captivated by the new style. It was repeated in other churches of Pisa, at Lucca, at Pistoja and at Arezzo. At S. Michele, Lucca, the western gable was carried up more than 30 feet above the roof proper, simply to provide more arcades. The whole of the ground storey of these Tuscan churches is generally arcaded, the arches springing from pilasters of slight projection, or from shafts of marble touching the walls. The arcading is carried across doorways, but emphasis is generally given to these by raising the arches above them. This was the rule in the churches of Pistoja and it was also adopted in the west front of Troja Cathedral in Apulia, in the south of Italy. The open galleries above at Lucca, as at Pisa, are not limited to the west front but are continuous along the sides and round the apse,

[1] *The Seven Lamps of Architecture.*
[2] *Mediaeval Art.*

producing fine effects of light and shade. At Pisa the clerestory windows are placed in alternate bays of external arcading, but this arcade bears no relation to the internal divisions. The same may be said of the aisle windows, which occur sometimes behind columns and sometimes between them. It was left for later architects to discover, with doubtful results, that everything in a church must be arranged symmetrically.

Florence. The Florentine architecture of the Romanesque period is different in many respects from that of the churches

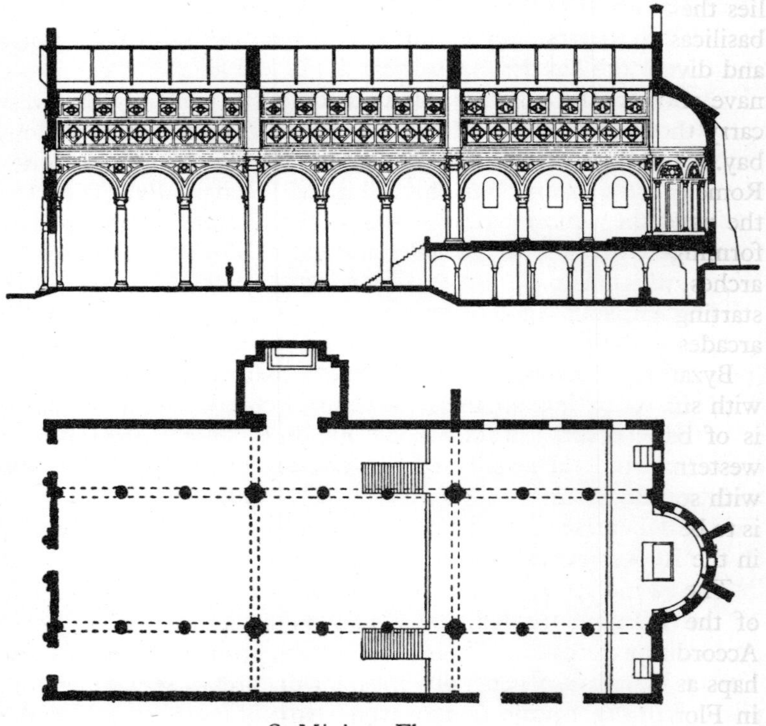

S. Miniato, Florence.
Scale 50 *ft. to* 1 *in.*

mentioned above, chiefly because of much closer adherence to Early Christian forms. There are only three monuments of the period—the Church of S. Miniato, built on a hill above the town, the Baptistery in the city, and the Badia at Fiesole. Of these the most important is S. Miniato (*c.* 1013), in which three influences—Early Christian, Byzantine and, to a lesser extent, Romanesque—

meet. In many respects it is an ordinary basilican church, except that its crypt is larger, and its chancel raised higher, than in Early Christian examples. There are no transepts whatsoever. Old columns and capitals—some of the latter much too small for the columns below—are extensively used; over the nave and aisles are open timber roofs; and in its general plan, construction, and proportions, there is little to distinguish it from the earlier churches in Rome. It was never intended to be vaulted, indeed, it could not be, and every part of the design proclaims that fact; but (and herein lies the main difference between this church and Early Christian basilicas) transverse diaphragm arches span both nave and aisles and divide the church longitudinally into three large bays. The nave and aisle ceilings are, in consequence, not continuous. To carry these transverse arches, piers are introduced at every third bay. These piers are not rectangular, like those in S. Clemente, Rome (p. 17), but are quatrefoil in plan. One quarter of each on the nave side is carried up above the crown of the nave arcade, forming a half-round pilaster to support the main transverse arches, while from the opposite side smaller arches span the aisles, starting from the same springing line as do the arches of the arcades.

Byzantine influence is shown in the decoration of the interior with simple patterns of brick and coloured marble. The outside is of brick and is extremely simple, with the exception of the western façade, which is cased in black and white marble panelling with somewhat unfortunate effect. The same style of decoration is to be found in the west front of the Badia at Fiesole (*c.* 1090) and in the Baptistery at Florence.

The Baptistery is a simple octagon, 90 feet across, and how much of the Romanesque structure remains is exceedingly doubtful. According to Cummings,[1] it was built originally as a church, perhaps as early as the sixth or seventh century; but the construction in Florence of a domed building of so great a span is unlikely at that time. The details throughout are classical, and the detached columns which decorate the interior walls are probably antique.

ROME

Because of the strong classical traditions, there is little genuine Romanesque architecture to be found in Rome. Only one church,

[1] *History of Architecture in Italy*, London, 1908.

dedicated to SS. John and Paul, is important. The portico, the tower (Pl. 11), the pavement and the apse certainly belong to the twelfth century, the last being enlivened by a typical Lombardic arcaded gallery. Nevertheless, it was during the Romanesque period that many of the Early Christian churches were restored, and many of the brick campanili, which have already been described (p. 172), built. This, too, was the time when the famous school of marble workers, the Cosmati, practised their art. To the Cosmati we owe much of the furnishing of Roman churches. Nearly all of the great marble candlesticks, the pulpits, the baldachinos, the bishops' thrones and the choir screens were their work. Their art spread to southern Italy and northern Europe. In Westminster Abbey, the Shrine of Edward the Confessor, carried out about 1268, was a product of this school. Its finest works are to be found in the cloisters of the basilicas of S. John Lateran and S. Paul Outside the Walls. They are very fanciful in design, and the unconstructional character of the shafts, most of which are either twisted or deeply fluted, is pardonable because the weight to be carried is but slight. The shafts are arranged in pairs, and those that are twisted or fluted are enriched with marble and glass mosaics. Mosaics are also inserted in the frieze, the bright colours being framed by the white marble of which the whole of the cloisters, except the plinth, are composed.

SOUTHERN ITALY

Romanesque architecture in the southern half of Italy is largely limited to two districts: the province of Apulia, with its centre at Bari, and the Norman kingdom of Sicily, with its centre at Palermo. Some of the buildings of the period, especially those with domes and a centralised plan, were derived from Byzantine sources and have already been discussed (pp. 90–92). Others are similar in construction or in plan to Norman or Lombardic buildings and, although built by Arab workmen and incorporating many features of Byzantine decoration, properly belong to this chapter.

Generally, the churches in Apulia have suffered considerably from neglect, ill-judged restoration, and additions and alterations in the Rococo style of the sixteenth and seventeenth centuries. Nevertheless, they deserve more attention from the student than they generally receive. Their fittings, often the work of the Cosmati, compare in beauty and interest with those of Rome and Florence; the pulpits in the cathedrals of Sessa and Ravello, with their inlays of glass mosaic, are especially notable. No part of Italy is so rich in bronze doors. This branch of industry, which was doubtless introduced here by the Byzantines, seems to have been practised by the local men to a considerable extent. The finest doors are in the cathedrals of Troja, Trani and Ravello. Those in the last two were the work of Barisanus of Trani and were executed about 1180. They are of solid cast bronze, after the old Roman-Byzantine method, and are very different from those at S. Zeno, Verona, in which bronze plates, and moulded and pierced bronze rails and stiles, are nailed to wood.

Stone carving is generally far superior to that in other parts of Italy, possibly owing to the district's having been for so many years under Byzantine rule. In most cases it is extremely delicate and refined. In the few examples where it is quite the reverse, the design is much the same, but the workmanship is clumsy and is probably the product of Norman workmen who copied the finer work of the Greeks. Byzantine influence is also conspicuous in the substitution of flush bands of glass mosaic for moulded drip-stones over the windows. Over each semi-circular-headed window of the crypt in the east end of S. Nicolo, Bari, instead of the usual projecting hood mouldings there is a concentric band of glass mosaic, flush with the stonework. The jewel-like effect is very telling, and all the more pleasing since it comes as a surprise. The pierced marble window slabs of Bari Cathedral are among the latest of their type, and there are many others in most of the churches of Bari and Trani, those of S. Gregorio, alongside S. Nicolo, being especially numerous and beautiful.

S. Nicolo, Bari. The prototype of the Apulian Romanesque is the Church of S. Nicolo, Bari (begun 1087). It is a large, aisled church with a transept, or bema, which, like that of Trani Cathedral, is continuous from north to south, being cut off from the nave by an arcade. The nave is divided into arcade, triforium and clerestory, in proportions similar to those in Jumièges, in Normandy (begun 1040). The roof is of timber. A peculiarity is the coupling of the columns of the three western bays; the inner columns carry transverse diaphragm arches which reach only as high as the string course below the triforium and support nothing whatsoever. These inner columns, though old, are manifestly additions, but it is difficult to say why they or the arches were added. In Trani Cathedral, the columns are also coupled, but there are no transverse arches.

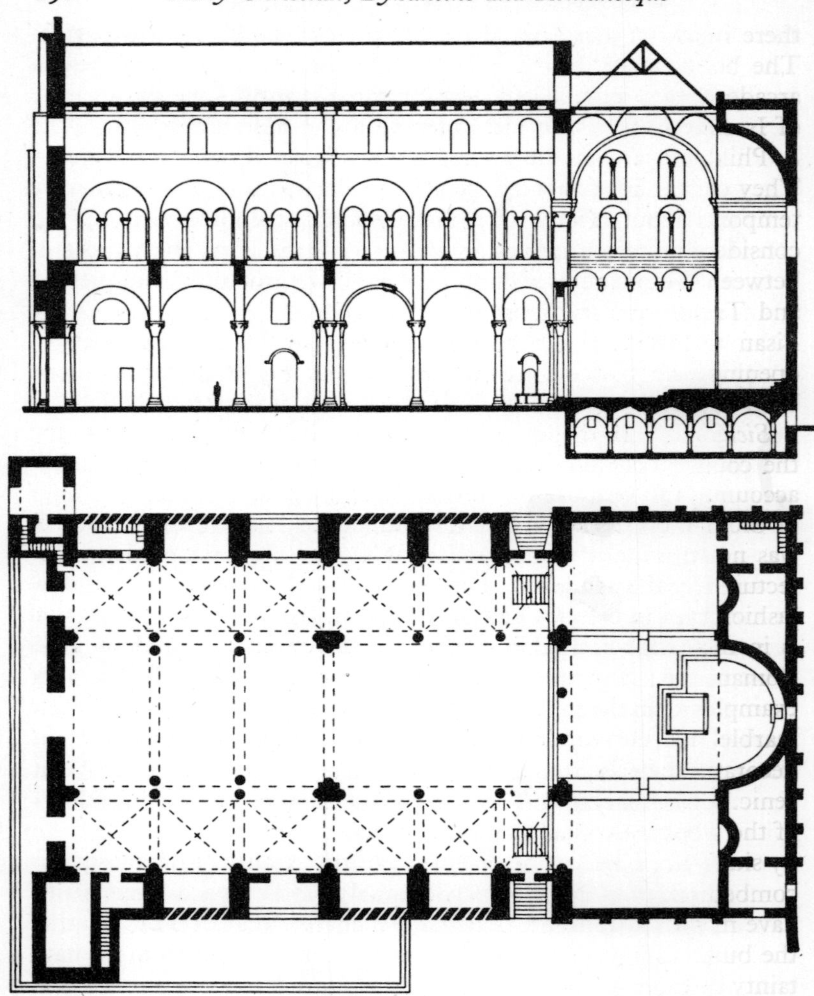

S. Nicolo, Bari.
Scale 50 ft. to 1 in.

The west end is severely plain, and the best external feature is the arcading of the aisle walls. Here the arches do not spring from pilaster strips or from slender shafts, as in Tuscany, but from wide buttresses projecting about 8 feet.[1] In Trani and Bari cathedrals

[1] The aisle walls have been brought forward to the face of the buttresses to provide side chapels inside, but these are evidently additions, and no attempt has been made to bond the new work with the old.

there is similar arcading, though the projection is a few feet less. The boldness of these buttresses is curious. There are similar arcades, but of less projection, along the aisle walls of the Cathedral of Issoire, Auvergne, and round the upper part of the chancel of S. Philibert, Tournus, Burgundy, but none in other parts of Italy. They cannot be due to Norman influence, because although contemporary churches of Normandy and England have buttresses of considerable width, these project only a few inches and the space between them is never arched. Above the outside arcading at Bari and Trani there was evidently originally an open gallery, as in Pisan work. In S. Nicolo the gallery still exists, though the openings are now walled up; in Trani Cathedral the gallery has been entirely swept away.

Sicily. Before the Norman conquest of Sicily, more than half the country was Moslem and the rest was largely Greek. This accounts, to a considerable extent, for the distinctive peculiarities of Sicilian churches. Norman influence in architectural matters was not particularly strong, with the result that the finest architecture of the Romanesque period is that which is domed in eastern fashion, and which has already been described (pp. 90–92). It is in the larger cathedrals of Cefalu, Palermo and Monreale that Romanesque features are most pronounced. But even in these examples there is much that is foreign to western eyes; the high marble dadoes that line the walls recall Byzantine methods of decoration, but much of the detail introduced into them is Saracenic. The mosaics that are used to decorate the upper surfaces of the walls are unmistakably Byzantine; but these are found side by side with Romanesque groined vaults (Cefalu) and with honeycombed and painted ceilings which only Saracenic workmen could have made. The crestings and battlements which crown some of the buildings outside (especially at Palermo) may with equal certainty be ascribed to the Saracens; they present forms unknown in Romanesque and Byzantine churches. The jambs of doorways and windows are often a curious mixture of Byzantine, Saracenic and Romanesque detail. The mouldings are very shallow, the orders of the arches of correspondingly slight projection, and zigzags, lozenges and other enrichments generally associated with Norman work are frequently carved side by side with more classical detail. All the arches of the Sicilian churches are pointed and stilted, a feature which was undoubtedly used in Sicily long before the Normans came.

A favourite method of decoration, on outside walls, is a kind of inlay in which stone is cut away and a black composition inserted. This composition sometimes forms the background in a pattern and sometimes the pattern itself. Another motif which is particularly popular for external decoration is the interlacing arcade which, using the pointed arch, results in an effect which closely resembles thirteenth-century geometric window tracery in England.

Monreale Cathedral (Pl. 12). The cathedral at Monreale, near Palermo, has by far the most striking interior of any Sicilian church. Its magnificent perspective is largely due to the way in which the eye is carried upwards, towards the east end, to the grandly-designed mosaic head-and-shoulders of Christ, which fills the semi-dome of

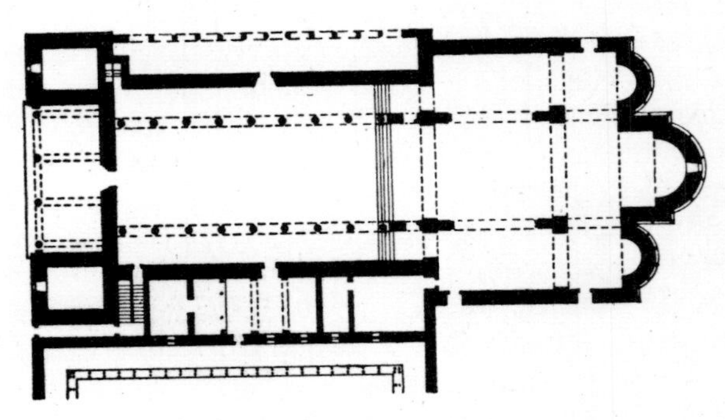

Monreale Cathedral.
Scale 100 *ft. to* 1 *in.*

the apse. The arch at the east end of the nave—which, by the way, is not stilted—springs from about the level of the crown of the arches of the nave arcade, but the arch and vault east of the crossing, and the semi-dome beyond, are much higher; simple abaci, covered with mosaics, mark the different springing lines. The choir vault and semi-dome over the apse, like all the arches in the church, are pointed. All these curved surfaces are covered with mosaic, and so are the long walls above the arcade. The sheer quantity of colour is overwhelming. There are some 70,000 square feet of illustrated matter, all composed of units seldom more than half-an-inch square. Counterchanging is freely employed in the decoration. The figures are always either white or many-coloured on a background of gold, but whenever conventional patterns are used, as in the window-jambs and arches, the patterns are in gold and the ground is in colour. The panelled marble dado, 23 feet high, round the aisle walls has its rails and cresting in coloured glass mosaic, the whole composition of the nave being surmounted by a richly-painted timber roof.

The outside of the church is very striking on all sides. At the west is a porch, sandwiched between the two western towers which stand almost clear of the church; on the north a loggia, in an almost unique position; at the east end the apses, decorated with intersecting arches (all of which are pointed), the upper piers being carried on detached marble shafts; and on the south, the cloisters.

The cloisters provide an interesting instance of the conflict between Norman and Saracenic ideas. The arches are moulded in true Norman fashion, with a somewhat rough semi-circular member as an inner order, but are stilted and pointed. Below these are extremely delicate shafts set in pairs, each alternate pair being inlaid with coloured mosaic. A single oblong abacus covers each pair of exceptionally well-carved capitals, but is not nearly wide enough to support the inner orders of the arches above, which consequently overhang in a most unfortunate way. This suggests that two sets of workmen were employed; one set designed the arches, the other the shafts and capitals, and no one made any attempt to bring the work of the two into relation with each other. Such an arrangement seems extraordinary and illogical, especially as there is no evidence to suggest that the columns and the arches were not built at the same time.

Other Examples. Two other cathedrals must be mentioned, both having similar plans. Palermo, which was ruthlessly restored in the eighteenth century and whose appearance was largely transformed by the superimposition of a Renaissance dome, retains a most elaborate cornice composed of bands of mosaic crowned by a single undulating battlement; and Cefalu (begun in 1131), where Romanesque feeling is stronger than at Palermo or Monreale, although it is the earliest of the three, has an eastern end much higher than the nave, and a mosaic figure of Christ even finer than that at Monreale. The greater portion of the interior has been modernised, but this cannot destroy the effect of the extraordinarily lofty pointed arch and vaulted choir, which is unlike any in Italy and whose proportions are almost identical with those of contemporary cathedrals in Normandy.

CHAPTER XIII

ROMANESQUE IN GERMANY

THE story of German architecture, from the time of the great achievement of Charlemagne at Aix-la-Chapelle in the eighth century (p. 133) until the beginning of the eleventh century, is almost blank as far as existing buildings are concerned; and after the middle of the twelfth century there is no major contribution made by Germany towards the development of Romanesque or mediaeval architecture. The period of our study is, therefore, limited to the eleventh century and the early part of the twelfth. To this historical limitation must also be added a geographical boundary; for nearly all the important buildings are to be found in a relatively small part of Germany—in that area of the lower Rhine which runs north-west from Worms to Cologne. At that time and in that place the Germans held their own with other nations in the importance, beauty and originality of their buildings. That they made little advance afterwards was because they were handicapped by their own creations. They could not shake themselves loose from the shackles of the style which, if they had not originated, they had undoubtedly done a great deal to foster.

The extent to which the workmen had lost the faculty of original design and the spirit of independence so essential for artistic advance, is shown in the church at Andernach, built at the beginning of the thirteenth century. It is a remarkably fine building, but, considering the hundred years or more which separate it from other equally fine churches in the country, it is evidence of the stagnation which unfortunately had set in. An undue craving for novelty and change is no doubt a curse, but the desire to improve on what had been done before, which animated the French and English builders in the twelfth century, was a laudable ambition. When, in the middle of the following century, the Germans awoke to the necessity for change, they had sunk too deeply into the rut of tradition to be able to extricate themselves unaided. They therefore turned to France, and there found models which they imitated with more or less success. There is little, however, that is characteristically their own in their thirteenth- and fourteenth-century work. The fame of German church architecture rests mainly on the early efforts of the eleventh century and on the few buildings of the twelfth.[1]

At the beginning the Germans, like all other nations, owed much to Italy, but their dependence on that country was linked with a boldness and strength, a sense of fine scale and simplicity in design, largely their own. They used ornament sparingly, but what little they used was good. The forms of their capitals and designs of their carvings were based on Byzantine work, but had a distinct character—less refined, no doubt, than the work farther south, but more in keeping with the solid quality of their buildings.

Double Apses. One of the most characteristic traits in German churches is the double apsidal ending, one apse being at the east end, the other at the west. Double apses were by no means unknown in earlier churches elsewhere, and in some cases they may have been due to the change in orientation (see pp. 19–21), which would necessitate the building of a new apse for the altar at the east end, and allow the retention of the original chancel apse at the west. This, however, fails to explain those churches which were built with an apse of the same date at each end. Some Early Christian churches in the East were constructed in the first instance with double apses, but the plan of these was probably due to special ritual requirements which can hardly have existed in Germany many centuries later.[2] The generally accepted reason for the two apses in Germany is that the eastern apse was for the abbot, or prior, and monks, and that the western one was for the bishop and the people. Each is presumed to have had its own choir. If this reason is the correct one, the arrangement, internally, at least, is far finer than that general elsewhere, which placed the people's altar at the east end of the nave and accorded it no specially treated surroundings.

In some churches, it is true, there is no western apse—Speyer (Speier) Cathedral is the largest exception to the general rule—

[1] It is unfortunate that the area of the lower Rhine, where most of the examples were built, was the one which suffered the most severely during the 1939–45 War. Not only were such cities as Aix-la-Chapelle and Cologne intensively bombed before the allied armies reached Germany, but the fighting during the crossing of the Rhine was most violent. The cathedrals at Speyer, Mayence, Laach and Worms were, in the main, fortunately undamaged, but the ancient cities of Hildesheim and Trèves suffered greatly.

[2] A more significant clue is provided in the manuscript plan of S. Gall, where there are altars at both east and west ends (see p. 119).

but in most examples the apse at the west end is equal in size and importance to that at the east. At Mayence (Mainz) Cathedral the western arm is far larger than the eastern. It was built *c.* 1200, that is, a hundred years later than the rest of the church, and although this may account partly for its extent, its size and beauty are also proof of the determination of the laity in the thirteenth century that their altar and their representative should have noble surroundings.[1]

There is never more than one apse at the west end, although not infrequently there are three side by side at the east end, as at Laach Abbey Church. These provided space for the additional altars

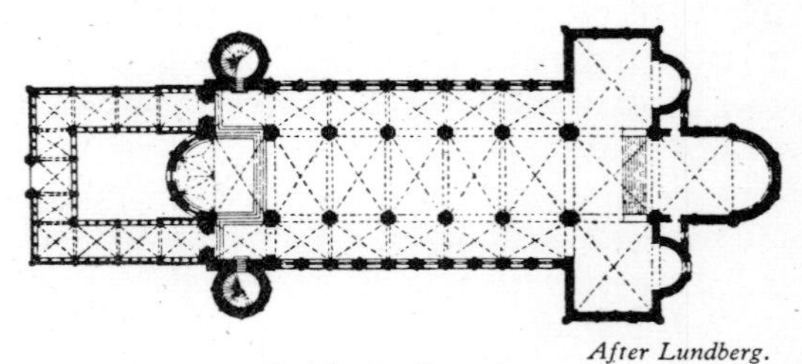

After Lundberg.

S Maria, Laach.
Scale 100 *ft. to* 1 *in.*

required by the monks, and further accommodation could be obtained in the crypts which, although by no means universal, are not uncommon under the eastern choirs, as at Mayence Cathedral.

Transepts. The crossing in front of each central apse, west as well as east, is generally covered by an octagonal tower or cupola, carried on squinch arches, which rises above the roof; on either side of it, in many churches, are transepts. These are usually of slight projection, if they project at all. There is more compactness about the plans of German churches as a whole than is generally found elsewhere. The main result outside is that there is little to show which is the west end and which the east. Each end has an apse, its pair of transepts (as a rule) and its cupola, while the unbroken line of the roof over the nave forms a connection. Considerable ingenuity is displayed in varying the designs, so that of no one church can it be said that east and west ends are identical. And yet, notwithstanding the striking effects which are frequently produced, a feeling of dissatisfaction arising out of the duality is not altogether unnatural. One misses the marked differences in

[1] The western altar is the one now used for service.

treatment between the west and east fronts that are so characteristic of many of the churches of other countries.

Towers and Turrets. The most effective feature of the German church externally is generally the skyline. This is due to the fine balance which the large cupolas give to the main central roof and to the subordinate towers or turrets which are appendages to nearly all the large churches. The Germans understood thoroughly the art of grouping these to the best advantage, and of placing them so that they should assist, and not conflict with, the larger features. There are generally two turrets at each end. In some

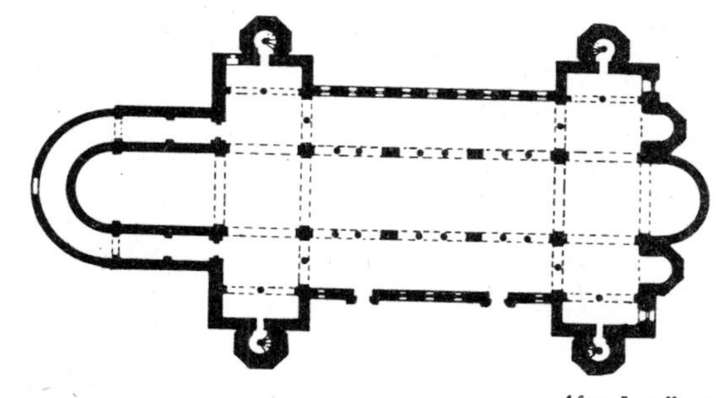

After Lundberg.

S. Michael, Hildesheim.
Scale 100 *ft. to* 1 *in.*

cases they stand out in bold projection from the transepts, as at Mayence Cathedral and the Church of S. Michael, Hildesheim. In others they flank the apses, as in the cathedrals at Speyer, Worms (Pl. 12) and Bonn. In other countries circular towers are rare; in Germany they were common in all the early centuries of church building. They appear on either side of the entrance to the octagon of Aix-la-Chapelle, and in the parchment plan of S. Gall two such towers are indicated at the west end (p. 119).

Lateral Entrances. One result of the double apse plan is that, as a rule, the entrances to the church are at the sides, and not at the west end. There are exceptions, of course, where there is no western apse, as at Speyer Cathedral, and in some cases also (Trèves, Mayence and Laach) there are doorways at the west end opening into the aisles; but the central western doorway is rare, not only in Germany, but also in churches in Switzerland built under German influence. It often finds no place even when there is no western apse, as in Zürich Cathedral. By its omission the Germans lost an opportunity for architectural display. A central west doorway affords some excuse for the exercise of the designer's and the sculptor's skill, and at the same time provides the most dignified entrance to a church. It might have been thought that the Germans would have transferred their energies to the lateral entrances, but with a few exceptions these, so far as can be judged from the original examples which remain, were small and unimportant. The transepts are too near the ends to accommodate entrances; the main doorways, therefore, in most examples, face one another about the middle of the church.

External Treatment. From Lombardy the Germans borrowed the arcaded galleries, pilaster strips and arched string courses. All were used in moderation. The galleries were formed in the thickness of the western walls, as at Trèves, where there are two, one above the other. Sometimes they ran along the sides, as at Speyer, and generally continued under the eaves of the eastern end and around the cupolas. Except for these galleries, the walls were treated with great severity. Thin pilaster strips and arched corbelled string courses were used round the smaller towers and turrets, but otherwise there was little attempt at decoration. In this respect there is a greater resemblance to the architecture of Lombardy than is found in Romanesque architecture elsewhere. It is true that in S. Philibert, Tournus, there is much in the design that is similar to the cathedrals of Mayence, Speyer, etc.; but Tournus is in Burgundy, and Burgundy belonged to the German Empire in the eleventh century. On a more primitive scale, the pilaster strips and arcading which form so distinctive a feature of Anglo-Saxon architecture in England obviously stem from the same source. In France and in England after the middle of the eleventh century, however, the pilasters are of quite different proportions, more structural and less merely decorative, and the string courses are of another character.

The east end of Worms Cathedral, with its octagonal tower behind the circular turrets, the galleries under the eaves and the pilasters and arcaded string courses, shows well the typical features of the style. It is an immense church, with two apses and only one transept. The eastern apse was finished square on the outside, and is masked to some extent by the turrets on either side. Each tower is panelled with pilaster strips and arcaded string courses, and a single gallery arcade links the towers to the apse, below the line of the gable and above the windows (Pl. 12).

Internal Treatment. In many large churches of the twelfth

century, only the aisles are vaulted, the naves being covered by timber roofs. It is not known when vaulting was first employed over naves. The three largest of the Rhenish Romanesque churches, Speyer, Mayence and Worms, may have been originally designed for vaulting, but if so the probability is that the vaults did not involve diagonal ribs. The nave vaults of Mayence and Worms are now ribbed, the ribs being moulded and the transverse arches plain. In all three churches the vaults are very domical. The aisle vaults of Mayence have no ribs, only transverse arches. This fact, coupled with the absence of projections on the nave side from which either diagonal or wall ribs could conveniently spring, seems proof that the nave vault of this church is a later addition. The transverse arches are slightly pointed, a further reason for doubting that the vault is the original one. In Worms Cathedral ribs may have been intended from the first, since the piers are large and there are projections. These, however, are not conclusive proof of such intention, for there are similar piers at Speyer, where the vaults, which date from the middle of the twelfth century, have no ribs.

Most of the vaults are quadripartite, but in two churches in Cologne, S. Maria and the Holy Apostles, where the vaulting is almost certainly later, the sexpartite plan is adopted. In nearly all German churches, late as well as early, one bay of the nave equals two bays of the aisle, but none of the bays in either nave or aisles is exactly square; those of Mayence Cathedral, in fact, are distinctly oblong.

The internal treatment generally is very simple. There are no triforiums; indeed the absence of inside galleries suggests that, whatever may have been the case elsewhere, there was no use for them in Germany. Access to the roof space over the aisle was usually effected from the turret staircases. It has been suggested that the desire not to increase the height may have had something to do with the omission of galleries. Nevertheless, the nave of Speyer Cathedral is 108 feet high and that of Mayence Cathedral is only 20 feet less. These dimensions far exceed many contemporary examples in France. The nave of the Abbaye-aux-Hommes, Caen, is almost as wide as that of Speyer and yet is only 70 feet high, although it has a tall and spacious triforium.

In the treatment of the nave arcades of Speyer, Worms and Mayence, there was evidently a strong wish to obtain a feeling of verticality. This was achieved by continuing the inner members of the piers the full height of the wall up to the springing of the vaulting. In all these churches the piers are alternately large and small, the latter being perfectly plain.

The effect of the interiors is stark and severe almost beyond compare for that time. Cushion capitals are the general rule, and the absence of ornament of any sort is quite remarkable. The blank walls between the clerestory and the nave arcade emphasise the bare effect. It is possible that they were painted originally, so that there might once have been plenty of colour, but today they are singularly bleak.[1]

Trèves. Trèves Cathedral is noted for being a remodelling of a much older building attributed to Helena, the mother of Constantine. It was originally a square enclosing a cross (as in Byzantine

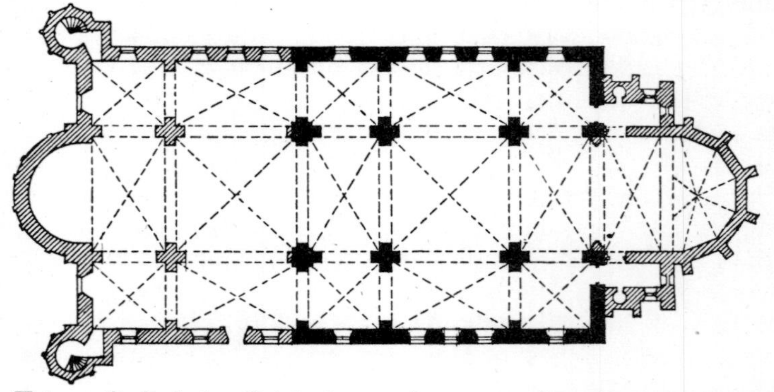

Trèves Cathedral. Original cross-in-square plan shown in black.
Scale 100 *ft. to* 1 *in.*

churches), the arms of which were probably the same height as the vault over the centre. The adoption of the cross-in-square plan resulted in the unequal spacing of bays. When, about the middle of the eleventh century, the nave was continued westwards, the rhythm of large and small bays was maintained. The original structure was not pulled down, and in the walls of the existing church are brick voussoirs of the old arches, and the capitals of four pilasters which may have belonged to the great piers that

[1] According to Jackson, the walls of the churches of Cologne were painted early in this century, with disastrous results, for the windows had already been filled with coloured glass. 'The colour by reflection in mural painting is killed by the overpowering brilliancy of colour transmitted through stained glass.' T. G. Jackson, *Byzantine and Romanesque Architecture*, Vol. II, p. 27.

marked the central square. The large bays are about 53 feet square and are covered with vaults larger than are to be found in any Romanesque church in Germany. Exactly when they were built is uncertain, but it was probably not before the end of the twelfth century or the beginning of the thirteenth. The vaulting is slightly domical and the transverse arches dividing the bays are pointed and of considerable width, while the diagonal ribs are by comparison exceedingly thin. The oblong vaults of the transepts on the north and south sides of the original central square are the same height as those of the nave, the other side vaults being lower. The church thus retains its cross-in-square form, although both the western and eastern arms have been lengthened. Altogether, whether viewed from the east or the west end, the interior is most unusual.

S. Maria in Capitolio, Cologne. There are a number of churches in Germany with apsidal endings to transepts as well as to choirs. At Cologne there are three—S. Maria in Capitolio, S. Martin and

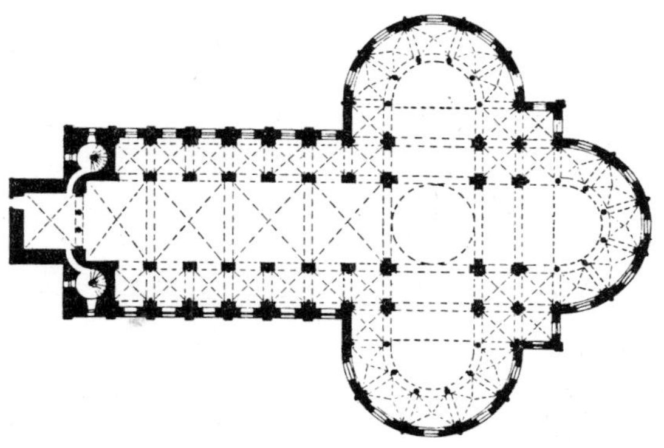

S. Maria in Capitolio, Cologne.
Scale 100 *ft. to* 1 *in.*

the Apostles' Church. All have suffered from war damage. In S. Maria the roof remains on only part of the apses, and because of the collapse of the central cupola the general devastation was very great. S. Martin still possesses apsidal ends, but the great tower over the crossing has fallen and with it most of the vaulting of the nave. The west tower of the Apostles' Church received a direct hit which cracked the whole structure and resulted in the collapse of all the nave vaulting.

S. Maria was the most interesting, because it had aisles round its apses. A similar arrangement is found in some Byzantine churches, and especially in the Church of S. Lorenzo, Milan (p. 66), from which it is possibly derived. S. Maria had to some extent lost its original character, since the nave vaulting and decoration were additions, but the eastern portion was much the same as it was when built some time in the eleventh century. It occupied the site of an older church (built *c.* 700), the foundations of which may have influenced its plan. The transept arms were covered by barrel vaults, the apses by semi-domes and the crossing by a low dome carried on true pendentives. Tapering columns with cushion capitals surrounded the apses and separated them from the ambulatory aisles. The whole of the eastern part was raised slightly above the nave, and under the chancel, approached by steps down from the two transepts, was a well-lighted crypt which has also suffered from war damage.

Tournai. Perhaps the finest cathedral in which the tri-apsidal plan was adopted is at Tournai, in Belgium. The original chancel apse has been destroyed, and the long choir belongs to a later date than the rest of the church, but the apsidal transepts remain practically unaltered. At the crossing is a large square tower with a steep slated roof, and smaller towers flank the two surviving apsidal ends. The tri-apsidal plan places it in the category of Rhenish churches, but the nave (dedicated in 1066), with its large, open-arched triforium and its grotesque, carved capitals, is more in harmony with the Romanesque architecture of northern France.

Lund. Before leaving this summary of German Romanesque architecture, mention must be made of one other church, the Cathedral of Lund, which, though in Sweden, comes rightly within this chapter. It was consecrated in 1145 by Archbishop Eskill, who had been educated at Hildesheim. The building consists of a nave and aisles, western towers, aisleless transepts, an apsidal choir, a large and lofty crypt—indeed, all that one might expect to find in a church of the region of the Rhine. It is the oldest and most important cathedral in Sweden, and its arcaded gallery round the apse seems to be earlier than any in Germany. The architect was Donatus, who is presumed to have been an Italian, and so it is possible that this feature, together with the richly-carved north porch which has columns carrying beasts, is directly inspired from Lombardy.

CHAPTER XIV

ROMANESQUE IN ANGLO-SAXON ENGLAND

THE history of architecture in England is still only imperfectly known. For a long time there was some doubt whether true Saxon architecture existed, most of the remains being ascribed to Norman times. The comprehensive researches of A. W. Clapham[1] have, however, conclusively settled the question in the affirmative. From the number of buildings which have now been ascribed to the period (seventh to mid-eleventh centuries), and from the carved stone crosses and tombstones, the illuminated manuscripts, the jewellery and metalwork of all sorts, there is much to indicate a high level of artistic ability. To what degree all this was the product of local genius, or the result of foreign importations, is still to some extent debatable. In every case, the larger monastic churches and cathedrals to which documentary evidence refers have been replaced by later buildings. Of what remains there is a close resemblance to contemporary or earlier work abroad.

All early churches in this country, whether built by the followers of S. Augustine, by the Saxons before the Danes arrived, by the Danes after their conversion, or by Edward the Confessor immediately before the Norman Conquest, are either offshoots of Roman tradition, or belong to the great school of Romanesque building which prevailed throughout Europe during the early centuries of the Middle Ages. That they possess some characteristics not generally found elsewhere does not make them any the less Romanesque. Other countries have other characteristic traits of their own. Whether the features of the style came direct from Italy, or by a circuitous route from the East via Scandinavia, or by filtering through Germany and Burgundy, is immaterial. The last two countries were certainly nearer to England, but the germ first appeared in Italy, and maturity had not been reached anywhere, except in the Byzantine Empire, when the English churches were built.

The connection between Rome and this country was fairly close

[1] *English Romanesque Architecture Before the Conquest*, Oxford, 1930.

in the days of Alfred the Great, and later under Canute. Both kings made pilgrimage to Rome and must have returned with ideas. Foreign craftsmen were imported to assist in the building of some churches. Who these workmen were is somewhat uncertain; for the term 'Franks', which was applied to them, might mean Germans, Burgundians, or simply foreigners. The literary records of the introduction of foreign artists are very varied, but they do show how close the contact was between England and the Continent. In Italy we know that in the eighth and ninth centuries a large number of carvers were Byzantine Greeks, and it is possible that some of these men found their way to this country. The world was surprisingly small in those days, despite the difficulties of travel. A design itself is no proof of the nationality of the craftsman, because many designs which in their origin were characteristically Byzantine—the interlacing vine scroll, for instance—had been adopted by Italian, German and French workmen, and had become almost universal. The skill shown in the execution of a design is a surer guide, and the roughness of some English work suggests a local carver. On the other hand, the Madonna at York, carved in a local stone, has an assurance and quality which, at that time (tenth century), could only have been produced by an eastern artist (Pl. 13).

Stone Crosses. The stone crosses which are to be found in many parts of England are among the earliest monuments of Anglo-Saxon times. Many were erected to mark religious meeting-places. In the *Life of St. Willibald*, a Saxon who left England in 720, there is a reference to one of these crosses: 'It being the custom of the Saxon people to erect a cross for the daily service of prayer on the estates of noble and good men where there was no church.'[1] The two finest crosses are at Ruthwell and Bewcastle, on the present borders of Scotland and England, and there has been considerable controversy over their date, but it seems most likely that they belong to the second half of the seventh century. It is certainly surprising that there should appear so suddenly such remarkable stone monuments, in form unlike anything elsewhere and executed with a skill far greater than any contemporary work in western Europe. It is the skill rather than the subject matter that is significant. The sculptured figures which appear on the two sides of the Ruthwell and Bewcastle crosses are all highly

[1] Quoted from Dorothy Whitelock, *The Beginnings of English Society*, London, 1952.

formalised and draped with classical simplicity. The remaining sides are enriched with motifs that were conventional throughout Christendom, the most important being the vine scroll intertwining birds and beasts. That these patterns came from Armenia via Scandinavia, as Strzygowski [1] suggests, seems unlikely. Almost identical patterns were common in Byzantine work of the sixth century, as numerous carvings in Constantinople and Ravenna testify, but none has yet been proved to have existed in Armenia so early. It is more probable that the motifs were copied from Byzantine ivories, which might easily have been brought into this country.

Timber Churches. It is possible that many of the earliest churches in England built by the Saxons were of timber construction. The Saxons, noted as shipbuilders, would have been skilled carpenters, and because of the plentiful supply of timber the builders simply cut down the number of logs required and fitted them together in the easiest way possible. Only one church remains in England to give an idea of what these timber churches were like. This is at Greenstead, in Essex. The outside walls are low and built of halved trunks of oak placed vertically, side by side, the rounded halves outside and the junctions covered inside with fillets of wood. The church has been much restored and altered, so that it is difficult to be certain how much of the original timbers remain, though the method of construction adopted may be taken as a fair example of Saxon workmanship. The technique is called 'stave-work', and in no other country is there preserved an example of such wood construction of so early a date.

Early Stone Churches. Owing more to the ravages of Sweyn and his predecessors than to time, one cannot expect to find many entire churches in this country earlier than the beginning of the eleventh century. The crypts of Hexham and Ripon are undoubtedly older, and probably date from 671–678. The greater part of Escomb Church, Durham, is also apparently about contemporary with these. Portions of S. Martin, Canterbury, may well be older still, but the church has been much altered. The difficulty in determining dates is complicated by the fact that windows and doorways have sometimes been re-used in later walls, and that in some walls which are evidently early, all the openings are later insertions. Roman bricks in bands, and herringbone coursing, whether in brick or stone, prove nothing, since both were used

[1] *Origins of Christian Church Art*, 1923.

after the Conquest quite as much as before. There was more church building in the seventh and eighth centuries than in either of the two following, and an attempt is made by archeologists to differentiate between eighth- and tenth-century detail. Their arguments are not always entirely convincing and are too fine to be discussed here. Generally speaking, there appear to have been two distinct schools of architecture in the second half of the seventh century, one in Kent, introduced by Augustine, and the other in Northumbria, largely due to the missionary activities of Benedict Biscop. Such remains as have survived of the Kentish group show Roman influence, and its characteristic features are an apse, semi-circular within and polygonal outside, and a chapel or *porticus* on either side of the nave. The Northumbrian group, of which the churches at Escomb and Monkwearmouth are the most important, have high and long naves, roughly coursed masonry and chancels of smaller proportions with square east ends.

The square termination is one of the most interesting features of English church architecture, particularly since other countries seem to have preferred an apsidal ending. This preference did not extend to England, except in the Kentish group of churches, which were built under Roman influence, and in those churches built during the century following the Norman Conquest. The plan adopted in Northumbria, and later in the Midlands, consists of two rooms, the larger for the congregation and the smaller for the altar and priest. Both are rectangular, and there is no need to speculate whether the Celts or the Saxons thought out this plan for themselves; it required no great effort of the imagination. The only point of importance to us is that the customary ending at the east in an English church is square rather than apsidal. Less than half the pre-Norman churches have an apsidal ending, and those were probably introduced by S. Augustine.[1] His church at Canterbury, on the site of the present cathedral, is stated to have had two apses, one at the east end, the other at the west. It was only natural that he and his followers should advocate the plan customary in Rome, and the remains of the seven surviving churches cited by Clapham all had the apsidal ending. After the death of this missionary group, however, the people returned to the traditional British form.[2]

[1] The earlier Roman church at Silchester had an apsidal ending (p. 117).

[2] There are two notable exceptions of the tenth or early eleventh century, at Wing and Deerhurst, where the apses were polygonal inside and outside.

Later Stone Churches. From the ninth century until the Norman Conquest, the architecture of England may be regarded as an offshoot of the Carolingian tree, although the greater Saxon churches of that time were much smaller than their Continental counterparts. Unfortunately, these greater churches have perished almost entirely, or have been superadded by Norman work, so that our studies are restricted to a few small and remote village churches which would have been regarded as second-rate even in Saxon times. The most important features were the towers, which normally were very high and narrow in proportion; they were devoid of any buttresses, though they sometimes had a slight batter or taper, and were relieved by strip decoration. At Durham and Ramsey there were two towers set axially, at the west end and over the crossing, in the Carolingian tradition, but the surviving contemporary churches have only a single western tower, a nave and a chancel. The churches of Worth and Dover have also transepts, which are narrower than the nave, and there are one or two examples with aisles. One peculiarity is that the naves are exceedingly lofty and narrow. In Deerhurst the nave is 38 feet long and 21 feet wide and 38 feet high to the wall plate, the chancel being of the same width and height with a length of only 20 feet. Structurally the towers are the most significant features. Vaulting is limited to crypts, and on the outside the structural decoration is reminiscent of timber technique, depending for its effect upon narrow string courses, pilaster strip decoration and a curious method of bonding known as 'long and short work'.

The pilaster and string course method of ornamentation probably belongs to the tenth century, and the richest example is to be found in the tower of Earls Barton (Pl. 13). Here the pilasters are of slight projection and placed at intervals of about 4 feet. This treatment has, of course, nothing whatsoever to do with joinery construction; it is masonry construction, and is especially valuable where, as in the majority of English examples, it frames in and provides a bond at regular intervals to walls of rough rubble. In its simplest form the strips and string courses form a network of panelling on the face of the wall, but this is often elaborated by arcading. At Earls Barton and Barton-on-Humber there are two ranges, one roundheaded and the other triangular.

Much has been said and written about the so-called 'long and short' work found in so many Anglo-Saxon churches. Blocks of stone are set up vertically like posts, alternating with slabs built horizontally. This technique, whether at angles or on the face of a wall, has been regarded as precious, and peculiar to this country, but in point of fact, in many countries and in most periods, from Italy in the days of the Roman Empire onwards, people formed their quoins in this way whenever the stone of the district was such that it broke up naturally into small stones, with occasional bigger stones which could be used as stiffeners without much squaring or chiselling. In Sussex and in other parts, such rubble and stones come out of small quarries to this day. All over Normandy similar long and short bonding is found in garden walls and walls of out-buildings—wherever, in fact, the work is rough. As a rule the horizontal stones go through the thickness of the wall, the uprights only halfway. It is ordinary, commonsense rough building, and is general where workmen are unskilled, or when the work is not of sufficient importance to justify the expense of labour on stone. Surrounding the precincts of the abbeys of Jumièges and S. Georges, Boscherville, at Caen and in the country around, at Chartres and elsewhere, are many such walls. The objection to this method of building is that the long upright stones are not on their natural bed, but this does not seem to have had a bad effect on Anglo-Saxon work. For the student, long and short bonding has one virtue: it differentiates Saxon work from Norman work in England,[1] and is therefore some guide to the date of a building. The simple explanation is that the Normans were better masons, and had learned at Caen to quarry bigger stones and to cut and square them.[2]

The double-splay window is one of the commonest features of later Saxon architecture. In a few instances, traces have been found of the pierced wooden boards with which openings were filled (for Saxon windows were probably not glazed). Alternatively, pierced stone slabs were built into the openings, such as have already been described in the chapters on Byzantine work and the Romanesque churches of south Italy (pp. 58 and 189). At Barnack Church, Northants, there are two especially good examples, the pattern being of the interlacing character which was

[1] So far as I know, there is no example of long and short work executed in England after the Norman Conquest.

[2] Saxon masonry is sometimes excellent, as at S. Laurence, Bradford-on-Avon, and Odda's Chapel, Deerhurst, but the latter was built, as the dedication stone shows, 'in the fourteenth year of the reign of Edward, King of the English', i.e., in 1056, when intercourse with the Normans was very close.

Earls Barton, Northants; tower

Sompting, Sussex

Plate 13

S. Mary, Deerhurst, Glos; interior

Madonna, York Minster

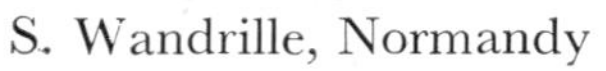

S. Wandrille, Normandy

Ver-sur-Mer, Normandy

Plate 14

S. Loup, Normandy

Thaon, Normandy

such a favourite with Byzantine craftsmen. The openings themselves were sometimes circular-headed, sometimes triangular-headed. When two or more lights were side by side, they were divided from one another by shafts in the centre of the wall, having capitals of the corbel type, with only slight projection at the sides, and a considerable projection front and back to carry the wall. The form of shaft most common in England is the baluster type, which is quite distinctive in character. It is turned on a lathe and has grooves and bands cut into the surface, with a considerable bulge too coarse to be called an entasis.

Bradford-on-Avon. The most complete early church in England is S. Laurence, Bradford-on-Avon. Its date is uncertain though a study of the twin angels above the chancel arch, which are obviously contemporary with the church, led Professor Baldwin Brown to place the building in the first half of the tenth century. In plan it consists of a nave and chancel, with a large porch on the north side, and there are indications that a similar porch also existed on the south. The opening between nave and chancel is only 3 feet 6 inches wide. Outside the treatment is more architectural than that of any other example, and the walls are faced with ashlar throughout. The upper part is arcaded, the arches being carried on short pilaster strips, many of which are roughly fluted. The arches and pilasters are not built independently of the walling but are bonded in, and project about 2 inches. This arcading is the most remarkable feature of the church. It is unlike anything which existed abroad at that time, and was never repeated after the Norman Conquest.

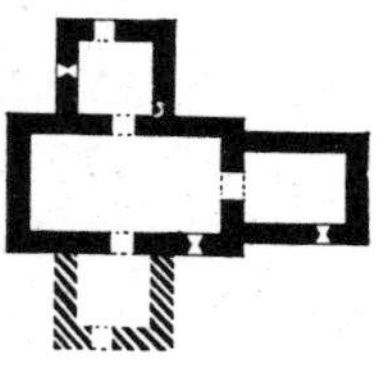

After Clapham.

S. Laurence, Bradford-on-Avon.

Scale 50 *ft. to* 1 *in.*

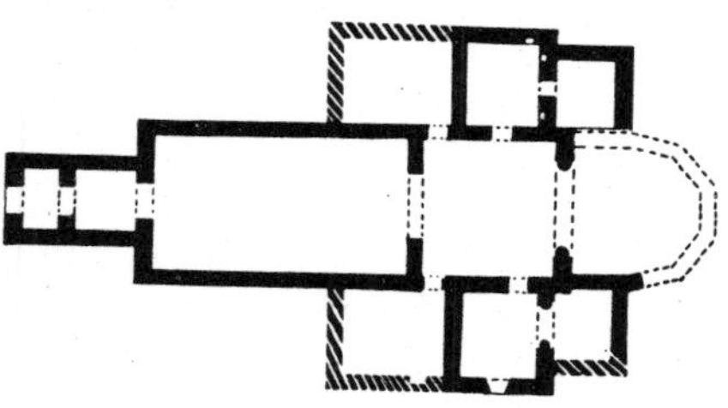

After Clapham.

S. Mary, Deerhurst. The shaded portions represent later additions.

Scale 50 *ft. to* 1 *in.*

Deerhurst (Pl. 13). The Church of S. Mary, Deerhurst, provides an example of an Anglo-Saxon church, of the same period but with the foundations of an apse which was polygonal externally and internally, and with a tower at the western end which is severely simple and without horizontal divisions. This must once have been still higher than it is now, for the original bell chamber has disappeared. Although much of the church has been added to and altered, it is still a remarkably interesting building, with its whitewashed walls and small, triangular-headed openings between the tower and the nave; with its font, which has a curious spiral ornamentation, and the remains of the two transeptal chapels which gave the building a cruciform plan.

Towers. Although there are very few relatively complete Anglo-Saxon churches, there are still a great many towers, to which are now attached Norman or Gothic edifices. Most are severely plain, but some are richly ornamented with long, thin pilasters and rough cornices or string courses and arcading, as at Earls Barton, Barnack and Barton-on-Humber. These are not likely to be earlier than the tenth century, and are more likely to belong to the first half of the eleventh. Their axial position at the west end is English, but their design has much in common with that of Germany and Lombardy, though the detail is much less refined. The tower at Earls Barton is by far the most decorative, even if that decoration is of a rather childish character. Except for the embattled parapet, it is still in its original condition.

The tower of Sompting Church is the only survival which retains the form of its original capping (Pl. 13). This consists of a steep gable on each face, from the apex of which rise the ridges of a pyramidal roof. It is indeed a simplified version of a type of tower termination which was common in Germany.

CHAPTER XV

ROMANESQUE IN NORMANDY AND ENGLAND

FOR nearly a hundred years after the Battle of Hastings, the architecture of Normandy and England proceeded on almost identical lines. The style had begun in Normandy with the building of the Abbey of Bernay (1017–50), and in England in 1050 with the foundation by Edward the Confessor of Westminster Abbey, which was built with the aid of continental craftsmen in the style which we now call Norman.

This style was the most advanced and progressive of all the branches of Romanesque architecture; for it was from the Norman that the Gothic ultimately developed. No doubt the inspiration came originally from Italy, but there is little about the style, other than the occasional use of the diaphragm arch, that can be directly attributed to that country. Norman architecture was a style in its own right. It was the product of a race of men who had, by the eleventh century, not only established themselves in France but had made themselves masters of Sicily and Apulia and become, with the conquest of England, a major European power.

So England was brought once more into the European framework, and much of her native architecture was destroyed and rebuilt on a more magnificent scale. There was little excuse for such rebuilding. Most of the Saxon churches must still have been in a reasonable state of repair, and the wholesale rebuilding that took place can only have been dictated by the ambition of the Norman prelates to impress the people of the conquered territories with the vaster and finer monuments of the new architecture; not, however, without protest. It was reported that Bishop Wulstan of Worcester, the sole surviving Saxon bishop, lamented as follows: 'We poor wretches destroy the Works of our Forefathers only to get Praise for ourselves: . . . we, neglecting the Care of Souls, labour to heap up Stones.' Within half a century the Normans had begun and nearly completed the great churches at Lincoln, S. Albans, Winchester, Gloucester and Norwich, and many others far larger than any the Saxons had built, and larger indeed than most of the abbey churches of Normandy. The cruelty of the Conquest was perhaps mitigated by such symbols of the culture of the conquerors; for England under Norman dominion led all Europe in the size and magnificence of her architecture.

NORMANDY

The earliest existing church of architectural significance in Normandy is the Abbey of Bernay, which lies on the road between Caen and Rouen. Originally it had a high nave of seven bays, subdivided into arcade, triforium and clerestory, and five of these are still intact. The choir and side aisles terminated in apses and had

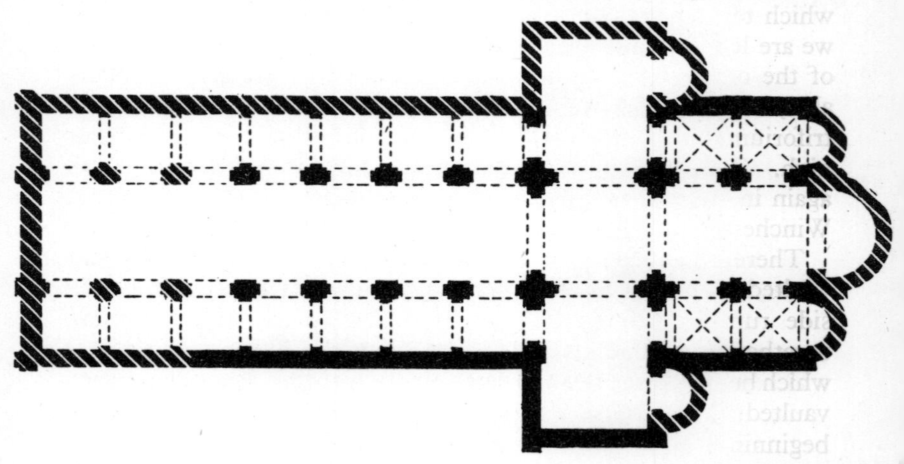

After Clapham.

Bernay Abbey, Normandy. The shaded portions are no longer standing. *Scale 50 ft. to 1 in.*

groined vaults. There were transepts, and over the crossing a tower. Here, then, is the prototype of the Norman Romanesque. It was to be followed in all essentials during a century of phenomenal building activity in Normandy and England. After Bernay, the next important church is at the ruined Abbey of Jumièges (1050), in which piers and columns alternated and two magnificent western towers terminated the aisles. Next come the two finest churches in Normandy, S. Etienne, or l'Abbaye-aux-Hommes, and La Trinité, or l'Abbaye-aux-Dames. Both were built at Caen in the years immediately before the Conquest, l'Abbaye-aux-Hommes by William the Conqueror, as an expiatory gesture to the Pope for his sin in marrying, without papal dispensation, his kinswoman Matilda; and l'Abbaye-aux-Dames by his wife. They stand at either end of the ridge upon which the city had grown. In 1944, following the landing of the 6 June, Caen was the principal objective of the Anglo-American armies, but although the city suffered almost a month of uninterrupted bombardment, these two churches have survived almost undamaged.

L'Abbaye-aux-Hommes (Pl. 15). This is one of the largest churches in France, but it has been a good deal altered. The choir, with its ambulatory and radiating chapels, was rebuilt in the thirteenth century. The existing sexpartite vaulting belongs to the twelfth century. The western towers are original, but the spires which terminate them were added in the thirteenth century. So we are left with little more than the nave arcades and triforium of the original building. The proportions of these are remarkable, and different from any other work we have studied; for the triforium arch is not only as wide as that below it, but almost as high. This is characteristic of much Norman work and occurs again in England at Ely, Peterborough, Norwich, Southwell and Winchester.

There has been much argument whether or not the nave was vaulted in the first instance, and the presence of shafts on the nave side running up the full height of the arcade and triforium, together with the ribbed half-barrel vaults over the triforium, all of which belong to the original work, suggests that the nave was indeed vaulted. *M.* Bouet[1] maintained that it was intended from the beginning to vault over the nave with quadripartite vaults, taking two bays each, but this view does not account for the intermediate shafts. There may have been a desire to cover the nave with stone, but the evidence is not strong enough to support *M.* Bouet's contention. Further, we know that when Lanfranc, the first Abbot of the Abbaye-aux-Hommes, began, after the Conquest, the building of Canterbury Cathedral upon a plan of similar proportions, the nave was covered with a timber roof, as were those of all the great churches in England.

Whether or not l'Abbaye-aux-Hommes in the eleventh century had a stone vault may be very interesting academically, but what is more important is that the twelfth-century vaulting which now

[1] *Bulletin Monumentale*, Vol. XXIX.

covers the nave was of an entirely novel form. Here for the first time we can see true sexpartite vaulting, still Romanesque in detail and in its use of round-arched forms. It was, in a sense, a step

After Pugin.

L'Abbaye-aux-Hommes, Caen.

ahead of the ribbed quadripartite vaults which covered the aisles. Two bays of the nave formed one compartment, approximately square, and an intermediate rib spanned the nave and lent support to the junction of the diagonal ribs. It was a solution, even if it was not a very good one, and it seemed to be the only solution as long as the builders were limited to round arches. Aesthetically it never produced an entirely satisfactory effect, even although mechanically it seemed reasonable. Thus far only did the Romanesque builders go, for it was not until the pointed arch was introduced into the vault that both the aesthetic and mechanical problems were overcome.

L'Abbaye-aux-Dames. The Church of l'Abbaye-aux-Dames has been so thoroughly restored to its early state that it now presents a very fair appearance of a twelfth-century church. It was dedicated some four months before the Battle of Hastings for nuns of the Benedictine Order, but it was not until the middle of the twelfth century that efforts were made to vault the nave and, in order to resist the thrust of the vaults, flying buttresses were thrown across the aisles. It seems, however, that they were placed too low to be effective, and instead, a series of diaphragm arches was built to span the nave and carry a timber roof. In 1692 a plaster vault

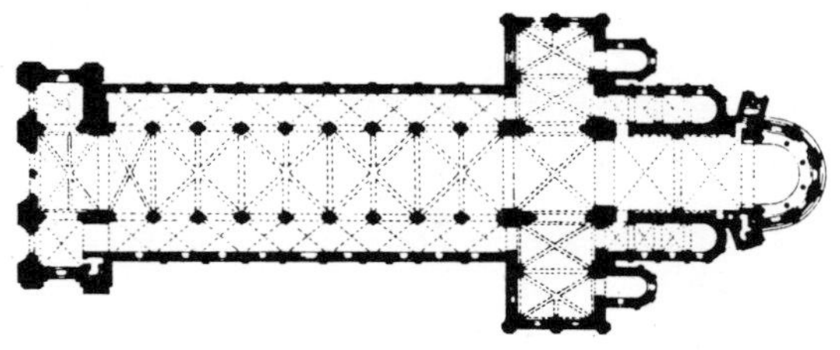

After Pugin.

L'Abbaye-aux-Dames, Caen.
Scale 100 *ft. to* 1 *in.*

was introduced, painted to represent stone. This was simply a quadripartite vault with the intermediate diaphragm arches supporting the apex of the web and the junction of the diagonal ribs. In 1859 this plaster construction was replaced by a vault of hollow bricks with light stone ribs.

L'Abbaye-aux-Dames is altogether a richer design than l'Abbaye-aux-Hommes. The great triforium gallery has been omitted, and in its place there is a passageway behind a continuous arcade underneath the clerestory windows. The aisles are higher and the piers lighter and the arches more ornate.

The plan is of the type called parallel-apsed. This consists of an apsidal choir with side aisles, also terminating in apses, and supported by additional apses off the transepts. All face east. It

After Pugin.

L'Abbaye-aux-Dames, Caen.

is of the same type as its predecessor at Bernay, and as its successors in England at Canterbury, S. Albans, Durham, Hereford and many other places.

The alternative eastern termination was the ambulatory, which is a later form and not common in Normandy, but characteristic farther south and east. It occurred in the Abbey at Jumièges in the form of a simple vaulted promenade around the apse, and in a fully-developed chevet with seven radiating chapels in the thirteenth-century alterations at l'Abbaye-aux-Hommes. In England the ambulatory type was followed at Gloucester and Norwich and in the twelfth-century extension of Canterbury.

Parish Churches (Pl. 14). In addition to the great abbeys mentioned above, there are in Normandy many smaller churches of great variety and charm. The earliest of these is the minute oratory in the Monastery of S. Wandrille, near Caudebec, which was built to house relics of S. Sernin of Toulouse. The original structure was of the seventh century. At the end of the tenth century it was rebuilt by the Normans, without doubt on the Carolingian foundations, as is evident from its curious trefoil eastern end. Nearly all the churches in Normandy have apsidal endings, and a few, like Bernières, Ouistreham and S. Georges, Boscherville, are vaulted. At Bernières, the vaults are quasi-sexpartite vaults, like those of the Abbaye-aux-Dames. At Ouistreham, there are two sexpartite vaults, and at S. Georges, Boscherville quadripartite ribbed vaults. The most interesting features of the many small churches are the towers, which occur either at the crossing or, more commonly, on the south side of the nave. They are in several stages, with arched openings often of several orders, richly decorated and culminating in pyramidal stone stepped roofs.

ENGLAND

Interesting though the above churches are, they were surpassed in almost every respect by the cathedrals and great monastic establishments built in England in the years after the Conquest. The number is astounding. Until the outburst of building in l'Ile de France a hundred years later, no country at any period could boast so many important churches in course of erection at one time. Little seems to have been attempted before 1070. The Conqueror and his nobles were otherwise engaged, and the priests had to accustom themselves to new surroundings, choose their sites and make the necessary preliminary arrangements. But once building operations had begun, there was little further delay. The following list gives the names of most of the cathedrals and larger churches, with the dates when building began and the *principal Romanesque features* that have survived.

BRISTOL. Augustinian. 1142. Of Norman work there remain only the north and south walls of the transepts and the large rectangular rib-vaulted Chapter House which, although restored, has much fine Norman decoration and elaborate arcading.

BURY ST. EDMUNDS. Benedictine. Completed 1095. Ruins; fine Norman gate-tower.

CANTERBURY. Benedictine. 1070. (p. 122.) First Romanesque building by Lanfranc, replaced Saxon cathedral. It was parallel-apsed and 'built of squared stones from Caen'. Nothing significant remains of this building. 1096–1107, eastern end replaced by a larger choir, with ambulatory, radiating chapels and additional transepts. 1174–84, this largely rebuilt and extended by curious apsidal termination called 'Becket's Crown'. 1390, nave, western and central towers rebuilt. Remains of the strictly Norman period include crypt which, with its richly-carved capitals, is among the finest in Europe, wall paintings in S. Anselm's Chapel, almost Byzantine in character, and the eastern transepts, with attached towers, which are arcaded in storeys like a Roman campanile.

CARLISLE. Augustinian. 1123. Nave originally of eight bays, of which only two survive complete with aisles, buttresses, windows, etc. Cylindrical columns nearly six feet in diameter with unusual leaf ornament to capitals.

CHESTER. Benedictine. 1092. Rebuilt 1211. Of the Romanesque church there survive only the north transept, the north wall of nave aisle and lower part of north-west tower.

CHICHESTER. Secular Canons. 1088. Burnt down and rebuilding begun 1114. Retains Norman nave of eight bays, which was only slightly modified after second fire, 1186; portions of south-west tower and north transept; two fine sculptured panels in south aisle of choir.

CHRISTCHURCH PRIORY. Secular Canons, later Augustinian. Late eleventh century. Nave, 118 feet long, is almost entirely Norman work. Arcade of seven bays with clustered columns carrying triforium gallery with much ornate carving. South transept still retains apsidal chapel, and north transept a richly-ornamented turret staircase, treated externally with intersecting arches, diaper work, etc., and capped by stone sloping roof.

DURHAM (Pl. 16). Benedictine. 1093. (pp. 230–3.) The finest, least altered and least spoilt by restoration of all Romanesque cathedrals. Retains Norman nave, aisles, transepts, choir (except apsidal end), western towers and considerable portion of cloistral buildings.

ELY. Benedictine. 1081. Nave, transepts and aisles provide an excellent example of Norman work with well-proportioned arcade and triforium gallery. Aisles have groined vaults carried on transverse ribs. Base of western tower and massive octagonal turrets at south-west corner remain. Beautiful, though restored, 'Prior's Door' on south wall leading to nave aisle.

EXETER. Secular Canons. 1117. Retains remarkable transeptal towers which are unique in England, though similar towers may have existed at Old Sarum. South tower Norman throughout, north modified in upper stages; both richly ornamented in storeys with blind arcades and circular openings.

FOUNTAINS (Pl. 18). Cistercian. 1135. (p. 130.) Although a ruin, preserves almost intact the plan of a typical Cistercian monastery. All the work is plain, even severe, in character. Of late Norman period there remain the dorter, parts of the Abbot's lodging, the nave aisles and transepts of the church. The nave has cylindrical piers with attached shafts on the aisle side. Aisles had remarkable transverse barrel vaults in the manner of Tournus (p. 146), of which portions survive (see Pl. 18). Square-ended chapels on east wall of transepts.

GLOUCESTER (Pl. 17). Benedictine. 1072. Ambulatory plan. Of the Norman church practically the whole structure remains, but much has been faced with later mediaeval work. Externally there remain the transepts, with their square corner turrets and eastern chapels; internally, the nave, with its massive cylindrical columns and minute triforium passageway. North aisle still preserves original Norman vaulting. Choir, with low arcade and spacious triforium gallery, has lost its original character by facing of Perpendicular tracery, but Norman work still evident in the vaulted ambulatory around the choir, with its groined vaults and two remaining radiating chapels. Well-preserved Chapter House and crypt.

HEREFORD. Secular Canons. 1079. Norman work chiefly limited to interior. Fine nave of eight bays, which has suffered from somewhat poor restoration to triforium and clerestory by Wyatt. Choir of three bays having Norman arcade and triforium; east wall of north transept with fine arcaded decoration.

LEOMINSTER. Benedictine. *Circa* 1130. Little remains; original Norman nave and north aisle, lower stages of north-west tower.

LICHFIELD. Augustinian. 1088. Nothing remains above ground of the Norman cathedral. Excavations indicated that in plan it was like, but smaller than, Peterborough.

LINCOLN. Secular Canons. 1072. Almost entirely rebuilt 1185–1200. Of the Norman church there remain central portion of western front and lower storeys of the two western towers.

LONDON (OLD S. PAUL'S). Secular Canons. 1087. Built in Caen stone. Retained until Fire of London its Norman nave, most of structure being later. Form of original east end uncertain, but Clapham considered ambulatory type most likely. No remains.

NORWICH (Pl. 18). Benedictine. 1096. (p. 228.) Magnificent, richly-ornamented tower with later crocketed spire. Nave and transepts original, but with later vault (1446–72) added to take the place of the original wooden roof. Apsidal choir and ambulatory retains two of the original radiating chapels.

OXFORD (CHRIST CHURCH (Pl. 17)). Augustinian. 1180. Retains original late Romanesque nave and choir; sixteenth-century timber roof over nave and pendant vault (1480) over choir. Unusual arrangement of arcade and triforium in which main arches are carried over triforium gallery, and subsidiary arches, bracketed from columns, spring at lower level to form arcade.

PETERBOROUGH. Benedictine. 1118. Parallel-apsed type. Preserves almost completely the whole of the Norman nave, choir and transepts. Apsidal choir is possibly the finest in the country. The aisles have early ribbed vaults, and the nave and choir are roofed with timber.

RIEVAULX. Cistercian. 1132. Ruins; nave and part of transepts, all of the plainest and most severe pattern. Arcade of square piers with angles splayed 5 feet from the ground, from which spring pointed arches; above, clerestory with round-headed windows.

RIPON. Secular Canons. 1154. Remarkable chiefly in that nave of original building was without aisles, and in place of triforium there was a range of windows below the clerestory. Only scanty remains. Late Romanesque transepts, and portion of apsidal end to chapel on south side of choir.

ROCHESTER. Benedictine. 1077. Scanty remains; outer walls of nave aisles and north tower. Rebuilt 1115. Of this period there survive west front, except for central window in gable; six bays of nave with clustered columns; an elaborately-decorated triforium which opens onto aisles; ruins of cloistral buildings.

ROMSEY (Pl. 17). Benedictine (nuns). 1120. (p. 123.) Retains almost unspoiled square east end, transepts with apsidal chapels, and large part of nave. Triforium arcade of great variety of treatment, consisting of round-headed open arches, some interlacing like tracery, and without tympanum or infilling. Externally, except for later west end and last three bays of nave, the abbey is an excellent example of Norman work.

S. ALBANS (Pl. 17). Benedictine. 1077. Built by Paul of Caen almost entirely of Roman bricks. Parallel-apsed plan with very long nave of rectangular piers, of which considerable portion survives, largely unaltered except by modern restoration. Originally plastered and whitewashed outside, plastered and painted inside. Considerable traces of frescoes remain on western face of nave piers. South aisle beyond crossing has plastered quadripartite vault, with red painted lines to simulate diagonal ribs and stone jointing. Magnificent brick tower.

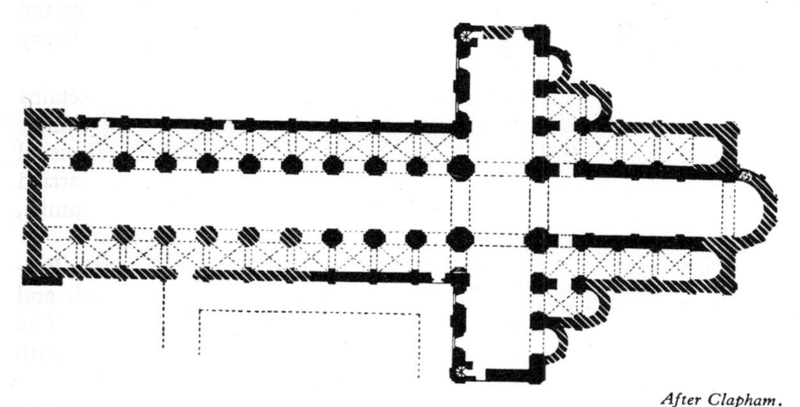

After Clapham.

S. Albans Cathedral.
Scale 100 *ft. to* 1 *in.*

SHERBORNE. Benedictine. Early twelfth century. Norman building largely converted into Perpendicular. Of Norman period there remain south porch, very much restored; north porch, rebuilt; lower stages of central tower.

SOUTHWARK. Augustinian. 1106. Scanty remains; portions of chapel of S. John the Divine (now used as vestry); prior's entrance to cloisters.

SOUTHWELL (Pl. 15). Secular Canons. 1108. Originally square-ended choir with side apses to aisles. Retains Norman nave with timber roof, aisles with ribbed vaults, and much characteristic decoration: scalloped capitals, billet, chevron, etc.; externally, central and western towers; barrel-vaulted north porch; unusual circular windows to clerestory.

TEWKESBURY (Pl. 18). Benedictine. 1087. Resembles Gloucester in many respects. Considerable remains in nave, transepts and choir. Nave arcade, of massive cylindrical piers over 30 feet high and 6 feet 3 inches in diameter, supports minute triforium and clerestory, the latter partly obscured by later vaulting. Apsidal vaulted chapel to south transept. Magnificent central tower and west front, with recessed arch of seven orders, 65 feet high and 34 feet wide.

WELLS. Secular Canons. 1061 and 1136. Entirely rebuilt after 1180. Possibly the only large church in England in which all traces of Romanesque are lost.

WESTMINSTER. Benedictine. 1055. Built at instigation of Edward the Confessor and completed after the Conquest. Of Norman work only significant survival is vaulted undercroft.

WINCHESTER. Benedictine. 1079. Retains original transepts, which have groined vaulted aisles on east and west sides, and a connecting gallery across the ends; crypt and central tower.

WORCESTER. Benedictine. 1084. Norman crypt and scanty remains in nave and transepts. An interesting feature is somewhat unusual three-light triforium openings in the two western bays of the nave, which are decorated with characteristic zig-zag ornament and circular paterae.

YORK. Secular Canons. 1080. Nave, transepts and perhaps choir built by Thomas of Bayeux. Considerable doubt about size and character of this church. Behind altar, the remains of exquisitely-carved Madonna and Child (see Pl. 13), but nothing structural now visible above ground. Below is crypt, which was built 1154–81, with elaborately-carved column shafts and capitals.

SCOTLAND AND WALES

While Scotland and Wales were outside Norman suzerainty during the years of Romanesque building activity, the Church was not restricted by national frontiers, and architecturally the work in Britain as a whole during the eleventh and beginning of the twelfth centuries can properly be called Norman. For that reason a summary is appended here of the important Romanesque remains outside England but within the British Isles.

DUNFERMLINE. Benedictine. 1124. Fine western doorway. Nave with cylindrical piers, having zig-zag, spiral and other ornamentation reminiscent of Durham. Simple triforium gallery and clerestory; aisles with ribbed vaulting.

JEDBURGH. Augustinian. 1147. Ruins; retains north and south transepts and two bays of choir with side aisles; choir built in style reminiscent of Romsey and Oxford, in which massive cylindrical columns are carried up to the height of the triforium arch, the lower arches being supported from corbels.

KELSO. Benedictine. 1128. Ruins; unusual cruciform plan with nave equal in length to transepts, and without aisles. Fine doorway to north transept.

KIRKWALL. Secular Canons. 1137. The most complete example of Romanesque architecture in Scotland, built when the Orkneys were part of the dominion of Norway. Retains nave arcade of eight cylindrical piers under a spacious triforium; three bays of choir, and transepts. A curious feature is the use of different coloured stones.

LLANDAFF. Secular Canons. 1121. Although the oldest episcopal See in Britain, little remains of the Norman period. Original cathedral probably aisleless. Archway and presbytery with uncommon paterae and other enrichments only found in one other place in Britain, viz. Malmesbury Abbey. Two richly-decorated late Norman doorways on north and south sides.

PEMBROKE, S. DAVID. Augustinian. 1180. Late Romanesque nave well preserved, with piers alternately cylindrical and octagonal with attached shafts. Triforium and clerestory curiously amalgamated under two arches to each bay of the arcade.

It will be seen that the earliest church building was largely in the hands of the Benedictine Order, and that the Order of Canons Regular of S. Augustine played only a subsidiary rôle. There was little to distinguish between the architecture of the two, although there was perhaps greater variety in the planning of the Augustinian churches. The Augustine canons resembled the Benedictine monks in so far as they lived in community and took religious vows; but their state of life remained strictly clerical and they did not undertake manual labour as prescribed by Benedict. The Cistercian Order only came into existence in 1098, largely because of the dissatisfaction of certain Benedictine monks with the manner and life of their fellows. The Cistercians endeavoured to follow more strictly the letter of Benedict's rule. They were extremely rigid in their outlook, and they began to build in England only towards the end of the Romanesque period. They avoided towns, and built their abbeys in remote districts. Secular Canons differed from the Augustinian Canons and the monks in that they did not live in community, but that each had one or more 'prebends', or livings, for which he was responsible, and his periods of residence were decided by the Chapter as a whole.

England and Germany seem to have been the only two countries in which a bishop's chair was placed in a Benedictine monastic church. In such cases the bishop was little more than a nominal head, all administrative power being in the hands of a Prior and Chapter. So many bishops in early days were 'half priests, half warriors', engaged in political intrigue, or in public duties for the good of the country, that they were often absentees from their churches for long periods. It seems to have made no difference whatsoever to the plan whether a church was monastic or was a cathedral ruled by secular canons or lay monks. Peterborough was only an abbey church, Ely an abbey church that was also a cathedral, while Chichester and Hereford had no monasteries attached to them; and yet the only difference that can be noted is that the last two have slightly shorter naves than the others. Even this is no real distinction, for the nave of Rochester—a cathedral served by Benedictine monks—is even shorter.

The Norman Conquest did something more than substitute one race of rulers for another. It introduced throughout the country new religious ideals, a new intellectual standard. The strict monasticism of the Benedictine Order had, it is true, been introduced into England a few years before; but it had found favour only in London and one or two other centres. Now it was carried all over the country, and beyond to Scotland and Wales. Many of the Norman nobles had spent some time in the University of Paris, then the chief centre of intellectual activity in western Europe; Thomas à Becket was educated there later. The Saxons, both priests and people, were far less advanced than the French. The Normans may have been rough and rude, judged by modern standards, but they were polished compared with the greater number of English thanes and nobles.

Nearly all the larger English churches have been altered through the centuries, so that there are very few in which the whole development of English mediaeval architecture, from Romanesque times up to the Reformation, cannot be traced. The necessity for a longer choir led to the destruction of the apses of Canterbury, S. Albans, Ely and many others. In no cathedral in England does the Norman east end remain exactly as it was when built; even Norwich, otherwise complete in plan, has lost the central chapel of its chevet. Peterborough retains the apse to its choir, but eastwards there is an addition of later date. The Durham apse had to make way for the Chapel of the Nine Altars. The naves and transepts have been less altered than the choirs. The later introduction of vaulting, however, has changed the appearance of many a nave, notwithstanding that the arcades, triforiums, and clerestorys remain much as they were originally. In the naves of Ely and Peterborough and in the transepts of Winchester, wooden ceilings remain, though of course they have been renewed. Elsewhere, at Gloucester, Tewkesbury, Norwich, etc., the wooden ceilings were replaced by stone vaults. Structural defects sometimes entailed whole rebuilding, as at Ely Cathedral, where the central tower fell, bringing down with it the neighbouring bays. Fire, which played such havoc all through the Middle Ages, also did as much damage in England as in France; although why it should have been so frequent and so disastrous in stone-vaulted churches is difficult to understand. In Chichester Cathedral, after the fire in 1186, the three-quarter attached shafts in the angles of the piers were replaced by more slender, detached shafts; the cushion capitals disappeared, lighter ones being substituted, and mouldings were worked on the wall faces of the arches to tone down their severity.

The disgust which the heavy proportions of Romanesque evidently aroused in the later builders, and the desire to have churches up to date, led to the entire remodelling of much of the work. Throughout the Middle Ages there was, apparently, little reverence for past endeavours. Buildings seem never to have been restored to their original state; they were rebuilt, and always in the most up-to-date and contemporary mode. At Gloucester the monks, unable to bear the cost of pulling down and rebuilding their choir, faced the whole with delicate pierced stone panelling, so that all they could see from their stalls was modern. From the aisles and triforiums alone were the solid piers and sturdy arches visible. At Winchester, Bishop William of Wykeham ordered the Romanesque piers on the south side of the nave to be carved into forms that pleased him better, and on the north side, finding this method too slow or too expensive, he had the facing stones of the piers removed, leaving only the cores, which were recased. The triforium was swept away, the arches of the main arcade raised and altered in shape, new windows inserted in the clerestory, and over the whole of the central area an elaborate ribbed vault built; so that only the transepts remained in the old style, and from the nave the church would appear quite new. At Exeter much the same thing had been done some fifty years before, but in a most drastic fashion, and at S. Albans, on two separate occasions with an interval between them of nearly a hundred years, determined attacks were made on the old work.

Naves. One of the most marked peculiarities of English Romanesque churches is the long nave. On the Continent, with very few exceptions, there are no churches which can compare in length of nave with English examples. The nave of Norwich has fourteen bays and is 260 feet long. Winchester, which now has twelve bays, originally had the same number as Norwich and is even longer. In the West of England, at Gloucester, Hereford and

Tewkesbury, the naves are shorter, but even so are greater than those of most churches on the Continent. Exceptions are the great basilican churches in Rome, S. Peter's and S. Paul's, which had naves 280 and 275 feet long; S. Sernin, Toulouse, is another, with twelve bays and a length of 210 feet; at Caen, l'Abbaye-aux-Hommes has eight bays, the same number as Gloucester, each nave being about 140 feet long; even at Durham, where the rapid fall of the ground at the west side rendered further extension impossible, the nave is 200 feet long.

In the naves of Ely, Peterborough and Durham, English Romanesque architecture can be seen to perfection. The naves of Tewkesbury, Gloucester and Norwich are spoiled to some extent by later vaults; but at Durham the vaults are almost contemporary with the nave. At Tewkesbury and Gloucester, the columns are perhaps too high and the capitals and arches exceedingly plain; at Hereford the columns are certainly too low, the capitals very elaborate and the arches unusually rich.

The piers of the main arcades in Romanesque churches are of three types: square, cylindrical and clustered. The square type is best seen at S. Albans, where the re-use of Roman bricks may have dictated its form. Cylindrical piers may be used either alone or alternating with clustered piers. At Gloucester, Southwell and Tewkesbury they occur alone; at Durham they alternate in the same way as at Jumièges Abbey in Normandy. Nave arcades of clustered piers, like those at l'Abbaye-aux-Dames, are found at Ely and Winchester.

In all large churches built by the Normans, whether in England or Normandy, the division of the nave wall into arcade, triforium and clerestory is the rule, but there is considerable variation in the height and proportion allotted to each. In the cathedrals of Norwich and Winchester (as originally built) all these divisions were approximately equal. At Durham and Tewkesbury the arcade is by far the highest of the three; at Oxford, Romsey and Jedburgh the arcade and triforium are combined under one arch, and at S. David's, Pembroke, the triforium is united with the clerestory. These variations show that there was no absolute rule of relative proportions and arrangement for the internal divisions of Romanesque churches. Of the two principal churches at Caen, l'Abbaye-aux-Hommes resembles Peterborough in its proportions, while the nave of l'Abbaye-aux-Dames is more like that of Gloucester, though the height of its triforium is even less than that of the English cathedral. Durham has the finest proportions of all. Its lowest storey considerably exceeds in height the two upper storeys together, and yet does not overwhelm them entirely, as happens at Gloucester.

The design of the triforium is as varied as its height and proportion. In Norwich and l'Abbaye-aux-Hommes each bay consists of a single arched opening about the same width as the opening below. At Winchester, Ely, Peterborough and Chichester, there is a pair of openings under a single arch with a solid tympanum above. The tympanums often have chevrons, triangles and other patterns roughly chiselled or axed on their faces, as at Christchurch and Rochester. Sometimes there are more openings underneath the main arches, as at Jumièges, Malmesbury and S. Bartholomew, Smithfield. A later development occurs at Romsey Abbey, where there are twin sub-arches which are free, and where a small shaft with a capital and base is inserted under the crown of the main arch. Generally the triforium storey extends over the aisle below and is covered by a sloping timber roof, but at Gloucester there is a half-barrel vault, and at S. John's Chapel in the Tower of London a complete barrel vault (Pl. 24).

The design of the clerestory is nearly always the same: on the inside face is a lofty arched opening (central with the window on the outside face), which is flanked by two smaller openings, each divided from the middle one by a shaft; behind these shafts there is commonly a narrow passage. The clerestory at Southwell is unusual in that it has a round window to each bay and a barrel-vaulted passage between it and the arched openings into the nave.

Transepts. All English Romanesque cathedrals are cruciform in plan, the transepts in most of them having the considerable projection which later became so marked a feature of English work. In Normandy, as a rule, they are equally strongly marked, the arms north, east and south of the crossing being, as at S. Georges, Boscherville, of the same length. The transepts of Ely and Winchester cathedrals have aisles on both west and east sides, and at Winchester the aisle passage is returned as an open gallery at the ends. A similar feature occurs at l'Abbaye-aux-Hommes, Caen. At Durham there are aisles on the eastern side but none on the west. The customary plan, however, is to have no aisles to the transepts, but instead one or two apsidal chapels opening directly out of the east wall of the transept, as at Norwich, S. Albans and l'Abbaye-aux-Dames.

Choirs. The eastern arms are short in comparison with the western, but longer in England than in contemporary churches abroad. From the first the tendency to lengthen this part of the church, so marked in later English examples, is evident. Norwich and Durham had four bays between the crossing and the apse, and so, originally, had S. Albans and Ely. Gloucester and Chichester had only three bays, but their naves were shorter. L'Abbaye-aux-Hommes had only two bays to the east, apart from the apse, and that is the number at S. Georges, Boscherville and S. Sernin, Toulouse, notwithstanding the great length of nave of the latter.

The termination of the eastern end provided opportunities for considerable variety of treatment. To begin with there were two alternatives. The first followed the plan of Bernay Abbey and of l'Abbaye-aux-Dames by having an apse at the end of the choir and smaller apses at the ends of the aisles. This was the plan that was adopted at Canterbury (originally), Peterborough, S. Albans, Ely and Durham. The second carried the aisles round the choir apse in the form of an ambulatory, from which chapels might radiate. This plan occurs at Jumièges, and it was followed in England at Worcester, Gloucester, Tewkesbury, Norwich and Chichester.

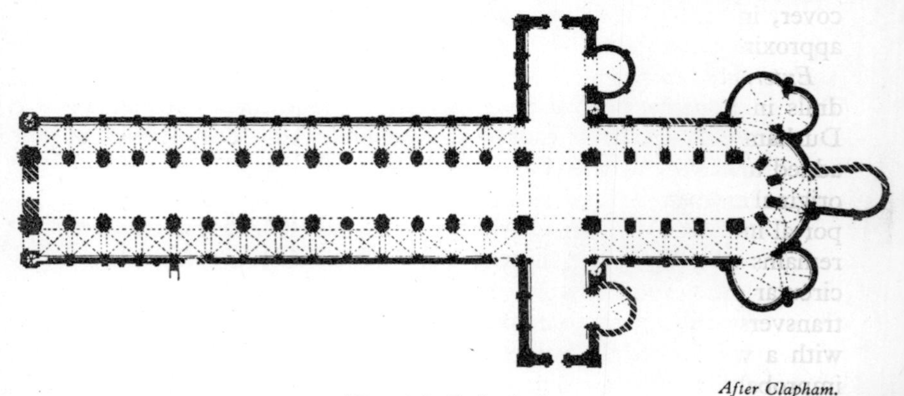

After Clapham.

Norwich Cathedral.
Scale 100 *ft. to* 1 *in.*

There is apparently no significance in the geographical distribution of these two types. Towards the middle of the twelfth century a third type was adopted, which has no precedent in France and may therefore be considered as an English characteristic, especially since it was the form to be followed in England with great consistency throughout the mediaeval period. This consisted of a square eastern end to the choir, and was adopted at Southwell, where there were apses to the aisles, and possibly at Hereford. A variation on this plan involved the carrying of the aisle along the back of the square-ended choir, as can still be seen at Romsey (p. 123).

Nearly all the eastern ends of our Romanesque cathedrals have been replaced by later additions. Norwich is perhaps the best preserved example of the ambulatory plan, for, with the exception of the eastern chapel, almost the whole structure survives. Peterborough, which had a parallel-apsed plan, still has its apsidal termination to the choir, but the side apses to the aisles have been removed to provide access to a late Perpendicular chapel or retro-choir.

The apsidal termination introduced problems which were never properly solved in Romanesque times. Almost inevitably it resulted in narrower bays, with the consequent stilting of arches; and where there was an ambulatory, the bays on plan were of such an irregular shape that they could not be vaulted satisfactorily as long as the round arch was the basis of the construction. For it was only the advent of the pointed rib that made it possible to cover, in an architecturally satisfying way, vaults that were not approximately square.

External Treatment. The west fronts of Romanesque cathedrals in England have suffered as severely as their eastern arms. Durham Cathedral retains its two towers, but the Galilee Porch, added towards the end of the twelfth century, has obliterated the original entrance. Tewkesbury Abbey has the finest Romanesque portal in England. On each side are six attached shafts, and the remains of a seventh. They are carried up to support a semi-circular arch of as many orders, which rises higher even than the transverse arches inside at the crossing. The arch is now filled with a window and door of later date,[1] but it is by no means improbable that originally the archway was but the entrance to a recessed porch. The responds inside at the end of the nave arcades are unusually deep, so there would have been room for an outer porch. Southwell, with its two towers, gives perhaps better than any other example a fair picture of what a Romanesque western front was like. Even this, however, has been spoiled by the introduction of a large central window of the fifteenth century.

[1] The window is dated 1686, but, except that its detail is curious, it is a very fair copy of fifteenth-century work.

It is in the design of towers that the greatest variety in exterior design is to be seen. There is little enrichment to the main walls of the greater churches, which are invariably extremely simple, with flat pilasters marking the divisions of the bays and round-headed windows in between. The doorways and porches, with their moulded orders and chevron ornament, provide minor points of interest, but there is little sculpture or refinement. The Romanesque cathedrals of England were impressive largely by their size, their apparent massive solidity. The term 'apparent solidity' is used advisedly, because the story of Norman building makes a sad tale of structural disasters. A great many of the Norman towers collapsed soon after they were built—Winchester in 1107, Worcester in 1175, Lincoln in 1240 and Ely in 1322. A. W. Clapham considered that the central tower of S. Albans was the only important eleventh-century tower to have survived. The central towers of Norwich and Tewkesbury and the western towers of Southwell and Durham are all of the twelfth century.

The towers are the greatest extravagance of the Norman builders, and are generally richly decorated with interlacing arcades and other superficial ornamentation, of little structural significance but great aesthetic importance. The central towers, especially, are far greater in size than their Continental counterparts, and provide a fitting climax to the long, low and almost monotonous composition of the nave, transepts and choir.

Durham Cathedral. Durham Cathedral was the supreme achievement of the Norman builders in England. It far surpassed anything that had been built in Normandy, and it remains to this day the greatest of all Romanesque buildings. It is, indeed, the epitome of Norman endeavour, the most brilliant testimony which has survived of Norman power and culture in these islands. The site, a precipitous rock almost encircled by water, was far superior to that of any other cathedral, and building was begun only after the structural possibilities of the Romanesque style were realised.

The county of Durham was among the last areas of England to fall before the conqueror, in that 'harrying of the North' which was described by Trevelyan as 'a vengeance Turkish in its atrocity'. Within one generation of the event, the cathedral and the castle alongside it were being built as a symbol of the might of Norman civilisation. Because of the lateness of the undertaking, Durham differs from other cathedrals in that its nave was vaulted at approximately the same date as was the rest of the church.

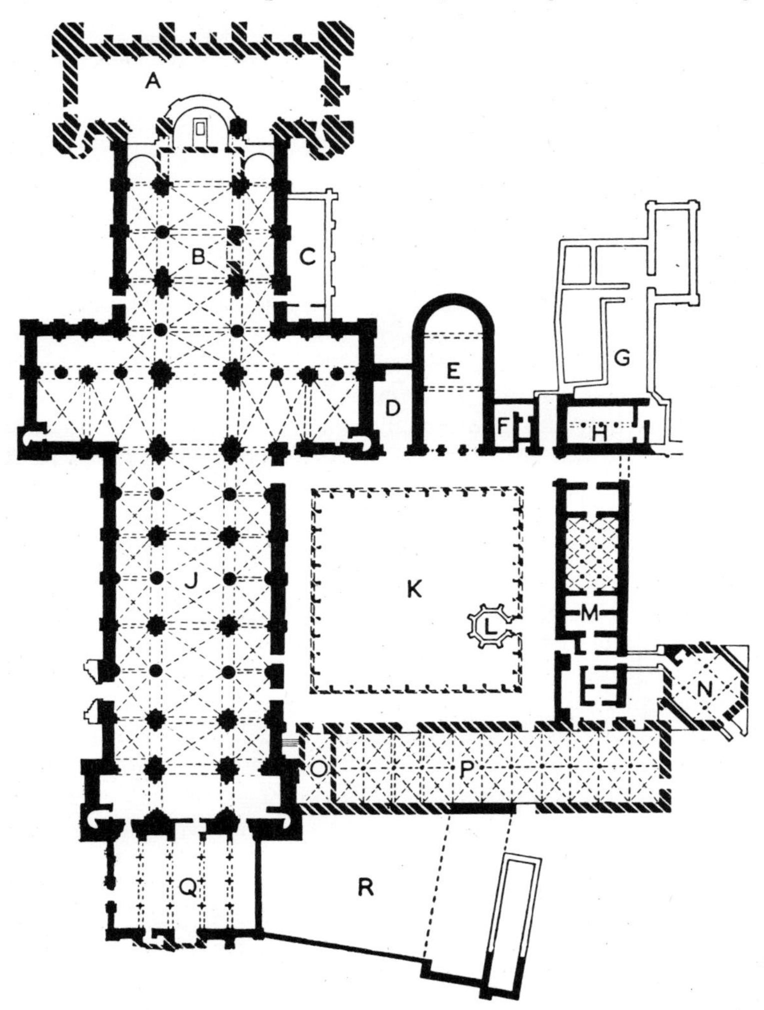

Modified from G. H. Cook, Portrait of Durham Cathedral, Phoenix House, Ltd.

Durham Cathedral.

KEY

A. Nine Altars Transept (1242–80).
B. Choir (1093–1109).
C. Revestry.
D. Locutorium.
E. Chapter House.
F. Prison.
G. Prior's Lodging.
H. Sub-dorter.
J. Nave (1110–38).
K. Cloister Garth.
L. Lavatorium.
M. Cellars, Frater over.
N. Kitchen.
O. Treasury.
P. Cellarer, Dorter over.
Q. Galilee Chapel.
R. Garden and Bowling Alley.

Scale 100 *ft. to* 1 *in.*

Building began in 1093 under the direction of Bishop William of S. Carileph, who had been at one time a monk of the Benedictine abbey of S. Calais in the old province of Maine, adjoining Normandy. Work was continued by his successor, Ralph Flambard (1096–1128), and by 1140 the whole cathedral, except for the upper parts of the towers, was finished. Architecturally it was superior to anything that had been done in the West before, not because of its size (for it was much shorter than Winchester or Peterborough), nor its plan (which conformed to the usual Benedictine arrangement), nor its detail (which had all the traditional barbaric enrichment), but because it incorporated in one building all those structural elements which ultimately were to revolutionise the whole history of building in western Europe.

The only unusual feature of the plan of Durham is the Galilee Chapel, which was added to the western front towards the end of the twelfth century. Durham consists of a nave of eight bays, a choir of four bays, and transepts (each having an eastern aisle) of three bays. The choir and the aisles terminated in apses. Apart from the central tower, and the parallel-apsed east end which was removed in the thirteenth century to make way for the Chapel of the Nine Altars, the cathedral is Norman throughout. In the nave and choir, great clustered piers alternate with cylindrical columns in the manner of Jumièges and S. Ambrogio, Milan. By the end of the eleventh century the eastern arm had been finished, and work had begun to the west. That the aisles were already vaulted with rib vaults seems certain, although it is doubtful if it was intended to cover any of the rest in the same way. In the transepts, there are shafts which start from the triforium level and run up to the apex of the present vault, suggesting that there was no intention of vaulting this part at all. The alternation of large and small supports is no positive proof that vaulting was to be carried throughout. In S. Zeno, Verona, and in many early churches in Germany, there is similar alternation, but no suggestion of any vaults to the naves. By 1104, however, structural knowledge was sufficiently advanced for an attempt to be made to vault the choir itself. These vaults, unfortunately, were so unsafe that they had to be rebuilt in the thirteenth century. By 1110 the transepts were successfully covered, and by 1135 the nave and aisles. All the vaults were ribbed, and the transverse arches which crossed the nave were pointed. A most curious feature of the Durham nave vault is the awkward way in which the diagonal ribs start from

Southwell Cathedral; west front

Abbaye-aux-Hommes, Caen; west front

Durham Cathedral;
nave

Durham Cathedral;
choir aisle vault

S Alban's Cathedral; nave

Romsey Abbey; nave

Plate 17

Gloucester Cathedral; nave

Christ Church, Oxford; north transept

Tewkesbury Abbey; west front

Norwich Cathedral; apsidal end

Plate 18

Castle Acre Priory

Fountains Abbey; south aisle

corbel heads, and not from the side vaulting shafts as might have been expected. If the transverse ribs were built before the vaults, this might provide the reason. Another peculiarity is that the clerestory windows are not central with the vault compartments, a fact which gives some colour to the theory that it was originally intended to cover the nave with sexpartite vaults, as at l'Abbaye-aux-Hommes, for if the diagonals had started from above the side shafts of the main piers and had been bisected by an intermediate transverse arch above each column, the windows would have centred exactly. Against this, it may be pointed out that each bay of vaulting between the great piers (especially the second and third bays west of the crossing) is far longer than its width, and the span of the diagonal ribs would consequently have been excessive. The truly significant fact, however, is that by 1135 (five years before the laying of the foundation of the choir of the Abbey of S. Denis, Paris) the Norman masons had built a ribbed vault over the wide span of the nave, using a pointed arch, and at the same time restraining the thrust of the vaults by quadrant arches which span the triforium chamber and constitute, in effect, flying buttresses.

Durham is notable not only for its cathedral but also for the conventual buildings associated with it. Here much of the Norman work still survives. The Chapter House, it is true, is only a replica, and the Norman cloisters have been replaced by much later work; but all around are the various buildings, the dorter or dormitory, the frater or refectory, the cellarium or cellarer's quarters, and beyond, the monks' garden and bowling green, the infirmary and the prior's lodging. Most of these buildings are Norman and, with the cathedral, remain today a remarkable monument to Norman endeavour.

Parish Churches. The list given of the greater churches is no mean record of the building achievements of the Norman conquerors. To it must be added the thousands of parish churches that were built either on new sites or in place of those which were deemed unworthy. Of all countries, England is the most remarkable for the number and variety of its parish churches. It has been said that the number at the time of the compilation of the Domesday Book practically equalled that at the close of the eighteenth century.[1] The great number of country examples we possess is due to some extent to our insular position, and to the kind of feudalism and the system of agriculture that developed, based

[1] *The Parish Churches of England,* Cox & Ford, 1935.

upon the village. The whole of England was dotted with villages and each had its own church. In France, Germany and other countries, villages were few and far apart. The majority of people were forced, for safety, to live in large communities. The farmers and agricultural labourers who lived outside had, in many cases, to trudge far to church, as they do in many parts of France to the present day, where a church serves a large outlying district. These widely dispersed churches were consequently larger; in England the parish church served a limited area and was as a rule small. From the wealth of material it is not possible to do more than classify the principal types and refer to a few. No two churches are alike, and nearly all have been modified and altered by subsequent additions, but there are still hundreds in which the main fabric is the work of the eleventh and twelfth centuries.

There would appear to have been four main types:

(a) *Aisleless.* This may consist of a single cell without any structural division, or may be divided into inter-communicating compartments (nave, choir and presbytery), and have a western tower in addition. It is by far the commonest type. The eastern ending may be apsidal, as at Kilpeck, Herts., Great Maplestead, Essex, and Moccas, Herefordshire, or it may be square, as at Iffley, Oxon., and Stewkley, Bucks.

(b) *Cruciform.* This has a central tower to mark the division of nave, choir and transepts, and may or may not have aisles. The finest example of the aisleless type is to be seen at Old Shoreham, Sussex, where evidence remains of apsidal chapels projecting east of the transepts. At Melbourne, Derby, there is a good example of the cruciform church with aisles. It is unusually large and has, in addition to the central tower, two western towers.

(c) *Aisled.* This type is generally confined to smaller towns rather than villages. It was in many cases a development of the aisleless plan, the aisles being added at a later date. At Little Munden, Herts., only one aisle, on the north side, has been added. However, the number of Norman arcades still remaining is evidence that many churches were planned with aisles from the beginning. At New Shoreham, Sussex, there was an excellent example of a late Norman aisled church, but in this case only the chancel end survives, where the aisles are continued on either side to form a square east end.

(d) *Circular*. Only three Romanesque examples survive: S. Sepulchre, Cambridge, S. Mary Magdalene in Ludlow Castle, and S. Sepulchre, Northampton.[1] There is no doubt that this plan was inspired by the Church of the Holy Sepulchre in Jerusalem, and similar examples exist in other parts of Europe (see pp. 132–4). As a rule they are arcaded, the outer ring

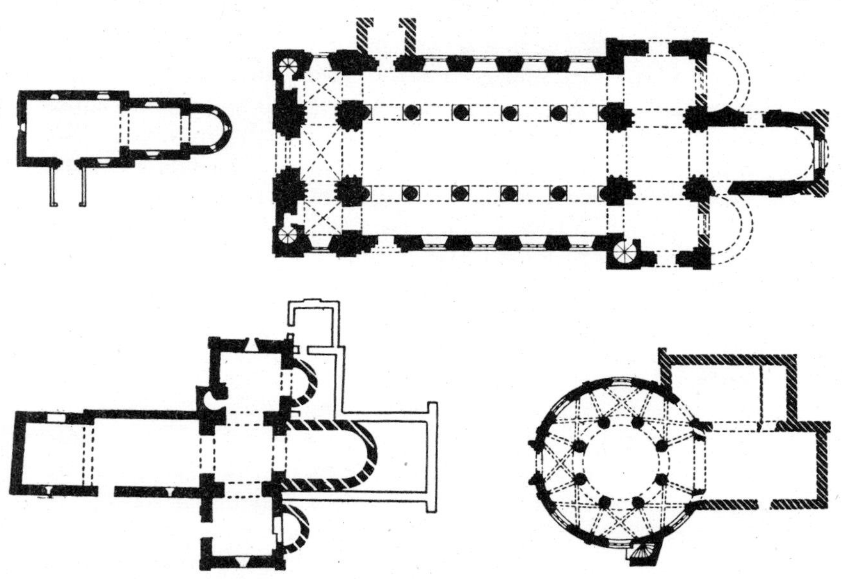

Plans of typical Norman parish churches.

(top left) Unaisled; Moccas, Herefordshire.
(top right) Aisled; Melbourne, Derby.
(bottom left) Cruciform; Old Shoreham, Sussex.
(bottom right) Circular; S. Sepulchre, Cambridge.

Scale 50 ft. to 1 in.

being vaulted, and have a triforium, clerestory and a projecting chancel. Ludlow is an exception, since there is no arcade. It was begun in 1095 and has been very much altered. The chancel extended east and was closed by a semi-octagonal apse.

In detail the smaller churches do not differ from the cathedrals and monasteries. The walls are extraordinarily thick, seldom less

[1] Two other round churches should be mentioned: the Temple Church, London, bombed in the last war and since restored; and the Church of the Hospitallers, Little Maplestead, Essex, which was the only circular church built in later times (fourteenth century).

than three feet, relieved externally by flat, pilaster-like buttresses which are largely decorative, for stone vaulting is exceptional and confined, as a rule, to the chancel. An important exception is S. John's Chapel in the Tower of London, where the nave has a barrel vault which finishes at the apse with a semi-dome and is supported by groined vaults over the aisles and the barrel-vaulted triforium. Internally, in aisled churches, there is normally a clerestory with a narrow mural passage, but no triforium. Towers and porches provided the principal opportunities for elaboration and decoration. The towers are enriched with many interlacings and arcadings, and porches, which are normally located on the south wall, are often richly carved with all the characteristic ornamentation of the period. Strangely enough, it is often in the smaller and more insignificant churches that the profusion of carving in porches is most striking. In the little church at Barfreston, Kent, for example, there is a splendid doorway which may have been carved by workmen from Canterbury, and which consists of an elaborate tympanum surrounded by scroll-work incorporating angels, kings, queens and other figures.

Churches were being built in the eleventh and twelfth centuries all over the country. The architecture was incomparably superior to the Anglo-Saxon endeavours, even although the sheer bulk of masonry employed often indicated an uncertain knowledge of constructional principles. There was much that seems cumbersome and crude when compared with the fine logic of subsequent Gothic formalism. The sculpture was often primitive in the extreme, and had little of the delicate humanism that followed when civilisation advanced. Nevertheless, there was about Norman architecture something magnificent in a monumental way which, in its finest examples, has never been surpassed.

CHAPTER XVI

ROMANESQUE IN FRANCE

THE study of the Romanesque architecture of France presents problems of classification which never occurred when we considered Britain. This is largely due to the fact that France, during the Romanesque period, was not a united country, but a number of semi-independent states. Nor was the population homogeneous; the north-west was peopled from Norman stock, the north-east was essentially Germanic, and the south Latin. The result was that there were wide variations in architectural expression in different areas. Further, the individual schools were not strictly confined by state boundaries, and features which we associate with a particular district often appear most disconcertingly in other districts which have apparently no connection whatsoever. In spite of these difficulties, and without distinguishing too minutely, four broad types may be determined. In the north we have the schools of Normandy and Anjou; the former, with its centre at Caen, we have already discussed in the last chapter; the latter, with its centres bordering the Loire, penetrated far into Aquitaine. In the east there is the Burgundian school, with its centres at Cluny and Citeaux; in the west, the school of Aquitaine, centring around Perigueux, with its churches of eastern plan and domical construction, which have been considered under Byzantine work (pp. 94–8); and in the south, the twin schools of Auvergne and Provence, with their centres at Clermont-Ferrand and Arles.

SOUTHERN FRANCE

Auvergne (Pl. 19). The churches in the old Province of Auvergne bear a remarkable family likeness. All might well have been designed by the same architect and built by one set of workmen.[1] The most important are Notre-Dame-du-Port, Clermont-Ferrand

[1] The Cathedral of Le Puy is an exception, but then it is southernmost of all and seems to have been built under other influences.

(1080), which is probably the earliest, the cathedrals of Issoire and Brioude, built in the first half of the twelfth century, and S. Nectaire, which, though small, is one of the most perfect. Many of their characteristics they share with churches of similar construction outside the province, such as S. Sernin, Toulouse, S. Etienne, Nevers, and the abbey church of Conques. In plan they

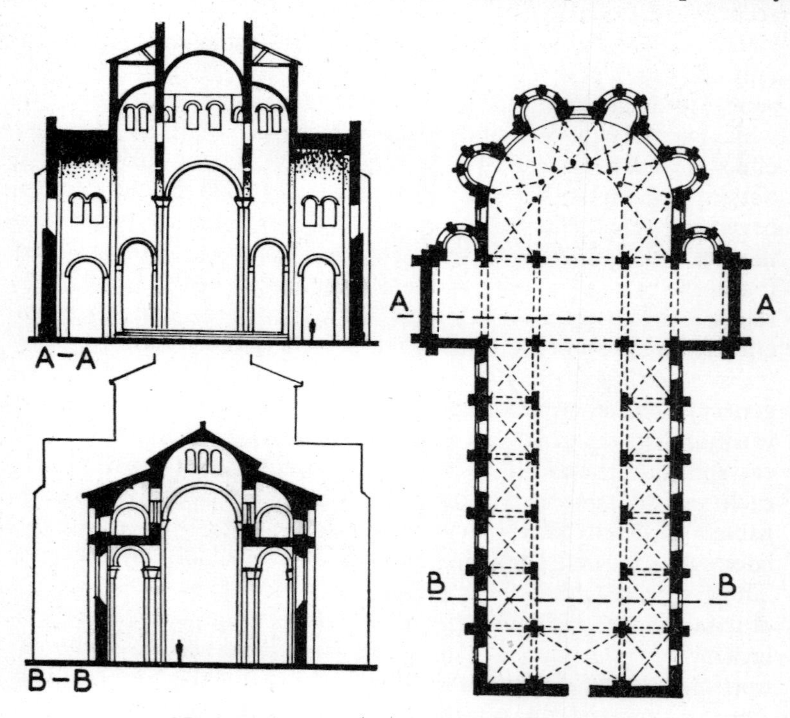

Notre-Dame-du-Port, Clermont-Ferrand.
Scale 50 ft. to 1 in.

are all aisled, have eastern chevets and, as a rule, apsidal chapels projecting from the eastern sides of the transepts. The chevets are remarkably well arranged, and their effect outside is in all cases most striking. At S. Nectaire there are three apses, at Clermont-Ferrand four, at Brioude and Issoire five. The naves are covered by semi-circular barrel vaults, and the aisles by groined vaults supported by transverse arches.[1] Over the aisles are spacious

[1] In the Church of Polignac, near Le Puy, the aisles as well as the nave are barrel-vaulted.

galleries covered by quadrant vaults which take the thrusts of the central vaults. There are no clerestory windows,[1] but the churches are adequately lit by large windows in the aisles and by light which filters through the triforium openings. The crossings are as well lighted as that of S. Ambrogio, Milan, but by the following method, which is peculiar to Auvergne. Two of the arches at the crossing terminate the eastern and western barrel vaults. The other two arches complete the crossing, but carry only the north and south walls of the cupola. Between the transepts and the cupola, in line with the aisles, are quadrant vaults which are raised high enough to allow for borrowed lights. The effect produced inside by this arrangement is very striking, and outside it is still more remarkable. The crossing itself is generally covered by an octagonal cupola, and the quadrant arches between the crossing and the transepts by lean-to roofs which butt against it and rise well above the other roofs of the church. The lean-to roofs, together with the cupolas and chevet, give an unequalled effect of breadth to the eastern façade.

External Treatment. The covering in Auvergne churches is generally stone, in big slabs, bedded on the sloping top of the vaults. The ridges are also of stone, elaborately pierced and carved, and many are two or three feet in height. The roof over each eastern apse at Issoire and Brioude stops against a small gable, which prevents it from cutting unpleasantly into the ambulatory roof. At the apex of each gable is carved a Greek cross. These crosses, the elaborate ridges, the delicately-carved capitals of many shafts round the apses—and above all, the diaper inlay of lava and red or white volcanic stone[2] in the gables and round the upper part of the apses—are all reminiscent of work in southern Italy and suggest some eastern influence. This is emphasised by the similarity between the arched recesses along the aisle walls of Issoire Cathedral and those at Bari and Trani (pp. 189–191).

Trefoil Arches. One curious trait found in many of the churches, generally inside, is the trefoil or cinquefoil arch, horseshoed at the springing. One hesitates to ascribe this to Saracenic

[1] In the Church of S. Etienne, Nevers, which belongs architecturally to the province, although it is some distance north of it, there are clerestory windows which come down unpleasantly upon the arches of the triforium openings, and would have been better omitted.

[2] The richest diaper work in Auvergne is in the Cathedral of Le Puy (the centre of a volcanic district), especially in the cloisters attached to the church.

influence, but it is difficult to account for the feature in any other way, unless, like the arched recesses, it filtered through from southern Italy.[1] In Issoire Cathedral all the openings in the triforium on the north side have trefoil heads, except in one bay, where they are semi-circular, while on the south side the arrangement is exactly reversed.

Barrel-vaulted Churches. Other churches of similar plan and construction outside Auvergne are S. Sernin, Toulouse (*c.* 1090), its Spanish sister, Santiago de Compostela, the abbey church at Conques, and S. Isidoro, León. They differ mainly from those in Auvergne in not having the crossing arrangement described above, and in the greater importance of their transepts. The similarity between the Spanish examples and those on the other side of the Pyrenees is easily accounted for. No churches of any size were built in Spain until Toledo was recaptured from the Moors in 1085, and the Spaniards, having no school of building of their own, naturally sought architects and workmen from southern France.

The church at Conques is in some respects finer than S. Sernin, although not so large. It is barrel-vaulted throughout, except at the crossing, which is covered by an octagonal lantern with a window on each of its sides, throwing a flood of light into the church. Its chevet has a fine appearance outside, but it lacks the decorative features which give such distinction to the chevets of Issoire and Brioude.

S. Sernin, Toulouse. S. Sernin is the largest of the barrel-vaulted churches in France.[2] Although the nave is narrow, being less than 30 feet wide, the total internal width of the western arm is not far short of 100 feet, because it has double aisles. The transepts have single aisles on both sides, and at the ends as well, as at Winchester. The crossing was probably originally covered by a low octagonal lantern, tower or cupola, as at Conques, but at a later period the present telescopic steeple was added, which necessitated the strengthening of the piers below it. The effect outside is striking, but this is only achieved by narrowing the openings of the crossing inside.

Provence (Pl. 20). The Romanesque architecture of Provence has

[1] Street, in his *Gothic Architecture in Spain,* shows a sketch of an extensively foliated arch inside S. Isidoro, León, Spain, which must have been suggested by some Moorish example, but the Saracenic occupation of Spain, of course, continued later than in Auvergne.

[2] The abbey church at Cluny was larger, but is now practically destroyed.

many features in common with that of Auvergne, but the churches
are smaller and workmanship is of exceptional delicacy. There is
one of the rugged quality of northern Romanesque; instead, there
refinement of detail which is undoubtedly due to the inspiration
sical remains in the district. The fluted pilaster so prevalent
ence is an example of a Roman feature translated into
ue work. This also accounts for many Corinthian
ch might appear to belong to the second century A.D.;
delicacy unknown in contemporary work in north-
land or Germany; and carvings on the mouldings
thus leaves, guilloches and fret patterns), differ-
those executed by Roman workmen in the
e.

barrel vaults, and these are generally
supporting aisles, others merely deep
nother by internal buttresses. They
ories are exceptional. S. Nazaire,
aisles covered by semi-circular
of the aisled type (see section,
ntfroide, and S. Trophime,
s the aisles have quadrant
mall clerestory windows
ignon and Orange, the
Dame de Nantilly,
e side recesses are
ntmajour church
ive of the side
o the width.
s attached
metimes
pitals
and
nt

ts-
, there

are a number of fortified churches with massive, buttressed walls, garnished with machicolations and crenellations and looking more like fortresses than churches. Their walls were thick enough to sustain a siege, and the roofs were sufficiently low-pitched to provide a platform which would accommodate the defenders and machines of war. One of the most impressive is the cathedral of Agde, which lies some two-and-a-half miles from the Mediter-ranean coast and which dates from the twelfth century. It is plain and forbidding crenellated structure with what appears to a donjon tower rising above the west end.

EASTERN FRANCE

Burgundy (Pl. 21). Burgundy was a large province, and its tudes, together with its extent, account for the variety o in its churches. Belonging to the German Empire of the century, it did not become an integral part of France centuries later, and for many years the Dukes of Burg the equals of kings. The real rulers of the Duchy, ho the monks. The abbots of Cluny, Citeaux and almost royal state. Their energies were unbounded the direction of church building. To them is superiority of Burgundian churches at the end century and the beginning of the twelfth, but to t must also be attributed the failure to take advanta ments which took place elsewhere.

From Sens in the north to Autun and Tourn through the hilly district in the centre whi Saulieu, Semur and Avalon, are many churches of great interest and considerable of these are barrel-vaulted. Of the except fine abbey church of Vézelay, which has

Vézelay. At Vézelay, in 1146, the Fr of S. Bernard, announced the Second Cr Richard Cœur de Lion and Philip Au the Holy Land. The nave, which was oblong bays. The transverse arches and all are stilted. There are no aisles. Vaulted aisles were commo vaults were a rarity and oblong The narthex of three bays was

vaults have pointed arches, but no diagonal ribs, except in the eastern bay.[1] The absence of diagonal ribs is one of the peculiarities of Burgundian intersecting vaults. Their omission at Vézelay is natural, since the church is early in date, but their absence from much later vaults in the Duchy is proof of the conservative spirit that reigned there. The church at Pontaubert, near Vézelay, built, it is stated, by the Templars towards the end of the twelfth century, is one instance out of many. It is vaulted throughout, and although the central bays are over 17 feet square, there are no diagonal ribs.

Narthex. Burgundian churches differ from all others in western Europe in the importance of the narthex. There are two types: open, as at Autun, Paray-le-Monial, Beaune, Semur and Notre-Dame de Dijon; and enclosed, forming ante-churches, as at Tournus, Vézelay and Cluny. Of the former, that of Autun (*c.* 1160) is by far the finest. The central bay in front is exactly double the width of each side bay and the porch is two bays deep. The striking effect produced is due to the general proportions and dimensions, which are very noble, and to the beauty of the sculpture in the tympanum over the central doorway.

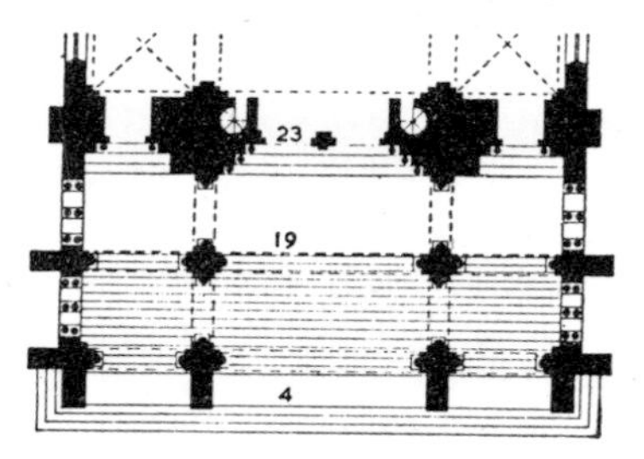

Autun Cathedral: Narthex.
Scale 50 ft. to 1 in.

The reason for the narthex in Burgundian churches is not clear. In the East, and in Early Christian churches in Italy, the narthex was for those who could not, by ecclesiastical law, be admitted into the church proper; but the regulations regarding admission in the West were different. The institution of infant baptism had destroyed the probationer class, and the rules preventing malefactors from entering were not so strict as in earlier days. Another reason, therefore, must be sought. It may be that there was a need for some spot under shelter where pilgrims, on days of high festival, could be marshalled. In the cases of churches belonging exclusively to a monastic Order, the narthex was generally enclosed, perhaps because the monks guarded zealously the right of entry into their churches; the open narthex was more commonly found in cathedral churches, into which people had the prescriptive

[1] Viollet-le-Duc says that these ribs are additions.

right of entry. Whatever the reason, no more were built after the thirteenth century. The open porches of later French and English cathedrals are very different from the narthex of either Vézelay or Autun.

Barrel-vaulted Churches. S. Philibert, Tournus, completed 1019 and the earliest of the barrel-vaulted churches in Burgundy, has already been referred to (p. 146). In the nave, instead of the rectangular piers or stumpy columns of most contemporary churches, there are fine, lofty, cylindrical columns built with many stones to each course. Their diameter is greater than the thickness of the walls which they support, and the projecting segments provide a seating on the one side for transverse arches across the aisles, and on the other for small attached shafts, from the capitals of which spring the main arches across the nave. Much the same arrangement exists in a church at Carcassonne. The chief peculiarity of S. Philibert, however, is that the transverse arches support barrel vaults which run transversely from north to south. This technique was adopted in other Burgundian churches, but was confined exclusively to aisles, and it was used by the Cistercians in England over the aisles of Fountains Abbey (Pl. 18).

The other barrel-vaulted churches in the Duchy are totally different in design, and are mostly one hundred years or more later in date. The first to be built was the great church at Cluny (the third on the site), which was begun in 1089, the nave being finished about 1130, and the narthex some fifty years later. Its total length, including the narthex, was 580 feet, which is about fifty feet longer than Winchester Cathedral. The peculiarities of its plan were double aisles, double transepts and an eastern chevet. The greater part of this church has disappeared.

The cathedral at Autun, consecrated in 1132, is a copy of Cluny on a smaller scale, and from it one may visualise the design of the parent church. All the principal arches and the barrel vault of the nave are pointed, and the arches are stilted, as was general in all southern examples. The vault is divided into bays by a transverse arch over each pier. The fluted piers (or rather, piers with fluted pilasters on their faces), the carving and the design of the capitals, the use of large stones and of keystones for the arches,[1] the delicate contours of many of the mouldings, all proclaim the strong influence exercised by the Roman remains in the town,[2] and contrast

[1] Keystones are found in pointed as well as semi-circular arches.
[2] There are two very fine Roman gateways at Autun.

curiously with the pointed arches and vault. The cathedrals of Paray-le-Monial and Beaune are very like Autun. Beaune has the same detached shafts immediately under the vault, nearly the same arrangement of triforium and clerestory, and similar fluted pilasters and vaulting shafts. The only variation of any importance is that the arches of the arcade spring from three-quarter columns instead of from fluted pilasters.

The main differences between the churches of Burgundy and those of the south of France are that the former have clerestory windows and the latter none, and that in Burgundy the triforium is unimportant and the openings in it small, since it is essentially a blind storey, whereas in Auvergne it is of considerable importance. Farther south still, in Provence, as a rule there was neither triforium nor clerestory, but only high aisles covered with barrel vaults supporting the nave.

NORTHERN FRANCE

Anjou. The architectural province of Anjou is difficult to define. On the north the boundary with Normandy is clear, but to the south the school of Anjou is inextricably mixed with that of Aquitaine. Nor are the examples of its work well known, because of the fame of the neighbouring great Gothic cathedrals of northern France. Everything has been judged by Amiens, Chartres and Beauvais; and because the earlier churches in the neighbourhood of the Loire have not such height and daring construction, they have been counted as inferior by the student of architecture. It is true that they cannot compare aesthetically with S. Ambrogio, Milan, Durham, and Notre-Dame-du-Port, Clermont-Ferrand. They belong in plan and general proportions to some of the aisleless domed churches of Aquitaine (pp. 94–98), except that they have ribbed intersecting vaults instead of domes. The most interesting are the cathedral and the Church of La Trinité, Angers, S. Pierre de la Couture, Le Mans (all *c.* 1150), S. Pierre, Saumur, and S. Radegonde, Poitiers (*c.* 1170). All these have aisleless naves. Angers Cathedral has transepts, which are additions, while the chancels of La Trinité, S. Radegonde and S. Pierre, Saumur, are earlier than their naves and date from the eleventh century.

Angers Cathedral. The nave of Angers Cathedral may be regarded as typical of the work of the school of Anjou. In plan it is almost identical with Angoulême, the great difference being the introduction of intersecting ribbed vaulting in place of domes. And yet the vaults are very domical, like most early French vaults, and the transverse arches, diagonal ribs and wall ribs are strong and bold. Each of the bays is nearly square, the span being over 50 feet and the height from floor to apex about 80 feet. These are no mean dimensions, but of course abutment was easy. There were no aisles over which the thrusts had to be transmitted, and the supports could be any size the architect chose to make them; in fact the whole of the continuous wall could be utilised. The difficulties to be surmounted were therefore far less than in later

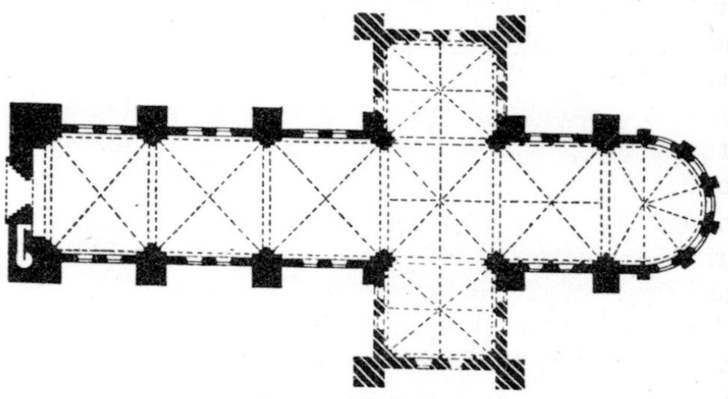
Angers Cathedral.
Scale 100 *ft. to* 1 *in.*

vaults, which were carried on thin piers and restrained by flying buttresses. Nevertheless, in the middle of the twelfth century it was a wonderful achievement.

Along the side walls are big pointed arches, one to each bay, which produce a much better effect than the smaller arcading in the later transepts and choir. Over the arches, partly carried by them and partly corbelled out, is a gallery, which runs round the church below the pairs of semi-circular-headed clerestory windows. It is a pity that the transepts were ever added; they detract from, rather than add to, the effect inside.

La Trinité, Angers. La Trinité differs from the cathedral in two important respects: a chancel arcade has been introduced to provide a clear definition between the nave and chancel; and the vaults are sexpartite, rather clumsily built and some 10 feet narrower than those in the cathedral. These are arranged in a rather curious manner in order to give a greater appearance of length to the interior. At the entrance the building is 80 feet high, but it gradually descends to only 65 feet at the eastern end. This is a trick of false perspective, and is only effective when viewed from the entrance. The range of semi-circular recesses in the lower part of the wall of the nave is very satisfactory; above, from the outside, these appear as strongly-projecting buttresses which take the thrusts of the main arches and ribs.[1]

Vaulting. There is no great disparity in size between S. Pierre, Saumur and S. Radegonde, Poitiers, and the Angers churches, but there is a marked difference in detail. This is most noticeable in the vaulting. The transverse arches are still bold, but the diagonal ribs are extremely slender. Strong transverse arches are a structural necessity when the vaulting is domical, and they possess also the great advantage of emphasising the rhythm of bays of the church. It is extremely doubtful if the later mediaeval builders, in their pride of craftsmanship, made any improvement when, with the adoption of a flat ridge line, they were able to reduce the transverse ribs to the size of other ribs. Many a vault of the thirteenth or fourteenth century looks flat and monotonous, owing to the absence of strongly-marked divisions. The effect of length induced by a rhythm of cross arches is lost; for it is the repetition of transverse arches that so often makes the vaults impressive. This is especially noticeable in barrel vaults, and possibly it was this knowledge that led the Burgundian architects, when building intersecting vaults, to dispense with diagonal ribs altogether. They preferred that nothing should weaken the effect which the transverse arches produced. The thin diagonal rib, consisting merely of a single three-quarter-round member, found in S. Radegonde and S. Pierre, is not confined to these two churches but occurs in nearly all the contemporary domical intersecting-vaulted churches in the district. Another local peculiarity is the ridge rib, of the same section and size as the diagonals. The presence of this feature is all the more curious, because ridge ribs were seldom employed in other parts of France (and never in early work), and the English vaults in which they appear are some fifty years later in date.[2]

S. Ours, Loches. The church which marks the conflict between the schools of Anjou and Aquitaine, between the vault and the dome, is S. Ours, Loches, to the south of Tours. This church

[1] La Trinité has been so extensively 'restored' that it is virtually ruined inside.

[2] Similar ridge ribs occur in the Cathedral of Trèves, Germany.

from the outside appears as nothing but four steeples in a row. The nave of two square bays is similar in plan to those of the domed churches farther south, such as Cahors Cathedral, and the ribbed-vaulted, aisleless churches to the north, of which those at Angers are typical. It seems probable that when the church was first planned, either vaults or domes were intended; but neither form was built. Each square of the nave is covered by a stone pyramidal spire which is octagonal inside and out. There is no inner ceiling nor shell; the corbelling for each octagon is treated decoratively and is visible from the inside as a dark, pyramidal recess. Outside, the pair of spires is sandwiched between two towers, each of which also has a spire. The skyline is remarkable, the combination of four abutting spires, allowing of no roof between, being unique.

Notre-Dame-du-Port,
Clermont-Ferrand;
vault at crossing

Plate 19

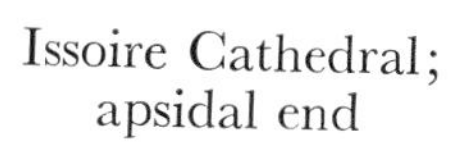

Issoire Cathedral;
apsidal end

S. Gilles, Provence; west front

Plate 20

S. Trophime, Arles; cloister

S. Philibert, Tournus; interior

Autun Cathedral; interior

Santiago Cathedral; interior

Salamanca Cathedral; cimborio

CHAPTER XVII

ROMANESQUE IN SPAIN

ROMANESQUE architecture developed only in the northern provinces of Spain, for to the south the Moslems were not expelled until the mediaeval period had passed. Even by the middle of the twelfth century, only one-third of the peninsula was in Christian hands. Our study, therefore, is very limited geographically. It is restricted, in fact, to the old kingdoms of Asturias, León and Navarre in the north and west, and to Catalonia on the Mediterranean coast, which was cut off from the rest by the Moorish kingdom of Zaragoza.

During the ninth and tenth centuries these kingdoms evolved an architecture which was in some respects in advance of other work in the West; but by the middle of the eleventh century the introduction of French culture resulted in a revolution in style almost as complete as had occurred when the Normans overwhelmed Anglo-Saxon England. There were two important reasons for the French migrations into Spain. The first was the discovery of the tomb of S. James the Apostle at Santiago de Compostela, which encouraged a steady stream of pilgrims to his shrine. The second was the Crusade against the Moslem conquerors, which was largely directed by French forces. The result was that the later Romanesque art of Spain was predominantly French in character and quite distinct from the earlier work.

EARLY ROMANESQUE

Asturias. The architecture of the ninth and tenth centuries in the early Visigothic kingdom of Asturias, which lies along the northern seaboard of Spain, is remarkable because it appears to have developed without stimulus from other countries and to have exerted little influence beyond its immediate locality. Even locally the distinctive way of building was supplanted in the eleventh century by the imported Romanesque technique from France. From what has survived, the Asturian style would seem to have been surprisingly complex. The churches, though small, are often cruciform and accompanied by a number of chapels disposed symmetrically on either side of the nave. The semi-circular apse is unknown, and barrel vaults are almost universal, sometimes with ribs and often supported by buttresses of considerable projection. There is much elaborate carved decoration and a frequent use of the horseshoe arch. This last feature, which we associate with the East, was, according to A. W. Clapham, a characteristic of Visigothic architecture, and indeed antedates its use by Islamic builders. The principal examples of the Asturian style are all in the vicinity of Oviedo, and date from the middle of the ninth century. At that time vaulted buildings were a rarity in western Europe, and for this reason it has been suggested that they might be the work of Syrian builders; but no convincing evidence to reinforce such a claim has as yet been produced.

S. Maria de Naranco, Oviedo. Among the more interesting of those buildings that have survived is the Church of S. Maria de Naranco, near Oviedo, which is said to have been built in A.D. 848. This building has a most unusual plan. At first glance it seems like a Roman amphi-prostyle temple, with a portico added on the north side. The exterior is plain, relieved only by buttresses, but the inside has much unusual decoration. For instance, the ribs, instead of coming down on to the attached columns of the nave, stop short and terminate in carved medallions, like medals on a ribbon. These medallions seem to be reproductions of Visigothic gold ornaments and have crude human figures and beasts carved within a foliage border. Below, the columns are carved in the form of twisted ropes and carry ornate carved capitals.

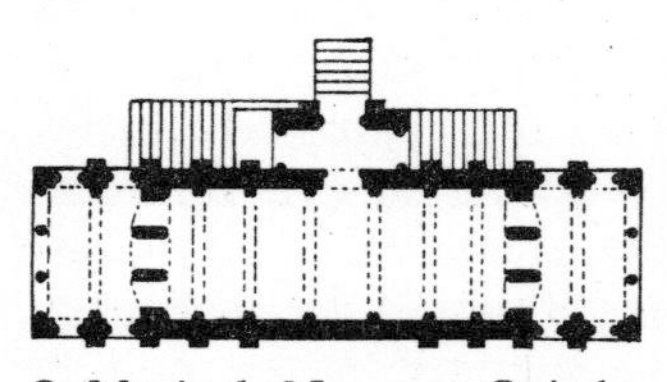

S. Maria de Naranco, Oviedo.
Scale 50 ft. to 1 in.

Catalonia. Catalonia forms the north-eastern corner of the Iberian peninsula, adjoining France and the Pyrenees on the north and the Mediterranean on the east. It was conquered by the Moors in A.D. 712 and freed by the troops of Charlemagne in A.D. 788. Subsequently it was ruled by French counts, who soon made themselves independent of France.

The earliest churches belong to the same tradition as those of Asturias, but after the middle of the tenth century an astonishing number of churches were built which show nearly every stage in the evolution of the Romanesque style. Their variety is remarkable.[1] There are barrel-vaulted basilicas, with transepts and without transepts; there are cross-plan churches and trefoil-plan churches; there are aisleless plans and circular plans; there are domed churches and, at Ripoll, a great double-aisled basilica with a T-transept, or bema, in the manner of the great Constantinian churches of Rome; there is a complete range of examples showing structural progress from the timber roof to the fully-vaulted building; and all this occurs within a country about the same size as Wales. All that is missing is the chevet, or ambulatory with radiating chapels, which is so characteristic a feature of the French Romanesque. But then, the stimulus did not come from France. The style is identical in many respects with the contemporary work in the region around Milan, although in its sculptured decoration it is distinctly inferior; in variety of plan, however, Catalonia surpasses the works of Italy, and from what has survived of fresco decoration it would seem that this small kingdom was superior in that art to any country in the Romanesque world.

The interiors of the Catalan churches appear to have been constructed according to a scheme which called for stucco and polychromatic rendering, and which in its fresh state must have appeared almost as rich as the mosaic decoration of the Byzantine Empire. Much has been lost, and only in the apses are the decorations unspoiled by later restorers. They have a rigid formalism almost Byzantine in character. In the centre of the semi-dome there is usually an enthroned Virgin and Child, with the three Magi in supplication; below, on the cylindrical apsidal wall, are the Apostles and the Prophets, carrying their appropriate symbols; all are painted in the brightest of colours.

Examples. The church at Ripoll, some fifty miles north of Barcelona, is perhaps the most remarkable of the Catalan churches, even if in plan it reflects the double-aisled basilicas of Early Christian Rome. It was built between 1020 and 1032, restored 1824–30, sacked and burned in the first Carlist War in 1835, and ruthlessly restored again 1886–93. The present structure has therefore little that can with any certainty be ascribed to the Romanesque original, other than its plan; but the plan is the surprising feature. Here is a nave arcade, some 200 feet long, of great Romanesque square piers which carry a barrel vault, and a

[1] The most fully-documented account of Catalan architecture is given in *Spanish Romanesque Architecture*, by W. M. Whitehill, Oxford, 1941.

second outer arcade of alternating piers and columns, which may have been intended to support some form of groined vaulting over the aisles. It is, in fact, an Early Christian plan in all its divisions, but modified by the introduction of piers in place of columns and a stone-vaulted ceiling instead of a timber roof.

Structurally, the highest level in Catalan architecture was reached with the building of S. Vincent de Cardona. Although contemporary with the church at Ripoll, it is fully-developed Romanesque, both in plan and in structure. It consists of a

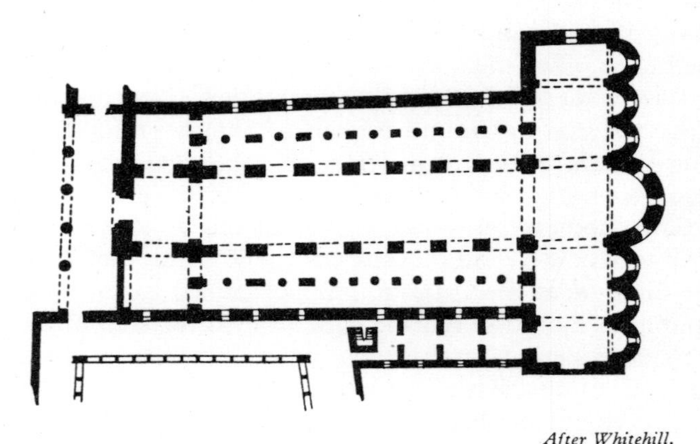

After Whitehill.

S. Maria, Ripoll.
Scale 100 *ft. to* 1 *in.*

barrel-vaulted nave with transverse ribs and groined vaults to the aisles. The transepts are barrel-vaulted, and at the crossing there is a dome set on squinches—the earliest in Spain. At this point stairs lead up to the chancel and down to a crypt. The piers are clustered, the arcade is built in two orders, and there are buttresses to withstand the thrust of the vaulting. There is here, indeed, at this early date (1020–40), every feature with which we associate the fully-developed Romanesque style, except the *ribbed* cross vault.

LATER ROMANESQUE

From the middle of the eleventh century French influence predominated. French monks, mostly of the Order of Cluny, were appointed to fill the principal Sees. The Court was Gallicised, and so was the crusading army. Frenchmen followed the pilgrimage road to the tomb of S. James at Santiago, and French offerings financed the major building operations. That there should be an identity of style on either side of the Pyrenees is not, therefore, surprising. Most of the churches have barrel-vaulted naves with quadrant barrel vaults over the aisles, and terminate in three apses in the manner of S. Nazaire, Carcassonne, and many Provençal churches. The most remarkable evidence of similarity, however, is to be found in the Cathedral of Santiago, which is identical in plan, proportions and general design to the Church of S. Sernin, Toulouse.

The most important monuments of the style are to be found at León, Santiago and Salamanca, but throughout Aragon, Navarre and Castille there are innumerable minor churches which follow the same tradition, though these have not yet been fully recorded. The principal difference between the Romanesque architecture of Spain and France and that of England is that the nave is roofed with a stone barrel vault with transverse ribs, as at Santiago and Toulouse, and there is no clerestory; whereas Ely, Norwich and Peterborough have clerestories and timber ceilings over the nave. Further, in place of the English and Norman central tower there is in Spain the 'cimborio', or lantern. Something similar in outside appearance is to be found in Auvergne, but it was in Spain that it was developed into a feature of outstanding importance. The cimborio is a domical structure designed, like the Renaissance domes, so that it should appear satisfactory from the inside as well as from the outside. This involved two domes—an inner dome set on a drum, and above this an outer shell, of the same diameter but of a steeper pitch, ornamented externally with curious crocketed ridges. From the outside it appears like a great stone mitre, and is much richer in effect than the simple, low, octagonal lanterns, with insignificant pyramidal tiled roofs, which are usual in Lombardy. Inside, a peculiar feature is the carrying of ribs up the sides of the drum and across the dome itself. This arrangement is to be found at Toro, Zamora, Plasencia and—the finest of all—Salamanca (Pl. 22).

S. Isidoro, León. The earliest examples of the fully-developed Romanesque are to be seen in the vicinity of León. Here was built in 1063 the Panteón de los Reyes, which adjoins the slightly later church of S. Isidoro. The Panteón from the beginning was a burial place for kings. It is unusually heavy in design and, though above ground, has the atmosphere of a crypt. The columns are low and squat monoliths, with richly-decorated capitals supporting groined vaults covered with exquisite twelfth-century paintings. The church is east of the Panteón and to one side of the main axis. The date of its foundation is doubtful, but it was certainly completed by 1149. The plan is that of a Latin cross with aisles, but there is no dome or cimborio over the crossing. Instead, the nave barrel vault continues without a break to the east end, and cusped arches lead to lower barrel-vaulted transepts. The nave of six bays has a clerestory immediately above the arcade; this was probably an afterthought, for during recent restorations traces of old vaulting capitals were discovered at a lower level. Apart from the choir which has replaced the original central apse, the church is Romanesque throughout.

Santiago (Pl. 22). The Cathedral of Santiago de Compostela marks the culmination of eleventh-century architecture in Spain.[1] It was here that the relics of the Apostle James were discovered in 835, and a small chapel was erected to enshrine them. In 997 this chapel was totally destroyed by the Moors who, however, respected the sacred relics. After the reconquest by Bermudo III, the roads were improved and pilgrims flocked to the shrine. Santiago became the focus of all the art and chivalry of western Christendom. It was the end of a great pilgrimage road, and a headquarters for the Crusade against Islam. The erection of the present cathedral was begun in 1078 by command of Bishop Diego Peláez and under the charge of Bernard the Elder and Rotbertus, or Robert. It is possible that Bernard was a Spaniard, and probable that Robert was a Frenchman. To these men is ascribed the general design of the church, and there is no doubt that its inspiration was French and not Spanish. Building operations seem to have been very slow, for it was not until 1188 that work was completed at the west end, and not until 1211 that the cathedral was consecrated. The plan is cruciform, with aisles to the transepts and apsidal chapels projecting on their eastern walls. The Sanctuary is apsidal and is surrounded by an ambulatory with radiating chapels—that is to say, a chevet, which was at that time a feature unknown in Spain. The nave is barrel-vaulted, and though without a clerestory there is a spacious, well-lit triforium which is roofed with a quadrant barrel vault.

[1] The most magnificent record of this cathedral is provided in *The Early History of the Cathedral of Santiago de Compostela*, by Professor Conant, 1926.

Very little of the original cathedral can be seen from the outside. The dome over the crossing is High Renaissance, and the western façade is a tremendous *tour de force* of the Spanish Baroque architect, Ferdinando Casas y Novoa. Behind this western portal, however, there still remains part of the original front, which exhibits some of the finest Romanesque sculpture in Spain. This is the Portico de la Gloria, which is dated 1188 and is the work of Master Mateo. In fact, it consists of three doorways whose ordered sides are lined with columns resting on the backs of prostrate monsters. Over the central doorway is a great figure of

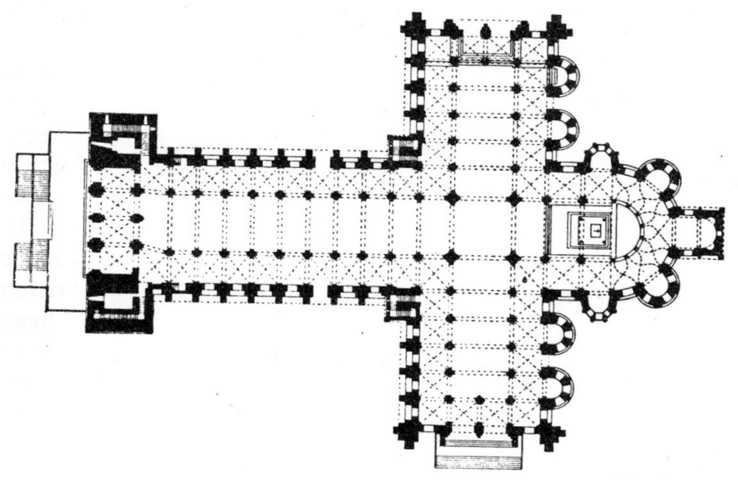

After Conant.

Cathedral of Santiago de Compostela.
Scale 100 *ft. to* 1 *in.*

Christ, King and Judge, more than fifteen feet high. Alongside are the Evangelists and twenty-four Elders of the Apocalypse. They are highly formal figures with elongated limbs, draped with almost classical refinement. Originally they were coloured, and faint traces still remain. Altogether, these sculptures represent the high-water mark of Romanesque endeavour.[1]

The Cathedral of Santiago provided the prototype for other cathedrals in the district. At Lugo and Túy there are the same banded barrel-vaulted naves, groined-vaulted aisles and quadrant-vaulted triforiums. Farther south, at Salamanca, Toro and

[1] There is a cast of these in the South Kensington Museum.

Zamora, the tri-apsidal plan prevailed, and the cimborio was the distinctive mark—for a time. But by the beginning of the thirteenth century French importations overwhelmed such features as might be considered original and national. At Toledo in 1227, seven years after the foundation of Amiens and Salisbury, the French Gothic style had totally supplanted the Romanesque. Thereafter, the architecture of Spain was Gothic, and French.

CHAPTER XVIII

SECULAR ARCHITECTURE

So far in this volume we have been concerned exclusively with religious buildings; and there can be no doubt that the most important architectural achievements in Europe over the period from A.D. 300 to 1200 were concerned with the Christian Church. Of the general run of domestic building of the period, very little remains. Town halls, guild halls, manor houses and the like all belong to a later period. Indeed, there were very few towns of any size, with a few notable exceptions such as Constantinople, Rome, Paris and London. Of the great palace at Constantinople only written records remain to furnish evidence of its character. The same applies to Charlemagne's palace at Aix-la-Chapelle. In France there are a few bridges, and in England two or three remnants of stone-built houses. We must assume that the homes of the vast majority of people in the West were crudely-built affairs involving little of the skill and ingenuity which was so evident in church architecture. Many were simple wooden shelters, and little more than that. There is, in fact, only one field of activity outside the Church in which architectural designers seem to have found opportunities to exercise their virtuosity. This is in the architecture related to the art of war: in the building of protective walls, castles and fortified dwellings.[1]

The principal conditions in the design of fortifications are to provide protection against the missiles of the enemy and to create obstacles to prevent an enemy from reaching the defences. The earliest fortifications consisted of a wall, or a rampart of earth

[1] A general history of the art of fortification in Europe from Roman to Romanesque times has yet to be written. Viollet-le-Duc's *Essay on the Military Architecture of the Middle Ages*, trans. by M. Macdermott, 1860, provides a useful introduction, but is limited to France and is more concerned with later mediaeval developments. There is, however, a large amount of material available on English fortified buildings from the earliest times, which provides the source from which the bulk of the present chapter is drawn. It may be, as a result, that this chapter appears rather parochial; but it should be borne in mind that because warfare is an international activity, features which occurred in one country were more or less duplicated elsewhere.

topped by a wooden palisade, with a moat or ditch in front to keep the enemy at a distance. It was also a necessity that the besieged should be able to protect their defensive screen in the event of the enemy's overcoming the ditch, and an advantage if the besieged could conduct their defence from a higher level than that of the enemy. All these conditions must be borne in mind when considering any system of fortification constructed before the invention of gunpowder.

Byzantine Fortifications (Pl. 23). A description of the walls of Constantinople indicates how these conditions were satisfied in the grandest manner. The city of Constantinople lies on a promontory roughly triangular in plan, two sides being bounded by water and

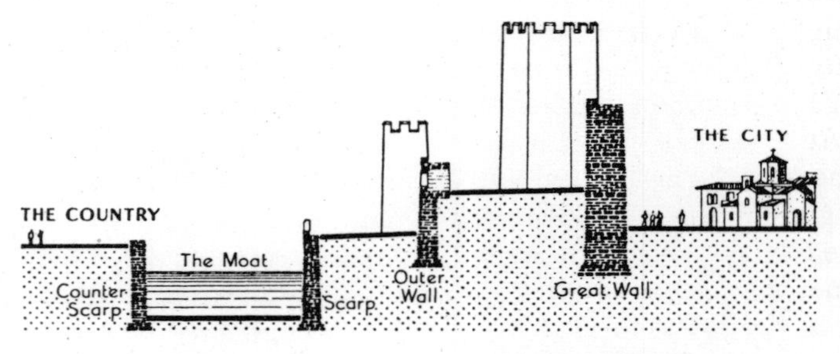

Section through land walls of Constantinople.
Scale 100 *ft. to* 1 *in.*

the third, the base, being the land connection with Europe. This landward side was the most obvious for attack, and here the main defences were constructed. First there was a moat, a buttressed walled channel 30 feet deep and 61 feet across, which could be filled when required. This was the first line of defence. Sixty feet inside this was a second line, a wall 25 feet high, reinforced with 35-foot towers which projected to provide cross fire should an enemy reach the base. Fifty feet farther in was a second and greater wall, 40 feet high, and strengthened by 60-foot towers. The walls were thick enough to provide a platform for the defenders. The outer face was carried up a few feet above the platform and crenellated to give protection against arrows and other projectiles, while at the same time providing safe viewpoints. The sight of these defences was enough to deter the Goths and the Huns. They were built in the sixth century and not breached by an enemy until 1453, when Mohammed II, with an army of 160,000 Turks against a garrison of only 8,000, attacked the city walls with the aid of huge stone cannon balls.

The defensive wall was the normal method of fortification for the great cities of the Byzantine Empire, and most of the principal works were undertaken by Justinian in the sixth century. In the countryside another method of defence was adopted: at strategic points, commanding a river crossing or guarding a pass or valley, isolated citadels were built. These would provide accommodation for a garrison, and were often rectangular in plan and reinforced by square towers which projected boldly at the corners and on either side of the entrance. The sight of these citadels or castles may have inspired some of the returning Crusaders to follow the lead of Byzantium and establish in the West similar structures for themselves. As in so many things, the Eastern Empire had kept alive the art of fortification long enough for the rest of the world to learn afresh what had been lost during the Dark Ages.

Although the First Crusade (1095) coincided with the beginning of the great period of castle building in western Europe, we cannot assume that the idea of castles came from the East, for the Château d'Arques, near Dieppe (1040) and the White Tower of London, which was begun in 1078, are prototypes; so it would seem that the West was not initially influenced by Byzantine models. Nevertheless, many of the characteristic features of Byzantine fortification were quickly adopted by the Crusaders in the citadels they built in the Holy Land and in the castles they built at home. The most important of these features were: (1) the development of the moat which, instead of being a narrow ditch, became a wide hazard which kept the enemy at such a distance that it was nearly impossible to reach the wall with a battering-ram; (2) the introduction of towers at intervals along the curtain wall to allow for cross fire; and (3) the development of machicolations which would allow for the dropping of missiles upon the heads of the enemy at the base of the wall. These features were all developed in the West in the twelfth century.

The Castle. A castle may be defined as a self-contained fortress intended for the purpose of residence and defence and, normally, as the stronghold of a feudal lord. The word 'castle' (*castel*) appears in England shortly before the Norman Conquest, when Edward the Confessor invited certain Norman knights to defend Herefordshire against the Welsh. A description of such a castle is given in *Acta Sanctorum*: 'The rich and noble of that region being much given to feuds and bloodshed fortify themselves. . . . They heap a mound as high as they are able and dig round it as broad a ditch as they can . . . round the summit of the mound they construct a palisade of timber to act as a wall . . . inside the palisade they erect a house, or rather a citadel, which looks down on the whole neighbourhood.'[1] This moated mound is called the *motte*, and in addition there was usually a base court, or *bailey*, to accommodate the garrison. This was of kidney shape, attached to the motte and also moated and palisaded to provide the first line of defence.

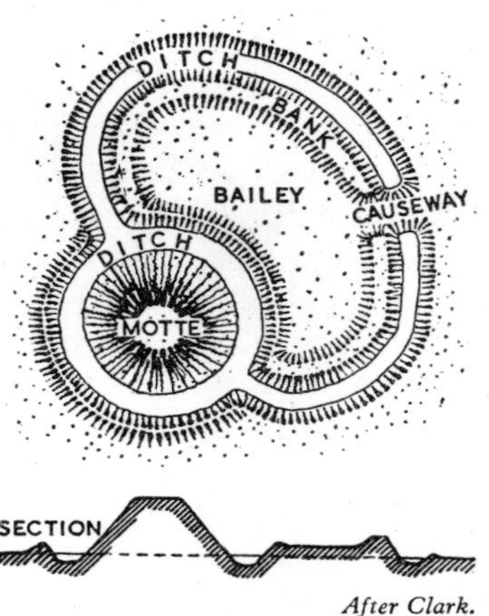

After Clark.

Motte and bailey fortifications, Laughton - en - le - Morthen, Yorks.
Scale 200 ft. to 1 in.

Castles of this type were quite new in England in the eleventh century, but they had already existed in France as early as the ninth. That the subjection of England by William the Conqueror was partly due to this innovation is evident from the remarks of Orderic Vitalis, who said: 'There was practically no fortresses such as the French call *castella* in the land, wherefor the English, though warlike and courageous, proved too feeble to withstand their enemies.' In the arts of war, as in the arts of religion, the advent of William the Conqueror was to revolutionise the English scene.

At first these castles were of the simplest sort, and it is unlikely that stone was used for either the dwelling or the surrounding fortification. This was partly because of the time necessary to build in stone, and partly because the newly-erected mound could scarcely be expected to withstand the load of a stone structure. Where a natural mound existed, stone might be used, but this was exceptional. Ninety per cent of the original castles in England were simply earthen mounds with timber palisades and a wooden citadel at the top. Up to 1100, at least eighty-five castles had been constructed, and only six or seven were masonry structures. Of

[1] Quoted by G. T. Clark, *Mediaeval Military Architecture*, London, 1884.

these the most important surviving are the Tower of London, Colchester, Pevensey, and Richmond, Yorks (Pl. 23).

The perishable nature of timber and its liability to destruction by fire made it suitable only as a temporary fortification. As soon as possible it would be replaced by stone, producing what is known as a 'shell' keep. This consisted of a ring of masonry round the plateau; inside there was room for small subsidiary buildings. Examples of this type are at Berkeley, Totnes, Launceston and Usk.

The alternative was a high, rectangular tower of masonry, of which the Tower of London, Hedingham and Rochester are typical. This provided a much more compact form of stronghold.

Geographical Distribution. The Normans, according to Viollet-le-Duc, were the first people in western Europe to build castles as part of a general scheme of defence. This system was introduced into England by the Conqueror, and although theoretically the building of castles was a prerogative of the Crown, practical needs made it essential to construct strong-points so quickly after the Invasion that William had to permit his followers to erect castles which became hereditary; a concession which his successors had occasion to regret.

The early castles should not be regarded as isolated fortresses but as units sited according to a carefully thought-out plan. They were sited alongside nearly all the larger communities to overawe the populace—simultaneously to threaten and protect. Along the south-east coast of England castles were placed at all convenient landing places—at Hastings, Folkestone, Dover, Saltwood, Romsey, etc. The great highway which leads from Dover through Canterbury and Rochester to London was defended by Norman keeps at each of these centres. In Essex the River Colne was protected at Colchester and Hedingham, and the former castle is one of the largest and the latter one of the most beautifully preserved of all the Norman keeps. The midland counties, being a safe distance from the seaboard, had relatively few castles. Bedfordshire has not a single example. On the Scottish borders, in Northumberland and Cumberland, on the other hand, the countryside was thickly studded with castles, and at Newcastle-upon-Tyne, Bamborough and Norham, Carlisle, Appleby and Brough, there are Norman keeps of the first rank.

Once the pacification of England had been accomplished, the Welsh border became the most important area of military activity. The outer line of defence was the River Wye from Chepstow to

Monmouth and Hereford, and north to Ludlow on the Teme. The inner line of defence was formed by the Severn and the Dee; on or near the Severn were the castles of Bristol, Berkeley, Gloucester, Worcester, Bridgnorth and Shrewsbury; on the Dee was the great Palatine castle of Chester, and numerous smaller castles stood along the riverside between Shotwich and Shockleach.

Castles offered one distinctive advantage over other fortifications: because they were built primarily as strongholds, the sites could be chosen purely for their natural strength. The defences of a town, on the other hand, had to follow the natural growth of the settlement, which was seldom along strategic lines. A steep hill, which vehicles of any kind would find difficult, would be unsuitable for a town but ideal for a castle. The more precipitous the sides of a hill, the more perfect the defences of the castle. When a site was fixed because of the existence of a town, the castle was generally placed at the highest or most exposed position, and if necessary the height was increased by artificial earthworks to ensure that the castle should dominate the town. As a rule, the castle would be located upon the line of *enceinte* and not within the town itself. Norwich and Newcastle were exceptions, but in these cases the town walls were built later. When the town stood on a river the castle would be placed on the bank, as at Richmond, Yorks, Barnard Castle, Hereford and Chepstow. If the river made a bend so that it almost encircled the town, the castle would be built at the isthmus so that it protected the town from hostile approach by land; such was the case at Bristol and Shrewsbury.

Many of the sites were of necessity low-lying or on flat ground. This was not necessarily a disadvantage, since an extensive plain reduced the danger of surprise attack and made possible the provision of wet moats and elaborate water defences which made mining operations by the enemy impracticable.

Technique of War. Some understanding of methods of warfare is necessary if we are to appreciate the significance of the castle as a piece of functional design. With the development of fortification there was a progressive improvement in the art of siegecraft. The one was a consequence of the other, and throughout the mediaeval period defensive methods seem to have been in advance of those of attack.[1] There were three dangers which the feudal lord had to

[1] Even with the invention of gunpowder at the close of the Middle Ages, this situation did not alter for a long time. The invention of the atom bomb appears to have reversed the position.

The walls of Constantinople

Richmond Castle,
Yorkshire

S. John's Chapel,
Tower of London

Castle Hedingham, Essex;
banqueting hall

fear in his castle. These were surprise attack, fire and treachery. Against the first two the massive stone keep, with its almost solid basement storey and its well-guarded entrance some 15 or 20 feet above ground level, was well protected. Against the third, a degree of security was afforded by the complex arrangement of passages and stairways within the castle itself. The shell keep on its lofty mound was almost equally impregnable. To capture a castle, an enemy had to be equipped not only with bowmen who could pick off the defenders as they appeared behind the battlements, but also with heavy pieces of equipment such as the mangonel and trebuchet, which could throw stone projectiles with considerable force against the walls. Alternatively, if the walls could be reached, the ram was a most important and useful weapon. This was a huge beam which was suspended by chains from a long, roofed-in timber structure, and which could be swung backwards and forwards by a team of men to batter a selected point of the wall until a breach was made. Another method of attack, which would be adopted if the site conditions allowed, was mining. This meant tunnelling underground to the foundations of the wall, removing the masonry above after supporting it by timber shores, and finally setting these beams alight so that when they burned the wall would collapse. This method was adopted at Rochester in 1215, when one angle of the keep was completely destroyed. To counter the advantage of the elevated position of the defenders, large timber towers were constructed, as high or higher than the defences; these were mounted on wheels and could be run up against the castle walls. All these methods were used, but seldom successfully.

Failing direct assault, there only remained the blockade. This theoretically should have been to the advantage of the attackers; practically, however, blockade did not often succeed. Castles were provisioned for at least six months; they had their own well and therefore a water supply. It was almost impossible, under the Feudal System, to keep an army in the field for as long as six months. Only mercenaries could be expected to stay at their posts for so long. A siege kept an army stationary, with the result that the ground was soon fouled and men swept off by sickness. No army could stay long without heavy losses by famine or desertion or disease. Nor was it easy over a long period to prevent the beleaguered garrison from making contact with friends outside. All the advantages seemed to rest with the defenders. Mining was possibly the most effective form of attack, if the site permitted, but other, and unsavoury, methods were occasionally adopted. Barrels of burning pitch thrown into the bailey could wreak havoc on the timber shelters which provided accommodation for men and livestock; but the stone walls and the keep itself were fairly safe. At one siege barrels of sewage were thrown to breed pestilence; this had the effect of forcing capitulation.

The means of defence were many. First in importance were the strength of masonry, and the advantage of an elevated situation. To prevent an enemy from reaching and scaling a wall, *bretasches* or *hourdes* were constructed. These were projecting galleries of timber which were built on the top of the wall and supported by wooden struts. From holes in the floor missiles could be dropped and boiling liquids poured on anyone foolhardy enough to attempt to scale the wall. In France these *bretasches* were common, but, it would seem from the absence of remains, less so in England. From them there developed, at the end of the twelfth century, machicolations which were much the same but constructed entirely of stone, the parapet wall projecting a couple of feet and being supported on corbels with openings between. Against the ram, bags of sand or wool were lowered to act as buffers, and attempts, often successful, were made with hooks to catch the beam itself.

The weakness of the Norman castle was that it was purely passive. It could contain only a small garrison, so that any effective sortie was difficult, and the rectangular keep did not provide for strong protective flanking fire. In Romanesque times this may not have mattered much, but in the thirteenth century the whole system had to be revised because of the increased efficiency of methods of attack and the greater power of the weapons that were used. This revision was largely the result of the Crusades, which made the western armies aware of the more scientific forms of fortification in the Byzantine world, which we have already described.

Castles with Rectangular Keeps (Pl. 23). The most compact form of stronghold was the rectangular keep, which provided a well-designed and secure dwelling-place for the feudal baron. As a rule such keeps were built on the firm ground of a bailey rather than on an artificial motte. Sometimes they stood free, as at London and Canterbury, and sometimes they were placed at a strategic point on the curtain wall, as at Kenilworth and Corfe. In England some forty-seven Norman rectangular keeps remain. They were always nearly square in plan, and generally a good deal higher than their width. Externally they were usually very simple, and ornamentation was limited to the pilaster buttresses and the treatment of doors and windows.

The walls were enormously thick, starting at ground level with 20 feet or more and diminishing a little by internal offsets to give a bearing for the timber floors. No original roof remains. The roof was a very vulnerable object of attack from burning missiles, and as a protection the walls were carried high above to form a screen. The general planning arrangement was to devote the ground floor to stores, the first floor to the guardrooms, and the second floor to the hall and public apartments; above this, where larger windows could be provided with some security, accommodation was available for private apartments. The entrance was always at first floor level and usually protected by a fore-building. Upstairs, the hall was generally the largest room, with deep window recesses and one or more fireplaces. It was at one and the same time the principal living- and dining-room, the administrative headquarters and the bedroom of the retainers. It was so large that it was sometimes divided, as at Hedingham, by a diaphragm arch, thereby halving the span of the timber floor above. Windows were mere slits, unglazed and fitted with wooden shutters. There was generally on this floor a small chapel, or at least an oratory, and this was the most enriched part of the building. In it one can usually find the characteristic decoration of the period.[1] Within the thickness of the walls were winding staircases, and many smaller rooms which served as garderobes, sleeping-chambers or oratories. Lastly, there was always a well within the keep, which often was accessible at each floor so that water could be drawn up easily to different levels.

Tower of London (Pl. 24). The earliest rectangular stone fortress in England was the 'White Tower' of London, construction of which began at the command of William the Conqueror in 1078; it was probably almost completed at the time of his death in 1087. When, having crossed the Thames, the Conqueror proceeded to occupy the city, he first established a camp at that point which is now the site of the Tower and constructed there a ditch and a palisade.

[1] At London, in the White Tower, the Chapel of S. John is a fully-fledged church, complete with vaulted aisles, triforium gallery, ambulatory and a barrel-vaulted nave. Ludlow is an exception in having no chapel within the keep; instead there is a detached circular chapel in the ward, or bailey.

The site had been carefully chosen on the eastern boundary of the city wall, where a castle could not only protect and overawe but, if necessary, effectively cut off trade between the city and the Continent.

The keep is the only part of that composite collection of buildings called the Tower of London which can be attributed to the eleventh century. It is rectangular, 107 feet by 118 feet, with a round stair-turret at the north-east corner and a bold, half-round apse, 42 feet in diameter, projecting on the east wall. The walls rise 90 feet from the ground floor to the crest of the battlements and diminish from 15 feet to 12 feet in thickness. They are built of rubble, with ashlar dressings at the corners and in the construction of the pilasters, which are the sole ornamentation. The entrance was probably on the first floor, protected by a fore-building, and from there one had access to a large hall, 92 feet by 37 feet, a smaller hall, 68 feet by 30 feet, and a third chamber with an apsidal end which is the crypt of the chapel. The staircase on the north-eastern corner, 11 feet in diameter, leads to the ground floor and the upper floors, which are all similarly divided into three main compartments. The second floor contains the great hall, the with-drawing room or solar, and the Chapel of S. John. The chapel rises from this level the full height of the keep, as probably did the great hall. The Chapel of S. John is one of the least altered examples of eleventh-century architecture in this country. It is the most complete Norman chapel in Britain and, although architecturally plain, its walls were probably painted or hung with tapestry, and in the thirteenth century, it was recorded, the eastern windows were filled with stained glass and the chapel with various ornaments. It is 55 feet long and 31 feet wide, with a nave 14 feet 6 inches wide and aisles which are continued round the apse to form an ambulatory. The aisles have groined vaults and the nave a barrel vault, terminating in a semi-dome. Over the aisles the triforium is also barrel-vaulted.

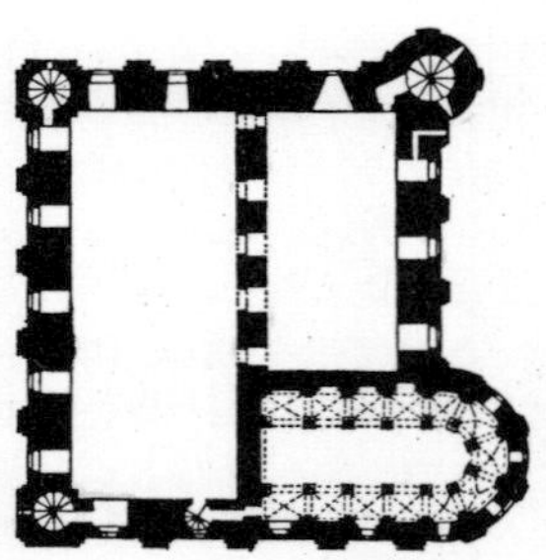

After Clark.

Tower of London: second-floor plan.
Scale 100 *ft. to* 1 *in.*

Castles with Shell Keeps. As the name implies, keeps of this type were mere rings of stonework open on the inside. They were invariably connected with earlier earthworks and were, in effect, stone replacements of the timber palisades on top of the mottes. Like the palisades, they were generally circular or oval in form and built on the edge of the platform. These rings of masonry, often 12 feet thick, 20 to 40 feet high and from 30 to 100 feet in diameter, were by far the most usual form of fortification in western Europe in Romanesque times. G. T. Clark[1] enumerates some 119 in this country, but only 40 actually remain, and these are all in a most imperfect condition; this is because they were less solid than the rectangular keeps, and because other means of defence were devised in the later mediaeval period, for the construction of which the stone provided a useful quarry.

The shell keep was never intended for residence, but only as a citadel or refuge after the capture of the bailey. At most there would be a circle of timber sheds against the ring wall and, at some point, a well. The entrance was by a wooden bridge over the ditch at the foot, and then by steps up the mound to a simple door in the wall, as at Arundel, Lincoln and Totnes. At York there was an imposing gatehouse incorporated in the shell, but this was unusual.

Totnes. The arrangement at Totnes in Devon is typical. The site is to the north-west of the town, the mound lying within the town, and the bailey, protected by a wide moat, beyond. The walls of the bailey connect with the town wall. An attacking force would have to breach the town wall, then the wall of the bailey, before making a final assault on the citadel. There was originally a second ditch around the base of the motte, but this has been

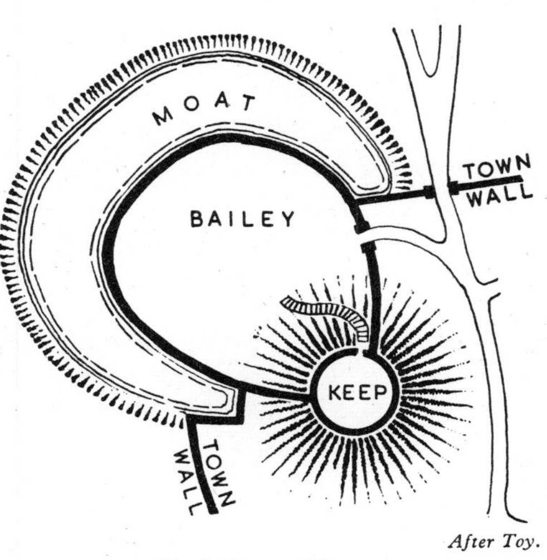

After Toy.

Shell Keep, Totnes.
Scale 200 *ft. to* 1 *in.*

[1] *Mediaeval Military Architecture*, 1884.

filled in. On top of the motte is the shell keep, having an internal diameter of 70 feet and consisting of a wall about 7 feet thick and 15 feet high. Two stairways are built in the thickness of the wall to give access to the parapet walk, and a small doorway leads by an internal passage to a latrine.

Walled Towns. The building of a wall around a settlement was a much earlier method of defence than the castle, and a much more popular one. At the time when the barbarians invaded Gaul and Britain, many of the towns preserved their Roman fortifications. These walled enclosures were for long the only defensive works of these cities. In France—Autun, Cahors, Auxerre, Poitiers and Bordeaux retained their Roman defences. In England, too, at the time of the Conquest there were still towns like Chester, Leicester and Gloucester, which retained their Roman walls, and many towns like Exeter, Hereford, Oxford and Stafford, which already had at least a ditch and a timber palisade to protect them. However, the majority of towns received their mural defences only after the Normans came. These protected the communities not only from outside invasion but also from the often hated 'protector' in his castle. The wall around the town was a constant reminder of the rights of the burgesses and their community of interests. It is true that in England these walls did not compare in size or dignity with similar fortifications in France or Italy. Nor in western Europe were there any great defences in depth and magnitude comparable with the land walls of Constantinople. The most impressive are at Carcassonne. They consist of a double line of ramparts, nearly a mile in circumference, protected at frequent intervals by towers having embrasures at different levels. To the north and within its own mural enclosure is the citadel, which was built in the eleventh or twelfth century. Beyond this is a great shell keep, which commanded the banks of the River Aude and provided, at the same time, a final refuge and a point from which sorties could be made by the garrison upon the besiegers. There is nothing in England to compare with Carcassonne. At most there would be a ditch and a wall 20 or 30 feet high, up to 6 feet thick, strengthened by small rectangular towers and interrupted at two or three points by imposing gatehouses. But of these Norman walls little survives, for obvious reasons. The English city is essentially an organic structure which, in nearly every case, has grown through the centuries far beyond the restrictive Romanesque girdle. Indeed, there are only five cities in England which retain really

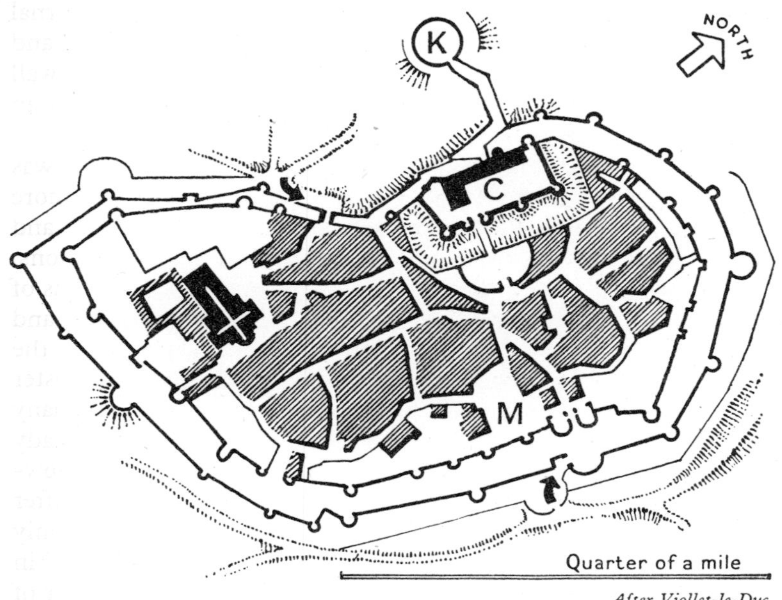

After Viollet-le-Duc.

Carcassonne.

KEY
C. Castle. K. Shell Keep. M. Market.

extensive mural defences. These are York, Chester, Chichester, Southampton and Chepstow. York has been particularly fortunate in preserving its four principal gatehouses, which are all of Norman foundation though encased and remodelled by later mediaeval work. At Southampton the remains are chiefly Norman, and at Chester and Chichester the walls follow the line of their Roman predecessors but are mediaeval. Chepstow is entirely fourteenth century.

The defences of York are the noblest and most perfect of their kind in England. Their circuit is a little over two-and-a-half miles, occupying both sides of the River Ouse and enclosing an area which was only exceeded by mediaeval London. On the north side the wall followed the line of the Roman city and incorporated the Roman 'multangular tower', and on the south it connected with the defences of the shell keep on the banks of the Ouse. The building of walls like those at York and Southampton must have been considerable undertakings. They were seldom less than 6 feet thick and always incorporated a rampart walk, or *allure*, protected by a parapet. At intervals towers projected to provide for flanking fire and the protection of the curtain wall. A passageway, the *pomoerium*, was always kept free of the wall on the inside, to allow for easy communication along its length.

The distinction between the town and the country was sharply defined by the wall. Outside were the open fields, and inside the congestion of small dwellings and churches. The shape of the town and the direction of the streets were dictated by the lie of the land. No doubt the result was picturesque in the extreme, but there was good reason for the twisting, tortuous nature of these early lanes; for in an age when glass was an unusual and valuable commodity, such twists ensured useful windbreaks; at the same time, the more labyrinthine the street pattern, the more confusing it would be to an enemy who had breached the walls.

Houses. There are so few remains of Norman houses that it is difficult to form an accurate picture of the domestic building of the period. The castle and the church would seem to be the limits of architectural endeavour in the West. Nowhere is there any indication of a standard of domestic comfort equal to that of Roman Britain. We must assume that the vast majority of people lived in wooden-built homes which have not survived, and although in 1189 the first Mayor of London introduced the first Building Act granting special privileges to those who built in stone, it would seem to have had little result. There are only two stone-built houses which can give us any idea of what a Norman town house may have been like; one at Lincoln and the other at Bury St. Edmunds. Both have two rooms; one, entered from the street, was probably used for storage, and another, above, was the living quarters and had a fireplace. Both these houses belonged to prosperous Jews in the twelfth century. Of the houses of the poorer citizens, none remains. They can have been little more than timber and clay shelters, without architectural distinction, roofed with thatch and providing in one room accommodation for the household and domestic animals.

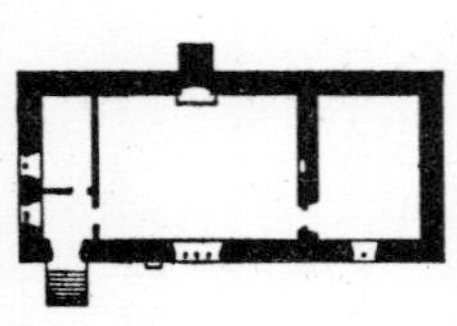

Boothby Pagnall: first-floor plan. *Scale 50 ft. to 1 in.*

In the country, at Boothby Pagnall, Lincs., there is a twelfth-century stone house which marks the first stage in the evolution of the English manor house. It is rectangular, 66 feet by 35 feet, with a ribbed-vaulted ground floor or undercroft, an upper floor reached by outside stone steps, and over this, within the roof space, a large dormitory lit at the gable ends. There was no internal communication between the undercroft and the hall on the first floor. The windows were not glazed, but would be provided with wooden or skin shutters, and on the ground floor, for defensive reasons, the openings were mere slits in the wall. The hall was the only dignified apartment. It had a fireplace on one side connecting with a large chimney. The entrance was probably screened by partitions, and at the far end there was a second chamber—the solar, or private retiring room. From such a simple arrangement of rooms the greater mediaeval manor house plan developed.

REFERENCES

The following list of books indicates the principal works referred to and the sources of many of the illustrations.

GENERAL

CLAPHAM, A. W. *Romanesque Architecture in Western Europe.* 1936.

FERGUSSON, J. *A History of Architecture of All Countries.* 3rd edition, edited by R. Phéné Spiers. 1893.

FLETCHER, SIR BANISTER. *A History of Architecture on the Comparative Method.* 8th edition, 1928.

JACKSON, T. G. *Byzantine and Romanesque Architecture.* 2 vols. 1913.

LETHABY, W. R. *Mediaeval Art.* 1904.

PEVSNER, NIKOLAUS. *An Outline of European Architecture.* 1948.

STATHAM, H. HEATHCOTE. *A Short Critical History of Architecture.* 1927.

EARLY CHRISTIAN ARCHITECTURE (Chapters I–III)

BUTLER, A. J. *The Ancient Coptic Churches of Egypt.* 2 vols. 1884.

CATTANEO, R. *Architecture in Italy from the VIth to the XIth Centuries.* 1896.

DAVIES, J. G. *The Origin and Development of Early Christian Architecture.* 1952.

DE ROSSI. *Roma Sotterranea.* 4 vols. 1864–77.

DE VOGÜÉ. *Syrie Centrale: Architecture Civile et Religieuse du Ier au VIIe Siècle.* 2 vols. 1865–77.

HUBSCH, H. *Monuments de l'Architecture Chrétienne depuis Constantin jusqu'à Charlemagne.* 1866.

KOLDEWEY AND PUCKSTEIN. *Die Griechischen Tempel in Unteritalien und Sicilien.*

LOWRIE, W. *Christian Art and Archeology.* 1901.

VAN DER MEER, F. and MOHRMANN, CHRISTINE. *Atlas of the Early Christian World.* 1958.

BYZANTINE ARCHITECTURE (Chapters IV–VII)

BUXTON, D. R. *Ecclesiastical Architecture in Russia.* 1929–30.

BYRON, R. *The Byzantine Achievement.* 1929.

CHOISY, A. *L'Art de Bâtir chez les Byzantins.* 1883.

DALTON, O. M. *Byzantine Art and Archeology.* 1911.
East Christian Art. 1925.

DIEHL, C. *Manuel d'Art Byzantin.* 2 vols. 1925–6.

HAMILTON, J. A. *Byzantine Architecture and Decoration.* 1933.

HAMILTON, J. A. *Byzantine Architecture and Decoration.* 1933.
HASLUCK, F. W. *Athos and its Monasteries.* 1924.
LETHABY, W. R. and SWAINSON, H. *The Church of Sancta Sophia, Constantinople.* 1894.
LOUKOMSKI, G. K. *L'Architecture Religieuse Russe du XIe Siècle au XVIIe Siècle.* 1929.
MILLINGEN, A. VAN. *Byzantine Churches in Constantinople.* 1912.
RICE, D. TALBOT. *Byzantine Art.* 1935.
RICE, T. T. *Russian Art.* 1949.
SALZENBERG, W. *Altchristliche Baudenkmäle von Constantinopel vom V. Bis XII. Jahrhundert.* 1854.
SCHULTZ, R. W. and BARNSLEY, S. H. *The Monastery of S. Luke of Stiris in Phocis.* 1901.
SPIERS, R. PHÉNÉ. *Architecture East and West.* 1905.
STEWART, CECIL. *Byzantine Legacy.* 1947.
STEWART, CECIL. *Serbian Legacy.* 1959.
STRZYGOWSKI, J. *Origin of Christian Church Art.* Trans. by O. M. Dalton and H. M. Braunholtz. 1923.
TEXIER, C. and PULLAN, R. P. *Byzantine Architecture.* 1864.

ROMANESQUE ARCHITECTURE
ITALY (Chapter XII)

CUMMINGS, C. A. *A History of Architecture in Italy.* 2 vols. 1901.
PORTER, A. KINGSLEY. *Lombard Architecture.* 1917.
RICCI, C. *Romanesque Architecture in Italy.* 1925.
RIVOIRA, G. T. *Lombardic Architecture.* Trans. by G. McN. Rushforth. 2 vols. 1910.
ROHAULT, DE FLEURY. *Monuments de Pise au Moyen Age.* 1866.
STREET, G. E. *Brick and Marble Architecture in North Italy.* 1874.

GERMANY (Chapter XIII)

LUNDBERG, E. *Arkitekturens Formspråk.* 1951.
Neuss. *Kunst der Alten Christen.* 1926.

ANGLO-SAXON ENGLAND (Chapter XIV)

CLAPHAM, A. W. *English Romanesque Architecture before the Conquest.* 1930.

NORMANDY AND ENGLAND (Chapter XV)

CLAPHAM, A. W. *Romanesque Architecture in England after the Conquest.* 1934.
MACGIBBON, J. and ROSS, T. *Ecclesiastical Architecture of Scotland.* 3 vols. 1896–7.
PUGIN, A. W. *Architectural Antiquities of Normandy.* 1828.

FRANCE (Chapter XVI)

BAUM, J. *Romanesque Architecture in France.* 1928.
DE LASTEYRIE, R. *L'Architecture Religieuse en France à l'époque Romane.* 2nd ed. 1929.
MARKHAM, V. R. *Romanesque France.* 1929.

SPAIN (Chapter XVII)

CONANT, K. J. *The Early Architectural History of the Cathedral of Santiago de Compostela.* 1926.
WHITEHILL, W. M. *Spanish Romanesque Architecture.* 1941.

SECULAR ARCHITECTURE (Chapter XVIII)

CLARK, G. T. *Mediaeval Military Architecture.* 1884.
LLOYD, N. *A History of the English House.* 1930.
OMAN, C. *Castles.* 1926.
QUENNELL, C. H. B. and M. *A History of Everyday Things in England.* Vol. I. 1918.
TOY, S. *Castles, a History of Fortifications.* 1939.

ARCHITECTURAL GLOSSARY

Note: This glossary is limited to words and terms used in this volume only.

Abacus. The top member of the capital of a column, generally square or rectangular in plan and in Romanesque work often moulded.

Abbey. A religious establishment governed by an abbot.

Aisles. The parts on either side of the nave of a church or basilica whose interior is divided by columns or piers; generally lower and narrower than the nave.

Ambo, or **Ambon.** A raised pulpit commonly found in Early Christian churches, from which the Epistles and Gospels were read.

Ambulatory. The aisle which surrounds the apse of a church at the eastern end.

Annulet. A ring around the shaft of a column.

Apse. A semi-circular or multangular termination of the chancel.

Arcade. A series of arches carried on columns or piers, either attached to or independent of a wall.

Architrave. The lowest division of the entablature (*q.v.*), spanning horizontally between columns.

Archivolt. The moulded face of an arch.

Ashlar. Stone walling, the exposed face of which is of squared and finished construction.

Atrium. The forecourt of a church, especially in Early Christian work.

Bailey. The fortified open courtyard of a feudal castle.

Baldachino. A canopy carried on four columns, generally placed over the principal tomb in a church.

Baptistery. A building containing a baptismal font; in Early Christian architecture, separated from the church.

Barrel Vault. *See* Vaulting.

Basilica. In Early Christian architecture, an aisled church with a long nave terminating in an apse.

Batter. The slightly inclined face of a wall.

Battlements, also called **Crenellations.** A parapet, having a series of embrasures.

Bema. The Sanctuary, or area generally raised above the level of the nave, which is reserved for the clergy in Early Christian and Byzantine churches. In Byzantine churches it is entirely screened from sight by the iconostasis (*q.v.*).

Billet. One of the characteristic Norman ornamental motifs, consisting of short cylinders or square sections at regular intervals.

Bowtell, or Boltel. In Norman architecture, a form of rounded moulding.

Campanile. A bell tower of Italian design, generally separated from a church.

Capital. The top feature of a column between the shaft and the entablature (*q.v.*).

Cathedral. A church which accommodates the Bishop's Throne, or Cathedra.

Cavetto. A moulding of concave profile, usually a quarter-round.

Centering. A framework in timber which is used in arch and vault construction to provide support until the mortar is set.

Chancel. That portion of a church, usually at the eastern end, which accommodates clergy and choir.

Chevet. The rounded eastern termination of a Romanesque church which includes the chancel, the ambulatory and radiating chapels.

Choir. The eastern portion of a church which accommodates the singers.

Cimborio. In Spanish Romanesque architecture, the cupola or lantern which rises from the roof immediately above the crossing.

Clerestory, or Clearstory. That portion of the nave of a church which rises above the aisle roof and is pierced by windows.

Clustered Pier. A pier composed of a number of shafts or angles. (See p. 155.)

Corbel. A block of stone, often elaborately carved, projecting from a wall and acting as a supporting bracket.

Corinthian Order. One of the five Orders of classical architecture, distinguished chiefly by its capital, which is formed by an arrangement of acanthus leaves.

Cornice. The crowning member of an entablature (*q.v.*).

Cosmati. The name of a family of marble workers in Rome during the 12th and 13th centuries. (See p. 188.)

Crenellation. See Battlements.

Cupola. A small domed turret built over the roof.

Curtain Wall. The wall between towers or bastions in defensive works.

Cushion Capital. A capital common in Romanesque work, having an approximately cubical form, the lower portion of which is rounded off to meet a circular shaft. (See p. 166.)

Diaphragm Arch. An arch normally spanning a nave or aisle and having a wall over it.

Domical Vault. *See* Vaulting.

Dorter, or **Dormitory.** Sleeping accommodation in a monastery.

Dosseret. A deep block with sloping sides, resting upon a sculptured capital in order to support an arch above. (See p. 56.)

Drum. The vertical wall, circular or polygonal in plan, which carries a dome.

Enceinte. The outer line or enclosures of a fortress.

Entablature. The upper horizontal parts of an Order of architecture, comprising architrave, frieze and cornice.

Entasis. The very slight convex curvature added to the taper of the shaft of a column.

Extrados. The outer curve or boundary of the face of an arch.

Frater, or **Refectory.** The dining-hall of a monastic establishment.

Flying Buttress. A structure of masonry, usually consisting of a quadrant arch springing from an independent pier to the wall of the nave of a church, to resist the thrust of the nave vault.

Fresco. Mural painting applied to plaster which is still wet.

Frieze. The horizontal division of an entablature (*q.v.*) between the architrave and the cornice. Also used to refer to any long horizontal decorative part of a design at a high level.

Groin. The arris formed at the intersection of vaulting surfaces.

Haunch. That portion of an arch, dome or vault between the crown or apex and the springing.

Herringbone Masonry. Bricks or stones laid diagonally in courses to form a zig-zag pattern.

Iconostasis. In Byzantine architecture, a screen covered with paintings which divides the Sanctuary from the main body of the church.

Impost Block. The stone in a wall from which an arch springs.

Infilling. In Romanesque work, the masonry of the vault between the ribs.

Intercolumniation. The spacing between columns.

Intersecting Vault, or **Cross Vault.** *See* Vaulting.

Intrados. The soffit or underside of an arch.

Ionic Order. One of the five Orders of classical architecture, distinguished chiefly by the spiral volutes in the capital.

Jamb. The upright side of a door or window opening.

Keep. The strongest part of a Norman castle, usually a tower detached from but surrounded by other defences.

Label. In Romanesque architecture, a projecting moulding over the head of an arched opening to throw off rain.

Long and Short Work. In Saxon architecture, the laying of dressed stones alternately flat and upright at the corners of a wall.

Machicolations. Stonework forming a projecting parapet, supported on corbels between which missiles could be dropped on an enemy.

Moat. A ditch, not necessarily filled with water, which was dug around fortified works.

Monastery. A group of buildings designed for the members of a religious order—monks or nuns.

Motte. The steep mound of early Norman castles.

Narthex. In Early Christian and Byzantine architecture, a porch or vestibule at the entrance to a church, provided for penitents.

Nave. The central and chief division of a church.

Niche. A semi-circular recess in a wall.

Opus Alexandrinum. A type of mosaic floor in which large slabs of marble are used together with smaller tesserae to form ornamental patterns, especially in Early Christian churches.

Order. In Classical architecture, signifies a column with base and capital, together with the entablature. In Romanesque architecture, each ring of an arch which consists of several rings of different thicknesses. (See p. 153.)

Palisade. A fence enclosing a fortified place, and consisting of stakes driven into the ground close together.

Paterae. Small flat circular ornaments on a panel or frieze.

Pediment. A low triangular gable above an entablature at the ends of a roof.

Pendentive. The concave, triangular, curved piece of masonry by means of which a circular dome can be carried over a square or octagonal space. (See p. 50.)

Peristyle. A range of columns surrounding the exterior of a building, especially in classical temples.

Phiale. The holy well in front of a church in a Byzantine monastery.

Pier. Any more or less isolated vertical mass of masonry, as distinct from a column, from which arches spring in an arcade.

Pilaster. A shallow engaged pier with a flat face.

Plinth. The projecting base of a building or pier.

Quadripartite Vault. *See* Vaulting.

Quatrefoil. A geometrical pattern consisting of four attached circular lobes.

Quoins. The corner stones of a building.

Rampart. The stone or earth wall surrounding a fortress.

Random Rubble. Masonry not laid in regular courses, and composed of stones of varying sizes.

Ribbed Vault. *See* Vaulting.

Rubble. Stones of irregular shapes and sizes.

Sacristy. A room in or near a church, reserved for vestments and sacred vessels.

Sanctuary. The place which accommodates the principal altar of a church.

Scalloped Capital. In Romanesque work, a development of the cushion capital (*q.v.*), having the plain faces cut into a series of convex lobes. (See p. 166.)

Severy. One bay or compartment of a vaulted structure.

Set-off, or **Offset.** In Romanesque architecture, the sloping horizontal surface used especially at the junction of the plinth and the wall over and on buttresses.

Sexpartite Vault. *See* Vaulting.

Soffit. The undersurface of an arch or lintel.

Spandrel. The roughly triangular space between two adjoining arches.

Springing. The horizontal level from which an arch, vault or dome rises.

Squinch. A series of arches across the angles of a square to form an octagon upon which a dome may be set. (See p. 50.)

Stilted. The term applied when the springing of an arch is raised higher than is normal.

Stucco. Any material like plaster used as a wall covering, generally applied to external work.

Tablinum. In Roman houses, a room, connected with the atrium, which accommodated the family altar.

Tempera. A medium for mural decoration consisting of water-colour with some binding substance, such as egg, gum, milk, etc.; inferior to fresco.

Tracery. Ornamental stonework in window openings.

Transverse arch. An arch spanning at right angles to the main walls of a church.

Trefoil. A geometrical pattern consisting of three attached circular lobes.

Triforium. In Romanesque architecture, the space between the arcade and the clerestory.

Triumphal Arch. In Early Christian architecture, the great archway spanning the end of the nave in front of the Sanctuary.

Tympanum. In Romanesque architecture, the slab or piece of walling which fills the space enclosed by an arch over the lintel of a doorway or window.

Undercroft. A vaulted room, generally in a monastery and often underground.

Vaulting. Arched covering in stone or brick.

Barrel Vault. The simplest type of vault, usually of semi-circular section, and covering a rectangular space.

Cross, or **Groined Vault,** also called **Intersecting.** Generally used over square bays and formed by the intersection of two equal barrel vaults at right angles. (See p. 139.)

Domical Vault. A vault the apex or ridge of which is not level but concave. (See p. 143.)

Ribbed Vault. A vault framed with ribs which carry light panel infilling. (See p. 144.)

Quadripartite Vault. A vault divided into four parts.

Sexpartite Vault. A quadripartite vault which is further divided by means of a transverse rib, thereby resulting in a vault of six parts. (See p. 145.)

Voussoir. One of the wedge-shaped stones used in the structure of an arch.

Wall Plate. In roof construction, the continuous horizontal member which rests on a wall and carries the ends of the rafters.

Wheel Window. In Romanesque architecture, a large circular window with radiating mullions in the pattern of a wheel. (See p. 164.)

Zig-Zag. In Romanesque architecture, the sculptured moulding of short, sharp turns; also called Chevron. (See p. 165.)

INDEX OF BUILDINGS AND PLACES

Illustrations in heavy type